Taste of Home, Mom's BEST MEALS

Taste of Home Books

Reader's Digest

The Reader's Digest Association, Inc.
Pleasantville, NY/Montreal

A READER'S DIGEST BOOK

© 2005 Reiman Media Group, Inc.
5400 S. 60th St., Greendale, WI 53129

Editor: Heidi Reuter Lloyd
Art Director: Nicholas Mork
Food Editor: Janaan Cunningham
Associate Editors: Jean Steiner, Beth Wittlinger, Julie Schnittka
Graphic Art Associates: Ellen Lloyd, Catherine Fletcher
Associate Food Editors: Diane Werner RD, Coleen Martin
Assistant Food Editor: Karen Wright
Test Kitchen Director: Mark Morgan RD
Senior Home Economist: Pat Schmeling
Test Kitchen Home Economists: Nancy Fridirici, Peggy Fleming RD, Erin Frakes, Tina Johnson
Test Kitchen Assistants: Rita Krajcir, Megan Taylor
Senior Recipe Editor: Sue A. Jurack
Set Stylists: Julie Ferron, Sue Myers
Food Photographers: Rob Hagen, Dan Roberts
Food Stylists: Kristin Arnett, Joylyn Trickel
President: Barbara Newton
Senior Vice President, Editor in Chief: Catherine Cassidy
Chairman and Founder: Roy Reiman

Cover Design: Jennifer R. Tokarski

Pictured on Front Cover:
Old-Fashioned Beef Stew, Carrot Cake, Bread Roll

Pictured on Back Cover:
Chicken and Dumplings, Old-Fashioned Green Beans,
Mother's Dinner Rolls, and Orange Dream Cake

International Standard Book Number: 0-89821-421-1
Library of Congress Catalog Card Number: 2004098031

For more Reader's Digest products and information,
visit our website at www.rd.com

Printed in China

3 5 7 9 10 8 6 4 2

Taste of Home Mom's Best Meals

Table of Contents

261 Recipes from the Best Cook Ever–Mom!

Sweet-and-Sour Spareribs, p. 94

Summer Berry Pie, p. 173

Let's hear it for Mom!

She helped us grow up, taught us table manners and kept us well-fed with her many comforting concoctions. Whether she worked outside the home or inside—or both—she worked hard. And still she managed to fill the kitchen with tantalizing aromas that called us to the dinner table before she'd even said a word.

Nothing smelled finer or tasted better than Mom's cooking.

This book is dedicated to moms everywhere who know their way around the kitchen. The ones whose chocolate cake can calm a 6-year-old who just fell off a bike or bring a smile to a neighbor who is having a bad day. The ones whose chicken soup seems to cure the common cold and just about every other minor ailment of youth. The ones whose joy in life comes from creating smiles on other people's faces with the wonderful dishes she makes.

Great recipes from those special moms are right here in this book—261 of them in total. Where did they come from?

> This book is dedicated to moms everywhere who know their way around the kitchen.

Taste of Home, the largest cooking magazine in North America, has a popular column in each issue that's similar to a brag book. In that section, called "My Mom's Best Meal," proud daughters and sons nominate their mom and her fine cooking for special honors. They share her recipes and her story.

Our panel of professional home economists, food editors and magazine editors taste-test the nominations and pick the winners. Only 6 moms receive this high honor each year. Their stories, recipes and photos are then featured prominently in *Taste of Home*.

This book is a collection of the first 10 years of those heartwarming stories and mouth-watering foods. Here's just a sampling of what's inside…

Nothing smelled finer or tasted better than Mom's cooking.

- **A trip to Provence, France** inspired Nancy Larkin to create an elegant Christmas dinner with a French flair. Her story and recipes for Raspberry Tossed Salad, Herbed Roast Beef, Roasted Root Vegetables and luscious Orange Chantilly Cream begin on page 14.

Sirloin Sandwiches, p. 172

- **Sunday suppers** were always something special at Maxine Haynes' house. She and her husband were restaurateurs in Louisiana, and their best Southern recipes always found a spot on the home dinner table, too. Turn to page 62 to share her story and her recipes for Sunday Pork Roast, Mom's Sweet Potato Bake, Country Turnip Greens and Dixie Pie.

- **When someone celebrated a birthday** at Cindy Robbins' home in Ohio, that person received the royal treatment at dinnertime. The birthday gal or guy got to choose the entire meal, including the birthday cake. Cindy's daughter Kim recalls the joy of eating Mom's Lasagna, Chive Garlic Bread, salad greens with homemade Thousand Island Dressing and a candle-studded Old-Fashioned Carrot Cake on her birthday.

Meatball Stew, p. 202

- **Comfort food at its finest** is what Ellen Gibson cooked on her wood-burning stove years ago. Her recipes for cozy Chicken and Dumplings, Old-Fashioned Green Beans, Mother's Dinner Rolls and Orange Dream Cake are treasured keepsakes that her daughter still makes often today. Enjoy her story and recipes on page 100.

You'll find these plus 55 other heart-felt stories in the pages of this classic recipe collection.

We hope you'll enjoy using this recipe treasury as much as we enjoyed making it. Perhaps it will inspire you to create your own special memories. Happy cooking—and eating—from the editors at *Taste of Home*.

Chicken and Dumplings, p. 102

Mom's Best Hints & Tips

What's the best cooking advice your mom ever gave you? Here's what the readers of *Taste of Home*, America's No. 1 cooking magazine, have to say. The hints & tips are organized by course.

Snacks & Beverages

Easy Meatball Glaze
For an effortless meatball glaze, combine equal amounts of ketchup and jellied cranberry sauce; heat until the sauce is smooth. Stir in cooked meatballs and continue to heat on low until they are warmed through.

Cool Ice Cube Idea
When serving fruit juices or punch, make ice cubes from the drinks. This will keep the drinks from becoming watered down.

Tasty Tea Sweetener
For a delightful difference, try sweetening your tea with maple syrup instead of honey or sugar.

Cinnamon Stick Stirrer
When serving hot beverages, offer cinnamon sticks as stirrers. Everyone will love the added flavor.

Fast Punch
Pour leftover juice from canned fruit into a container and freeze. Thaw later for an easy-to-make punch.

Main Dishes

Keeping Meat Loaf Moist
For tender, juicy meat loaf, first mix all ingredients except ground beef. Then add meat and mix lightly. When shaping loaf, handle only as much as necessary.

Sweet Spaghetti Sauce
If you like your spaghetti sauce a little sweeter, try adding 1 tablespoon of grape jam to your favorite sauce.

Sneak in Spinach
Lasagna takes on a different twist if you spread a 15-1/2 ounce can of well-drained spinach on the middle layer. It's a delicious way to sneak vegetables into your family's diet.

Stew Thickener
Like your stew a little thicker? Just before serving, try adding instant potato flakes (about 1/2 cup at a time) until the gravy is the right consistency.

Fabulous Future Meal
Not a fan of leftovers? Try freezing small amounts of leftover chicken until you have enough for a pot pie or casserole. Your family will be glad you did!

Don't Brown Butter
If you see that the butter you are melting for sauteing or stir-frying is browning too quickly, add a small amount of oil to the butter.

Cutting Meat
When a recipe requires you to cut raw meat, partially freeze the meat beforehand. You'll find it's easier and faster to slice.

Cooking Perfect Pasta
Your pasta will turn out wonderfully every time if you cook it uncovered at a fast boil. A rapid boil helps circulate the pasta for consistent results. Also, be sure to stir frequently. As soon as the required cooking time has elapsed, drain the pasta to prevent further cooking.

Breakfast
Fluffier Scrambled Eggs
Light and fluffy scrambled eggs are easy! Just add a small amount of cream when beating the eggs.

Better Pancake Batter
For extra light pancakes, use club soda in place of the usual liquid in the batter.

Savory Pancakes
Add leftover sausages, thinly sliced, to your pancake batter to make a new breakfast treat.

From-Scratch Syrup
Out of pancake syrup? Make your own! Mix 1-1/2 cups brown sugar and 1 cup water in a small saucepan; boil 1 minute. Add 1 tablespoon butter, 1/4 teaspoon vanilla extract and 1/4 teaspoon maple flavoring.

Soups & Salads
Add Zip to Soup
Cayenne pepper (added a pinch at a time!) adds real zip to soup.

Dress Up Chili
For a unique flavor, try adding leftover jellied cranberry sauce to your favorite chili recipe.

Soup Seasoning
Add a little curry powder and a large slice of lemon to the pot of your favorite vegetable soup when simmering. You'll get rave reviews about the soup's special taste.

Potato Soup Pronto
Leftover mashed potatoes make delicious and easy potato soup. Just simmer some chopped onion and celery in a little water until tender. Then add leftover mashed potatoes, milk and salt and pepper to taste. Minced parsley or a shake of Parmesan cheese adds a nice touch.

Storing Lettuce
Wrap your washed lettuce in paper towel when storing it in the refrigerate to prevent "rust."

Second-Day Salad
Use leftover meat as the base for a main course salad the next day. Add salad greens or chopped fresh vegetables, and you'll have a meal in minutes.

Salad in a Snap
Speed up salad making by washing, cutting and drying all ingredients as soon as you buy them. Then store in a plastic bag. At mealtime, just pull out the bag and make the salad.

Side Dishes & Condiments
Bake Potatoes Faster
Bake potatoes in half the time by letting them stand in boiling water for 15 minutes before popping into a hot oven.

Keep Veggies Vibrant
For a lovely looking vegetable dish, add a bit of vinegar to the water when cooking. This trick helps all vegetables hold their fresh, bright color.

Creamy Mashed Potatoes
Do you want creamy mashed potatoes? Try this. After beating the potatoes with butter, salt and pepper, drop in small pieces of cream cheese while whipping.

Using Celery Leaves
Don't throw away celery leaves. They're wonderful in soups, salads and stuffing; they also make an attractive garnish.

Desserts
Fast Chocolate Frosting
For fast, fabulous frosting, break up two and a half chocolate candy bars and place them on top of a still-warm cake. When the chocolate has melted a bit, spread it evenly over the cake. If you like, sprinkle with nuts or coconut.

Frosting Final Touches
For easy frosting decorations, use the back of a spoon to swirl circles and wavy lines in the frosting. Lift the spoon to form peaks.

This roasted chicken dinner is certain to satisfy your family. Recipes are on pp. 40-41.

Memorable WINTER MEALS

Fresh from the Farm Kitchen

By Rosemary Pryor, Pasadena, Maryland

Ah, the precious memories of youth. I can still see the kitchen table in the farmhouse where I grew up as though it were yesterday. The table is meticulously set, and the glorious scent of baking ham fills the kitchen and spills into the rest of the house.

In reality, the 150-year-old house where I spent my childhood is long gone. But wonderful memories of the many meals our family spent together gathered 'round our huge kitchen table still remain fresh in my mind.

I grew up believing my mom was the best cook in the world, and I haven't changed my mind over these many years.

Mom hardly ever used a recipe—she'd add a dash of this or a dab of that and end up with a delectable work of art. Nothing was as fabulous as Mom's Sunday dinners.

How I remember the aroma of her Old-Fashioned Baked Ham baking…her Sauerkraut Casserole brewing…her Glazed Sweet Potatoes cooking. Waiting for dinner to be ready, I felt suspended between bliss and agony. It all smelled so good, it was nearly impossible to hold off. I wanted to sneak at least a bite or two, but, of course, I didn't.

Pineapple and cloves added sweet flavor to the canned ham. Apples and sausage made the sauerkraut special, so that it blended perfectly with the ham. The maple glaze over the sweet potatoes was pure heaven.

And, oh, Mom's Hot Milk Cake! That was the ultimate ending to a perfectly wonderful meal.

I can't bring back those days, but I can keep the memories alive every time I make Mom's special Sunday dinner.

Mom started a tradition of making family time special—with good, home-cooked food and lots of love—and I'm proud to say I've carried on the tradition with my own family. She's helped me do it.

Old-Fashioned Baked Ham, Sauerkraut Casserole, Glazed Sweet Potatoes and Hot Milk Cake (recipes are on pp. 12-13).

Sauerkraut Casserole

Mom brewed her own sauerkraut and, of course, the cabbage was from our big farm garden! Blending the kraut with spicy sausage and apples was Mom's favorite way to fix it, and I still love this country dish. It's a staple at my house now.

 1   **pound mild Italian sausage links, cut into 1-inch slices**
 1   **large onion, chopped**
 2   **medium apples, peeled and quartered**
 1   **can (27 ounces) sauerkraut, undrained**
 1   **cup water**
1/2   **cup packed brown sugar**
 2   **teaspoons caraway seeds**
Fresh parsley, optional

In a skillet, cook sausage and onion until sausage is brown and onion is tender; drain. Stir in apples, sauerkraut, water, brown sugar and caraway seeds.

    Transfer to a 2-1/2-qt. baking dish. Cover and bake at 350° for 1 hour. Garnish with parsley if desired. **Yield:** 6-8 servings.

Glazed Sweet Potatoes

Sweet potatoes fresh from Mom's garden disappeared quickly at our family table when she served them with this easy, flavorful glaze. She still makes them this way. They've become favorites with her grandchildren as well.

 2   **pounds medium sweet potatoes *or* 2 cans (18 ounces *each*) sweet potatoes, drained**

Old-Fashioned Baked Ham

Whenever I make a ham, I think of my mom—who was, in my opinion, the best cook ever! This combination of sweet and tangy is so delightful, but not at all hard to make.

 1   **can (8 ounces) pineapple slices**
 1   **canned ham (5 pounds)**
1/2   **cup packed brown sugar**
1/4   **teaspoon ground cloves**
 1   **teaspoon ground mustard**
 1   **tablespoon vinegar**
Maraschino cherries

Drain pineapple, reserving 2 tablespoons juice, and set aside. Place ham in a baking pan; bake at 350° for 30 minutes. Combine brown sugar, cloves, mustard and vinegar in a small bowl; stir in reserved pineapple juice.

    Score ham. Place pineapple slices and cherries on top of ham; spoon glaze over fruit and ham. Bake ham for another 40-45 minutes, basting occasionally. **Yield:** 8-10 servings.

Hot Milk Cake

This simple, old-fashioned cake tastes so good it will surprise you! As I remember my mom's delicious meals, this dessert was always the perfect ending. Mom always used "a dash of this and a dab of that" to come up with what we thought was "the best"!

- **4** eggs
- **2** cups sugar
- **2-1/4** cups all-purpose flour
- **2-1/4** teaspoons baking powder
- **1** teaspoon vanilla extract
- **1-1/4** cups milk
- **10** tablespoons butter

In a mixing bowl, beat the eggs at high speed until thick, about 5 minutes. Gradually add the sugar, beating until mixture is light and fluffy.

Combine the flour and baking powder; add to batter with vanilla and beat at low speed until smooth. In a saucepan, heat the milk and butter just until the butter melts, stirring occasionally. Add to batter, beating until combined.

Pour into a greased 13-in. x 9-in. x 2-in. baking pan. Bake at 350° for 30-35 minutes or until a toothpick inserted near the center comes out clean. Cool on a wire rack. **Yield:** 12-16 servings.

- **1/4** cup butter
- **1/4** cup maple syrup
- **1/4** cup packed brown sugar
- **1/4** teaspoon ground cinnamon

If using fresh sweet potatoes, place in a kettle; cover with water and cook, covered, for 25-35 minutes or just until tender. Drain; cool slightly. Peel and cut into chunks.

Place cooked or canned sweet potatoes in a 2-qt. baking dish. In a small saucepan, combine butter, syrup, brown sugar and cinnamon; cook and stir until mixture boils. Pour over potatoes. Bake at 350° for 30-40 minutes or until heated through. **Yield:** 8 servings.

Storing Sweet Potatoes

Store sweet potatoes in a cool, dry, well-ventilated place for up to 1 week. If kept dry and about 55°, sweet potatoes will keep for up to 4 weeks. Do not refrigerate.

French Cuisine For Christmas

By Kerry Sullivan, Maitland, Florida

My mom, Nancy Larkin (left), is a true artist—both on canvas and in the kitchen. When she's not painting watercolors in her studio, she's busy creating in the kitchen.

So it was no surprise that when Mom returned from a 2-week watercolor workshop in Provence, France a few years ago, she was all enthused about the meals she'd enjoyed there.

Our holidays are usually celebrated at her house, and the meals are always a real feast. That Christmas, Mom wanted our family to experience the same country cuisine she'd relished in France. So she fashioned an unforgettable table feast with a French accent.

On Christmas Eve, the dining room table was aglow with candles, crystal and good china. Mom explained a little about each dish as she served it.

Her Raspberry Tossed Salad was a refreshing blend of mixed salad greens and sweet fresh raspberries, drizzled with a light vinaigrette dressing enhanced with raspberry juice.

Because some of us like our beef well-done and others prefer it medium-rare, Mom prepared not one Herbed Roast Beef, but two. She coated the roasts with a fragrant herb rub and covered them in onions before baking, then served the meat with horseradish sauce.

Roasted Root Vegetables showcased homey potatoes, turnips and carrots seasoned with garlic and rosemary. They were the perfect complement to the roast beef.

The finale was Orange Chantilly Cream, a recipe Mom found in a French cookbook. She scooped out the oranges and filled them with a fluffy orange-flavored whipped cream.

I'm thrilled to share Mom's French-inspired Yuletide menu and hope you'll enjoy this feast as much as our family did. *Joyeux Noel!*

Raspberry Tossed Salad, Herbed Roast Beef, Roasted Root Vegetables and Orange Chantilly Cream (recipes are on pp. 16-17).

Raspberry Tossed Salad

Bright red raspberries star in this tossed green salad, making it the perfect ingredient for a festive Yuletide menu. Raspberry juice brings a special touch to the light oil and vinegar dressing.

✓ Uses less fat, sugar or salt. Includes Nutritional Analysis and Diabetic Exchanges.

- 9 **cups torn mixed salad greens**
- 3 **cups fresh *or* frozen unsweetened raspberries, *divided***
- 2 **tablespoons olive oil**
- 2 **tablespoons cider vinegar**
- 4 **teaspoons sugar**
- 1/8 **teaspoon salt**

Dash pepper

In a large salad bowl, gently combine the salad greens and 2-3/4 cups raspberries. Mash the remaining berries; strain, reserving juice and discarding seeds. In a bowl, whisk the raspberry juice, oil, vinegar, sugar, salt and pepper. Drizzle over salad; gently toss to coat. **Yield:** 12 servings.

   Nutritional Analysis: One serving (3/4 cup) equals 47 calories, 3 g fat (trace saturated fat), 0 cholesterol, 32 mg sodium, 6 g carbohydrate, 3 g fiber, 1 g protein. **Diabetic Exchanges:** 1 vegetable, 1/2 fat.

Herbed Roast Beef

A savory herb rub flavors this juicy roast, which makes an impression every time my mom serves it for dinner. The creamy horseradish sauce adds a kick to the crispy-coated slices of beef. It's delicious served over the tender meat.

- 2 **bone-in beef rib roasts (4 to 6 pounds *each*)**
- 2 **teaspoons fennel seed, crushed**
- 2 **teaspoons dried rosemary, crushed**
- 2 **teaspoons *each* dried basil, marjoram, savory and thyme**
- 2 **teaspoons rubbed sage**
- 2 **medium onions, sliced**
- 6 **fresh rosemary sprigs**

HORSERADISH SAUCE:

- 1-1/2 **cups (12 ounces) sour cream**
- 1/4 **cup prepared horseradish**
- 2 **tablespoons snipped chives**
- 3 **tablespoons lemon juice**

Trim and tie roasts if desired. In a small bowl, combine the fennel seed, crushed rosemary, basil, marjoram, savory, thyme and sage; rub over roasts. Place with fat side up on a rack in a roasting pan. Top with onions and rosemary sprigs.

   Bake, uncovered, at 350° for 2-1/2 to 3-1/2 hours or until meat reaches desired doneness (for rare, a meat thermometer should read 140°; medium, 160°; well-done, 170°).

Discard onions and rosemary. Let roasts stand for 10-15 minutes before slicing. Meanwhile, in a small bowl, combine the sauce ingredients. Serve with beef. **Yield:** 10-12 servings.

✳ ❄ ✳

Roasted Root Vegetables

Pleasantly seasoned with rosemary and garlic, this appealing side dish showcases good-for-you turnips, carrots and potatoes. We think it's a nice homey addition to our family's holiday meal.

✓ Uses less fat, sugar or salt. Includes Nutritional Analysis and Diabetic Exchanges.

- 5 medium red potatoes, cubed
- 4 medium carrots, cut into 1/2-inch slices
- 2 small turnips, peeled and cubed
- 1 garlic clove, minced
- 2 to 4 tablespoons olive oil
- 1 tablespoon minced fresh rosemary
   or 1 teaspoon dried rosemary, crushed
- 1/2 teaspoon salt
- 1/4 teaspoon pepper

Place the potatoes, carrots, turnips and garlic in a greased 13-in. x 9-in. x 2-in. baking dish. Drizzle with oil; sprinkle with rosemary, salt and pepper. Stir to coat.

Bake, uncovered, at 350° for 35 minutes. Increase temperature to 450°; bake 10-15 minutes longer or until vegetables are tender. **Yield:** 10-12 servings.

Nutritional Analysis: One 3/4-cup serving (prepared with 2 tablespoons olive oil) equals 55 calories, 3 g fat (trace saturated fat), 0 cholesterol, 144 mg sodium, 7 g carbohydrate, 2 g fiber, 1 g protein. **Diabetic Exchanges:** 1 vegetable, 1/2 fat.

✳ ❄ ✳

Orange Chantilly Cream

Mom first tried this recipe from a French cookbook years ago. She decorated the top of each light, fluffy dessert cup with a slice of orange from our trees! Everyone loved it.

- 12 medium navel oranges
- 4-1/2 cups heavy whipping cream
- 1 cup confectioners' sugar
- 2-1/4 teaspoons orange extract
- 1/3 cup orange juice

Cut a thin slice off the top of each orange. With a grapefruit spoon, scoop out the pulp. Invert oranges onto paper towels to drain. Remove and discard membranes from orange pulp; set pulp aside.

In a mixing bowl, beat the whipping cream until it begins to thicken. Add the confectioners' sugar and extract; beat until stiff peaks form. Beat in the orange juice. Fold in reserved orange pulp. Spoon into orange shells. Cover; refrigerate until serving. **Yield:** 12 servings.

A Southern New Year's Meal

By Ruby Williams, Bogalusa, Louisiana

All 10 of my sisters and brothers agree that our mom's best meal was the one she always cooked on New Year's Day. This memorable menu sure started the year off right!

With such a large family, Mom cooked simple, nourishing meals for the most part. No matter what she prepared, it was always delicious (and never lasted long in our house of hungry kids).

We were brought up to appreciate family and friends, and Mom made sure we were generous with our hospitality. So when we rang in the New Year with guests, this is the meal she'd prepare.

Mom never followed recipes. And I was always amazed that she knew just how much of everything to add to make meals taste terrific. After watching her cook this special-occasion meal from scratch for years, I finally decided to record the recipes.

The aroma of Garlic Pork Roast as it bakes is absolutely heavenly. It turns out moist and tasty every time and is a no-fuss favorite.

In the South, no New Year's celebration is complete without hearty helpings of traditional Black-Eyed Peas with Bacon.

Cabbage Casserole is a comforting side dish that gets its mild flavor from cream of mushroom soup and American cheese.

Dotted with raisins and pecans, Pumpkin Raisin Cake is surely one of Mom's best dessert recipes.

Of course, now when I make this dinner for my family, I also add the "special" ingredient Mom generously added to every recipe...love!

Garlic Pork Roast, Black-Eyed Peas with Bacon, Cabbage Casserole and Pumpkin Raisin Cake (recipes are on pp. 20-21).

Black-Eyed Peas with Bacon

A real Southern favorite, black-eyed peas are traditionally served on New Year's Day to bring good luck. My mother's recipe with bacon, garlic and thyme makes them taste extra special.

- **1 pound black-eyed peas, rinsed and sorted**
- **1/2 pound bacon, cooked and crumbled**
- **1 large onion, chopped**
- **1 garlic clove, minced**
- **1 tablespoon butter**
- **1/2 teaspoon dried thyme**
- **Salt to taste**
- **Additional crumbled bacon, optional**

Place peas, bacon and enough water to cover in a large kettle; bring to a boil. Boil for 2 minutes. Remove from the heat; cover and let stand for 1 hour. Do not drain.

In a skillet, saute onion and garlic in butter until tender. Add to pea mixture with thyme and salt. Return to the heat; simmer, covered, for 30 minutes or until peas are soft. Top with crumbled bacon if desired. **Yield:** 6-8 servings.

Cabbage Casserole

Even those who don't care for cabbage will enjoy it made this way. This tangy, creamy, comforting side dish goes exceptionally well with pork roast. When the roast is done, just turn up the temperature and pop the casserole in the oven for about 20 minutes.

Garlic Pork Roast

Mom cooked for 11 children, so her menus usually featured basic, simple foods. But on New Year's Day, she always treated us to this special pork roast. All of us kids agree this was our mom's best meal!

- **1 pork loin roast (about 5 pounds), backbone loosened**
- **1/2 medium green pepper, finely chopped**
- **1/2 cup thinly sliced green onions**
- **1/2 cup chopped celery**
- **8 garlic cloves, minced**
- **1 teaspoon salt**
- **1/4 teaspoon cayenne pepper**

With a sharp knife, cut a deep pocket between each rib on meaty side of roast. Combine green pepper, green onions, celery and garlic; stuff deeply into pockets. Season roast with salt and cayenne pepper.

Place roast, rib side down, in a shallow roasting pan. Bake, uncovered, at 325° for 2-3 hours or until a meat thermometer reads 170°. Let stand for 15 minutes before carving. **Yield:** 6-8 servings.

1 large head cabbage, shredded (about 12 cups)
1 onion, chopped
6 tablespoons butter, *divided*
1 can (10-3/4 ounces) condensed cream of mushroom soup, undiluted
8 ounces process cheese (Velveeta), cubed
Salt and pepper to taste
1/4 cup dry bread crumbs

Cook cabbage in boiling salted water until tender; drain thoroughly. In a large skillet, saute onion in 5 tablespoons butter until tender. Add soup and mix well. Add cheese; cook and stir until melted. Remove from the heat. Stir in the cabbage, salt and pepper.

Transfer to an ungreased 2-qt. baking dish. In a small skillet, melt the remaining butter. Cook and stir bread crumbs in butter until lightly browned; sprinkle over casserole. Bake, uncovered, at 350° for 20-30 minutes or until heated through. **Yield:** 6-8 servings.

Separating Bacon Strips

To easily separate packaged bacon strips, first roll up the whole package as tightly as you can the long way. You'll be amazed at how easily the strips come apart.

Pumpkin Raisin Cake

This nutty, golden cake is one of my mom's best. It's a wonderfully different use for pumpkin. With a holiday taste and beautiful look, it's bound to become a favorite with your family, too.

2 cups all-purpose flour
2 cups sugar
2 teaspoons pumpkin pie spice
2 teaspoons baking powder
1 teaspoon baking soda
1/2 teaspoon salt
4 eggs
1 can (15 ounces) solid-pack pumpkin
3/4 cup vegetable oil
2 cups bran cereal (not flakes)
1 cup chopped pecans
1 cup raisins
Confectioners' sugar, optional

Combine the flour, sugar, pumpkin pie spice, baking powder, baking soda and salt; set aside. In a large bowl, beat eggs. Add pumpkin and oil; stir in cereal just until moistened. Add dry ingredients and stir just until combined. Fold in pecans and raisins.

Pour into a greased 10-in. tube pan. Bake at 350° for 60-65 minutes or until a toothpick inserted near the center comes out clean. Cool in pan for 10 minutes before removing to a wire rack to cool completely. Dust with confectioners' sugar before serving if desired. **Yield:** 12-16 servings.

Salmon Supper Is Sure to Please

By Mary McGuire, Graham, North Carolina

My mother, Irene Isley (left), has a reputation for good cooking in our community.

It's no wonder she's often asked to bring some of her best dishes to various potlucks and gatherings. I'm proud to say that she's been an inspiration for me in the kitchen my whole life.

Although Mom would often serve salmon when I was growing up, what I looked forward to most were special occasions when she would treat the family to her wonderful Salmon Croquettes. (It was my job to debone the salmon.) Topped with a specially seasoned tartar sauce, each bite is so delicious.

With the croquettes, Mom would be certain to serve Hush Puppies, an absolute "must" on most dinner tables in the South. Crisp and brown, they're an extra-special treat. We'd eat every one, often as soon as they were cool enough to handle.

Another typical Southern dish is coleslaw, and we sure enjoyed Mom's version. Her Marinated Slaw smelled so good while marinating that it was hard for us to wait to dig in. We were always thankful the recipe made a big batch!

And Mom's best meal wouldn't be complete without her signature Coconut Pie. A rich slice of this succulent pie is true comfort food that brings back fond memories for me of spending time with my mother in the kitchen.

Of all the lessons I learned from Mom through the years, the most important thing I remember is to add tender loving care to everything I cook.

Salmon Croquettes, Hush Puppies, Marinated Slaw and Coconut Pie (recipes are on pp. 24-25).

Salmon Croquettes

Mom frequently served salmon when I was a girl. Learning the ropes in the kitchen as I grew up, I got the chore of deboning the salmon. I didn't mind because these light, crisp croquettes are absolutely delicious.

- 1 **can (14-3/4 ounces) pink salmon, drained, bones and skin removed**
- 1 **cup evaporated milk, *divided***
- 1-1/2 **cups cornflake crumbs, *divided***
- 1/4 **cup dill pickle relish**
- 1/4 **cup finely chopped celery**
- 2 **tablespoons finely chopped onion**

Oil for deep-fat frying

TARTAR SAUCE:
- 2/3 **cup evaporated milk**
- 1/4 **cup mayonnaise**
- 2 **tablespoons dill pickle relish**
- 1 **tablespoon finely chopped onion**

In a medium bowl, combine salmon, 1/2 cup milk, 1/2 cup crumbs, relish, celery and onion; mix well. With wet hands, shape 1/4 cupfuls into cones. Dip into remaining milk, then into remaining crumbs.

Heat oil in a deep-fat fryer to 365°. Fry croquettes, a few at a time, for 2 to 2-1/2 minutes or until golden brown. Drain on paper towels; keep warm.

Combine tartar sauce ingredients in a medium saucepan; cook over medium-low heat until heated through and slightly thickened. Serve warm with croquettes. **Yield:** 4-6 servings.

Hush Puppies

Mom is well known for her wonderful hush puppies. Her recipe is easy to prepare and gives tasty results. The chopped onion adds to the great flavor.

- 1 **cup yellow cornmeal**
- 1/4 **cup all-purpose flour**
- 1-1/2 **teaspoons baking powder**
- 1/2 **teaspoon salt**
- 1 **egg, beaten**
- 3/4 **cup milk**
- 1 **small onion, finely chopped**

Oil for deep-fat frying

In a medium bowl, combine the cornmeal, flour, baking powder and salt; mix well. Add the egg, milk and onion; stir just until mixed.

Heat oil in a deep-fat fryer or electric skillet to 365°. Drop batter by teaspoonfuls into oil. Fry 2 to 2-1/2 minutes or until golden brown. Drain on paper towels. Serve warm. **Yield:** 4-6 servings.

Marinated Slaw

This is a delectable dish that looks as good as it tastes. Mother usually saved this recipe for special occasions, but when she did make it, we sure enjoyed it. The mouth-watering dressing always tempted us while it cooked. It smelled so good.

8 cups shredded cabbage (1-1/2 to 2 pounds)
2 tablespoons chopped pimientos
1/2 cup chopped green pepper
3/4 cup chopped onion
1 cup sugar
1 cup vinegar
1/2 cup water
1 tablespoon mustard seed

In a large bowl, combine the cabbage, pimientos, green pepper and onion. Toss lightly; set aside.

Combine the remaining ingredients in a medium saucepan; bring to a boil. Reduce heat; simmer, uncovered, for 20-25 minutes or until slightly thickened. Pour over cabbage mixture. Cover and refrigerate 4 hours or overnight. Slaw will keep in the refrigerator for several days. **Yield:** 8-10 servings.

Coconut Pie

Watching my mother cook from scratch, I hardly knew that anything was available "pre-made" until I'd left home. One of Mom's best desserts is her old-fashioned coconut pie. (I use a convenient store-bought crust.) A rich, creamy slice is true comfort food.

1-1/2 cups milk
1 cup sugar
3/4 cup flaked coconut
2 eggs, beaten
3 tablespoons all-purpose flour
1 tablespoon butter, melted
1/4 teaspoon vanilla extract
1 unbaked pie shell (9 inches)

In a large bowl, place milk, sugar, coconut, eggs, flour, butter and vanilla; stir until combined. Pour into pie shell. Bake at 350° for 50 minutes or until a knife inserted near the center comes out clean. Cool to room temperature. Refrigerate leftovers. **Yield:** 6-8 servings.

Basic Pie Crust Recipe

To make a single-crust pie, combine 1-1/4 cups all-purpose flour and 1/2 teaspoon salt in a bowl; cut in 1/3 cup shortening until crumbly. Gradually add 4 to 5 tablespoons cold water, tossing with a fork, until a ball forms. Roll out pastry to fit a 9-inch pie plate; transfer pastry to pie plate. Trim and flute edges.

Hearty Midwest Holiday Fare

By Linda Nilsen, Anoka, Minnesota

My mother was a busy teacher when my younger brother and I were children. She was always on the go. But that didn't stop her from making luscious meals for our family…or from teaching me the importance of offering family and friends delicious foods made with lots of love.

We lived in California, but Mom was from a Swedish Minnesota farm family. When she got homesick for the farm, she'd make hearty meals with Midwestern flair. We always looked forward to those meals more than any others she prepared!

I especially remember Mom's Best Meat Loaf. The zesty seasoning featuring horseradish gives the meat a little zip. And the wonderful aroma while baking was unbeatable. Now I often capture that mouth-watering fragrance in my own kitchen.

Creamed Peas and Potatoes is an old-fashioned, hearty side dish that also adds appealing color to the dinner table.

My mom and her cousin came up with the original recipe for Favorite French Dressing many years ago. We'd look forward to a big green salad served with this tangy dressing. Mom got lots of requests for this recipe.

To top off her meal, Mom liked to prepare a special, traditional dessert from an old recipe that had been handed down in the family. Swedish Creme is thick, rich, beautiful and tasty.

I guarantee your family will favor this mouth-watering menu, no matter where you live!

Mom's Best Meat Loaf, Creamed Peas and Potatoes, Favorite French Dressing and Swedish Creme (recipes are on pp. 28-29).

Creamed Peas and Potatoes

Nothing beats this comforting side dish to go with Mom's meat loaf. The peas and potatoes combined with a creamy white sauce make a hearty dish.

- 4 medium red potatoes, cubed
- 1 package (10 ounces) frozen peas
- 1 teaspoon sugar
- 2 tablespoons butter
- 2 tablespoons all-purpose flour
- 1/2 teaspoon salt
- 1/4 teaspoon white pepper
- 1-1/2 cups milk
- 2 tablespoons minced fresh dill

Place potatoes in a saucepan; cover with water and cook until tender. Cook peas according to package directions, adding the sugar.

Meanwhile, melt butter in a saucepan; add flour, salt and pepper to form a paste. Gradually stir in milk. Bring to a boil; boil for 1 minute. Add dill; cook until thickened and bubbly. Drain potatoes and peas; place in a serving bowl. Pour sauce over and stir to coat. Serve immediately. **Yield:** 6-8 servings.

Favorite French Dressing

My mom and her cousin developed this tangy dressing many years ago. It really perks up salad greens and holds together well when mixed. Everyone wants the recipe once they try it. You'll soon understand why.

Mom's Best Meat Loaf

This is no ordinary meat loaf—the recipe is so good it's been passed down in our family for three generations. The zesty seasoning gives the flavor a spark. I remember Mom's delicious meals. She loved to serve this meat loaf.

- 1 cup milk
- 1 egg, lightly beaten
- 3/4 cup soft bread crumbs
- 1 medium onion, chopped
- 1 tablespoon chopped green pepper
- 1 tablespoon ketchup
- 1-1/2 teaspoons salt
- 1 teaspoon prepared horseradish
- 1 teaspoon sugar
- 1 teaspoon ground allspice
- 1 teaspoon dill weed
- 1-1/2 pounds lean ground beef
- Additional ketchup

In a large bowl, combine the first 11 ingredients; add beef and mix well. Press into an ungreased 8-1/2-in. x 4-1/2-in. x 2-1/2-in. loaf pan. Bake at 350° for 1 hour. Drizzle top of loaf with ketchup; bake 15 minutes more or until no longer pink and a meat thermometer reads 160°. **Yield:** 6-8 servings.

Swedish Creme

This thick, creamy dessert is a great finale to one of Mom's hearty meals. It has just a hint of almond flavor and looks spectacular with bright-red berries on top. The recipe calls for either fresh or frozen raspberries, making this a perfect year-round treat.

- **2 cups heavy whipping cream**
- **1 cup plus 2 teaspoons sugar, *divided***
- **1 envelope unflavored gelatin**
- **1 teaspoon vanilla extract**
- **1 teaspoon almond extract**
- **2 cups (16 ounces) sour cream**
- **1 cup fresh *or* frozen red raspberries, crushed**

In a saucepan, combine cream and 1 cup sugar. Cook and stir constantly over low heat until candy thermometer reads 160° or steam rises from pan (do not boil). Stir in gelatin until dissolved; add extracts.

Cool for 10 minutes. Whisk in sour cream. Pour into eight dessert glasses or small bowls; chill at least 1 hour. Before serving, combine raspberries and remaining sugar; spoon over each serving. **Yield:** 8 servings.

- **1 cup vinegar**
- **3/4 cup sugar**
- **1/4 cup grated onion**
- **1-1/2 teaspoons salt**
- **1-1/2 teaspoons ground mustard**
- **1-1/2 teaspoons paprika**
- **1 bottle (12 ounces) chili sauce**
- **1 cup vegetable oil**

In a bowl or jar with tight-fitting lid, mix vinegar, sugar and onion. Combine salt, mustard, paprika and 2 tablespoons chili sauce to form a paste.

Add remaining chili sauce and mix well. Pour into vinegar mixture; add oil and mix or shake well. Store in the refrigerator. **Yield:** 3-1/2 cups.

Thermometer Testing

It is recommended to test your candy thermometer before each use by bringing water to a boil; the thermometer should read 212°. Adjust your recipe temperature up or down based on your test.

A Memorable Christmas Meal

By Becky Brunette, Minneapolis, Minnesota

I treasure the memory of growing up with a home-cooked meal every evening and enjoying Mom's extravagant feasts for the holidays.

My mom, Julie Brunette (left), from Green Bay, Wisconsin, is well known as both a wonderful cook and baker. Her talent has long been appreciated by more than just my dad, my brother, Nick, and me. She is a super hostess and shares dishes for many gatherings.

Mom often used to make a little extra for supper, just in case our friends happened to stop by. It's no surprise that they did so frequently, enjoying the good food and company. Mom always made them feel welcome. When I went away to college, her cooking was one of the things I missed the most.

Our Christmas dinners have always been a collection of our family's favorite recipes, including Rice-Stuffed Cornish Hens.

The golden hens are stuffed with a flavorful dressing made from scratch with wild rice, long grain rice, savory pork sausage, onions and celery, just like Mom learned it from her own mother. The Cornish hens are topped with a delicious and pretty apricot glaze.

Green beans are one of the most-requested veggies in our family, and Mom's recipe for Crunchy Green Beans makes them taste even better.

Christmas Wreath Salad is a festive and colorful gelatin side dish that looks as good as it tastes. The deep red color is so pretty sitting on a blanket of fresh lettuce leaves.

To this day, all of us still make sure to save room for dessert when Mom is baking her yummy Pistachio Cake.

Since I live a distance away now, I can't just pop in for one of Mom's dinners. Recipes like these are truly a taste of home for me. Mom and I hope you enjoy them, too.

Rice-Stuffed Cornish Hens, Crunchy Green Beans, Christmas Wreath Salad and Pistachio Cake (recipes are on pp. 32-33).

Rice-Stuffed Cornish Hens

My mom prepares this impressive-looking entree for the holidays and for other "company's coming" occasions. The savory rice stuffing goes wonderfully with the moist golden hens and sweet apricot glaze. She is often asked for the recipe.

5-1/2   cups water, *divided*
  2   teaspoons chicken bouillon granules
1-1/2   teaspoons salt
  3/4   cup uncooked wild rice
1-1/2   cups uncooked long grain rice
  1   pound bulk pork sausage
1-1/2   cups chopped celery
  3/4   cup chopped onion
  6   Cornish game hens (20 ounces *each*)
  1   jar (12 ounces) apricot preserves

In a large saucepan, bring 5 cups water, bouillon and salt to a boil. Add wild rice. Reduce heat; cover and simmer for 20 minutes. Add long grain rice; cover and simmer 25-30 minutes longer or until rice is tender and water is absorbed.

Meanwhile, in a large skillet, cook the sausage, celery and onion over medium heat until meat is no longer pink and vegetables are tender; drain. Stir in rice mixture. Spoon about 3/4 cup stuffing into each hen. Place remaining stuffing in a greased 2-qt. baking dish; cover and set aside. Place hens breast side up on a rack in a shallow baking pan; tie drumsticks together. Bake, uncovered, at 350° for 45 minutes.

In a small saucepan, bring preserves and remaining water to a boil. Pour over hens. Bake 35-40 minutes longer, basting occasionally, until a meat thermometer reads 180° for hens and 160° for stuffing. Place baking dish of stuffing in the oven for the last 35-40 minutes of hens' baking time. **Yield:** 6 servings.

Crunchy Green Beans

Green beans taste terrific all by themselves, but my mom has managed to improve on Mother Nature! She adds mushrooms, celery and crisp slivered almonds to dress up the popular green vegetable.

  4   cups fresh *or* frozen green beans, cut into 2-inch pieces
1-1/2   cups diced celery
1-1/3   cups sliced fresh mushrooms
  3   tablespoons vegetable oil
  1   tablespoon cornstarch
  1   cup cold water
  1   tablespoon soy sauce
  1   teaspoon beef bouillon granules
  1/2   cup slivered almonds

Place the beans in a large saucepan and cover with water. Bring to a boil; cook, uncovered, for 8-10 minutes or until crisp-tender.

Meanwhile, in a skillet, saute celery and mushrooms in oil until tender. Combine the cornstarch, cold water and soy sauce until smooth; stir into celery mixture. Stir in bouillon. Bring to a boil over medium heat; cook and stir for 1 minute or until thickened. Drain beans and add to the celery mixture. Stir in almonds. **Yield:** 6 servings.

Christmas Wreath Salad

It's a jolly holiday when Mom makes this cool eye-catching salad. Pecans, pineapple and maraschino cherries are sweet surprises in every serving of this pretty side dish.

- 1 **package (6 ounces) strawberry gelatin**
- 1 **cup boiling water**
- 1 **can (20 ounces) crushed pineapple**
- 1 **cup (8 ounces) plain yogurt**
- 1 **cup chopped pecans, optional**
- 1/2 **cup red maraschino cherries, halved**

Lettuce leaves and additional cherries, optional

In a bowl, dissolve gelatin in boiling water. Refrigerate until partially set, about 30 minutes. Drain pineapple, reserving juice; set pineapple aside. Add enough cold water to juice to measure 1-3/4 cups; stir into gelatin mixture. Whisk in yogurt until smooth. Fold in nuts if desired, plus cherries and reserved pineapple.

Pour into a 2-qt. ring mold that has been coated with nonstick cooking spray. Refrigerate until set. Unmold onto a lettuce-lined serving plate and garnish with additional cherries if desired. **Yield:** 6 servings.

Pistachio Cake

Mom is well-known for her holiday cookies, candies and cakes. This delicious dessert starts conveniently with a cake mix and instant pudding. You're sure to get requests for second helpings when you serve it.

- 1 **package (18-1/4 ounces) white cake mix**
- 1 **package (3.4 ounces) instant pistachio pudding mix**
- 1 **cup lemon-lime soda**
- 1 **cup vegetable oil**
- 3 **eggs**
- 1 **cup chopped walnuts**

FROSTING:
- 1-1/2 **cups cold milk**
- 1 **package (3.4 ounces) instant pistachio pudding mix**
- 1 **carton (8 ounces) frozen whipped topping, thawed**
- 1/2 **cup chopped pistachios, toasted**

Whole red shell pistachios and fresh mint, optional

In a mixing bowl, combine the first five ingredients. Beat on medium speed for 2 minutes; stir in walnuts. Pour into a greased 13-in. x 9-in. x 2-in. baking pan. Bake at 350° for 45-50 minutes or until a toothpick inserted near the center comes out clean. Cool on a wire rack.

For frosting, in a mixing bowl, beat milk and pudding mix on low speed for 2 minutes. Fold in the whipped topping. Spread over cake. Sprinkle with pistachios. Refrigerate for about 30 minutes before cutting. Garnish with whole pistachios and mint if desired. Refrigerate leftovers. **Yield:** 12-15 servings.

Savory Stew Is Always a Hit

By Anne Heinonen, Howell, Michigan

My 10 brothers and sisters and I grew up with cold Minnesota winters. One of my fondest memories is coming in from the frigid walk from the school bus stop to the comforting aroma of my mother's hearty cooking.

Mom, Lorraine Torola (above left), is known for her Old-Fashioned Beef Stew, which she made often to warm us up. She never uses a recipe, but after numerous requests from my seven sisters and me, she finally wrote one down. I still think it tastes best served at *her* table.

To go with the stew, Dad pitched in and made the flavorful Flat Bread. It was an easy job for his big, strong hands.

Mom's Glass Bowl Salad moved quickly around the table. We loved the tasty combination of creamy and crunchy ingredients.

Her delectable Ice Cream Sundae Dessert is still one of my favorites. It makes me think of special occasions since that's when Mom always served it.

Now I make this meal for my husband and our 12 children. Mom and I hope you enjoy it, too!

Old-Fashioned Beef Stew, Glass Bowl Salad, Dad's Flat Bread and Ice Cream Sundae Dessert (recipes are on pp. 36-37).

Glass Bowl Salad

Crisp refreshing ingredients topped with a creamy dressing and crumbled bacon assured there'd be no leftovers when this salad bowl made its way around the table.

- 1   medium head iceberg lettuce, shredded
- 1/2 cup chopped celery
- 1   cup shredded carrots
- 1   package (10 ounces) frozen peas, thawed
- 5   green onions, sliced
- 1   medium green pepper, chopped
- 1   cup mayonnaise
- 2/3 cup sour cream
- 6   bacon strips, cooked and crumbled

In a 3-qt. clear glass serving bowl, layer the first six ingredients in order given. Combine mayonnaise and sour cream until smooth; spread evenly over salad. Cover and chill overnight. Sprinkle with bacon just before serving. **Yield:** 8-10 servings.

＊　＊　＊

Dad's Flat Bread

While Mom was busy with the rest of the meal, Dad helped by making this flat bread. There's no mistaking that this flavorful bread is homemade. It has a wonderful texture and lovely golden color.

 Uses less fat, sugar or salt. Includes Nutritional Analysis and Diabetic Exchanges.

- 1   package (1/4 ounce) active dry yeast
- 2   cups warm water (110° to 115°), *divided*
- 1/3 cup sugar
- 2   tablespoons vegetable oil

Old-Fashioned Beef Stew

This hearty beef stew has a garden full of flavor with vegetables like cabbage and carrots. Mom knew this main dish is one that would suit us 11 kids. When all of us were home, she'd throw in extra vegetables to stretch it.

- 1   boneless chuck roast (2 pounds), cut into 1/2-inch cubes
- 1   tablespoon vegetable oil
- 1   large onion, chopped
- 5   cups water
- 1   teaspoon seasoned salt
- 1/2 teaspoon pepper
- 2   to 3 teaspoons salt
- 5   to 6 medium potatoes, peeled and cut into 1/2-inch cubes
- 5   medium carrots, cut into 1/4-inch slices
- 1   medium rutabaga, peeled and cut into 1/2-inch cubes
- 1   cup sliced celery (1/2-inch pieces)
- 1/2 medium head cabbage, finely sliced
- 1/4 cup all-purpose flour
- 3/4 cup cold water
- 2   teaspoons browning sauce

In a Dutch oven over medium-high heat, brown meat in oil. Add onion, water, seasoned salt, pepper and salt; bring to a boil. Reduce heat; cover and simmer for 2 hours. Add vegetables; cover and simmer for 30 minutes or until meat and vegetables are tender.

Combine flour, cold water and browning sauce. Stir into stew; bring to a boil, stirring constantly. Boil for 1 minute. **Yield:** 8 servings.

Ice Cream Sundae Dessert

We kids couldn't wait to dig into this tempting ice cream dessert. It's cool and smooth, with a ribbon of fudge inside. Whenever I make it for my family, I think of Mom.

 2 cups (12 ounces) semisweet chocolate chips
 1 can (12 ounces) evaporated milk
 1/2 teaspoon salt
 1 package (12 ounces) vanilla wafers, crushed
 1/2 cup butter, melted
 2 quarts vanilla ice cream *or* flavor of your choice, softened

In a saucepan over medium heat, melt chocolate chips with milk and salt; cook and stir until thickened, about 25 minutes. Remove from the heat; set aside. Combine the wafer crumbs and butter; set aside 1 cup.

Press remaining crumbs into a greased 13-in. x 9-in. x 2-in. pan. Chill 10-15 minutes. Pour chocolate over crumbs. Cover and freeze for 20-25 minutes or until firm. Spread ice cream over chocolate. Sprinkle with reserved crumbs. Freeze at least 2 hours before serving. **Yield:** 12-16 servings.

 1 tablespoon salt
 1/2 cup rye *or* whole wheat flour
 5-1/2 to 6 cups all-purpose flour

In a large mixing bowl, dissolve yeast in 1/2 cup water. Add sugar, oil, salt, rye or whole wheat flour, 3 cups all-purpose flour and remaining water; beat until smooth. Add enough remaining flour to form a soft dough. Turn onto a floured surface; knead until smooth and elastic, about 6-8 minutes.

Place in a greased bowl, turning once to grease top. Cover and let rise in a warm place until doubled, about 1 hour. Punch dough down. Divide in half.

On a greased baking sheet, flatten each half to 1-in. thickness. Pierce each loaf several times with a fork. Cover and let rise in a warm place until nearly doubled, about 30 minutes. Bake at 375° for 25-30 minutes or until golden brown. **Yield:** 2 loaves (32 slices).

Nutritional Analysis: One slice equals 116 calories, 220 mg sodium, 0 cholesterol, 23 g carbohydrate, 3 g protein, 1 g fat. **Diabetic Exchange:** 1-1/2 starch.

Garnish with Flair

Try grating a chocolate candy bar over the top of Ice Cream Sundae Dessert. It's a quick and easy way to decorate. Plus, it's pretty and tasty, too.

Sunday Supper Sure to Satisfy

By Sandra Melnychenko, Grandview, Manitoba

My mom has a reputation among our family and friends for being an excellent cook and baker. It comes as naturally to her as it did to my grandma.

Looking back, I'm sure cooking for four children wasn't easy, but my mother, Peggy Chapman (above left), always had something delicious for us to eat. I give her lots of credit now that I have to plan tasty menus and prepare appealing recipes for my own husband and four children. Sometimes it can be a real challenge!

All the years I lived at home, we'd look forward to having company for Sunday supper. It was my job to set the table with our best china. Mom felt it was important for everything to be just right. She believed in treating guests like royalty.

One dish Mom often served was Roasted Chicken and Potatoes with dressing. I can still recall the wonderful aroma of this dish as it cooked. We couldn't wait for Mom to announce that dinner was ready.

Along with the chicken, Mom would make comforting Cheesy Turnips and Carrots. I'm convinced it's the best way to eat these vegetables. Our company must have felt the same way, because the serving bowl was usually empty at the end of the meal! It was a rare occasion when there were any leftovers.

Mom would round out the meal with her tender Parker House Rolls. I've yet to meet a person who can eat just one.

But the best part, as far as we kids were concerned, was the Old-Fashioned Rice Pudding. Its country-style flavor appeals to everyone.

Why not make a special supper for your family by serving my mom's best meal?

Roasted Chicken and Potatoes, Cheesy Turnips and Carrots, Parker House Rolls and Old-Fashioned Rice Pudding (recipes are on pp. 40-41).

Roasted Chicken and Potatoes

My mom's tender roasted chicken with potatoes and sage dressing is even more wonderful than its aroma while baking. My children now enjoy this main dish as much as I did when I was young.

- 1 cup chopped celery
- 1 medium onion, chopped
- 1/2 cup butter
- 2 tablespoons poultry seasoning
- 1/2 teaspoon rubbed sage
- 8 cups cubed day-old white bread
- 1/2 cup chicken broth
- 1 roasting chicken (5 to 6 pounds)
- 1/2 teaspoon paprika
- 1/4 teaspoon salt

Pinch pepper
- 6 medium baking potatoes, peeled and quartered

In a skillet, saute celery and onion in butter until tender, about 5 minutes. Add poultry seasoning and sage. Place the bread cubes in a large bowl. Stir in celery mixture and chicken broth; mix lightly.

Just before baking, stuff the chicken. Place on a rack in a roasting pan; tie the drumsticks together. Combine paprika, salt and pepper; rub over chicken. Bake, uncovered, at 350° for 1-1/2 hours, basting every 30 minutes.

Place the potatoes around chicken; cover and bake 1-1/2 hours longer or until potatoes are tender and a meat thermometer reads 180°-185°. Thicken pan drippings for gravy if desired. **Yield:** 4-6 servings.

Cheesy Turnips and Carrots

Mild-tasting turnips and carrots are wonderfully enhanced by ginger, onion and a mouth-watering creamy cheese sauce in this super side dish. The serving bowl is always empty at the end of the meal.

- 3 cups diced peeled turnips
- 2 cups sliced carrots
- 1/4 teaspoon ground ginger
- 3/4 cup water
- 1 teaspoon salt, *divided*
- 1/2 cup chopped onion
- 1/2 cup diced celery
- 3 tablespoons butter
- 3 tablespoons all-purpose flour
- 1/4 teaspoon pepper
- 1-1/2 cups milk
- 1 cup (4 ounces) shredded cheddar cheese

In a saucepan, combine the turnips, carrots, ginger, water and 1/2 teaspoon salt. Cover; cook over medium-high heat for 10-15 minutes or until vegetables are tender. Drain and reserve liquid; set vegetables aside.

In a skillet, saute onion and celery in butter until tender; stir in flour, pepper and remaining salt. Add the

milk and reserved vegetable liquid; bring to a boil. Cook and stir until thickened and bubbly. Stir in the cheese until melted; stir in the vegetables and heat through. **Yield:** 4-6 servings.

Parker House Rolls

Mom is especially well-known for the delectable things she bakes, like these moist, golden rolls. When that basket comes around the table, we all automatically take two—one is just never enough.

- 1   package (1/4 ounce) active dry yeast
- 1   teaspoon plus 6 tablespoons sugar, *divided*
- 1   cup warm water (110° to 115°), *divided*
- 1   cup warm milk (110° to 115°)
- 1   tablespoon salt
- 5-1/2   to 6 cups all-purpose flour
- 1   egg
- 2   tablespoons plus 2 teaspoons vegetable oil
- 3   tablespoons butter, melted

In a mixing bowl, dissolve yeast and 1 teaspoon sugar in 1/2 cup water; let stand for 10 minutes. Add milk, salt and the remaining sugar and water. Gradually add 2 cups flour; beat until smooth. Beat in egg and oil. Stir in enough of the remaining flour to make a soft dough.

Turn onto a floured surface; knead until smooth and elastic, about 6-8 minutes. Place in a greased bowl, turning once to grease top. Cover and let rise in a warm place until doubled, about 1 hour. Punch dough down.

Divide in half; roll each half on a floured surface to 1/3- or 1/2-in. thickness. Cut with a floured 2-1/2-in. round cutter. Brush with the melted butter.

Using the dull edge of a table knife, make an off-center crease in each roll. Fold along crease so the large half is on top. Press along folded edge. Place 2-3 in. apart on greased baking sheets. Cover and let rise until doubled, about 30 minutes. Bake at 375° for 15-20 minutes or until golden brown. Remove from pans and cool on wire racks. **Yield:** 2-1/2 dozen.

Old-Fashioned Rice Pudding

This comforting dessert is a wonderful way to end any meal. As a girl, I always waited eagerly for the first heavenly bite. Today, my husband likes to top his with a scoop of vanilla ice cream.

- 3-1/2   cups milk
- 1/2   cup uncooked long grain rice
- 1/3   cup sugar
- 1/2   teaspoon salt
- 1/2   cup raisins
- 1   teaspoon vanilla extract

Ground cinnamon, optional

In a saucepan, combine milk, rice, sugar and salt; bring to a boil over medium heat, stirring constantly. Pour into a greased 1-1/2-qt. baking dish.

Cover and bake at 325° for 45 minutes, stirring every 15 minutes. Add raisins and vanilla; cover and bake for 15 minutes. Sprinkle with cinnamon if desired. Serve warm or chilled. Store in the refrigerator. **Yield:** about 6 servings.

German Fare Warms the Heart

By Karin Cousineau, Burlington, North Carolina

I was just 18 when I married and came to America from Germany so my husband and I could begin our life together.

Since it was my first time away from my family, I was very homesick. One thing I found that helped to ease my longing for home and my mother, Annelies Hupfeld (above), was to cook some of her special Sunday dinners.

My favorite has always been her tender, flavorful Beef Rouladen, fluffy Mom's Potato Dumplings, Spiced Red Cabbage and delicious Apple Date Crisp. This traditional German meal always brings back warm memories of my family.

My parents had to rebuild after World War II. Our family was quite poor, so we grew most of our food in our large garden. Since we had lots of fresh vegetables on hand, Mom made mostly soup.

My father worked out of town during the week. On Sunday, when we were all together, Mom would prepare a truly great meal with meat. My older brother and I couldn't wait—we were so tired of vegetable soup!

My parents still live in Germany. Mom is proud to share these wonderful family recipes.

Beef Rouladen, Mom's Potato Dumplings, Spiced Red Cabbage and Apple Date Crisp (recipes are on pp. 44-45).

Mom's Potato Dumplings

These moist dumplings are an extra-special way to serve potatoes. The bread centers add a comforting touch, and the potato taste really comes through. They go so well with the Beef Rouladen and gravy.

- 5 to 6 medium potatoes
- 5 tablespoons all-purpose flour
- 1 egg, beaten
- 1-1/2 teaspoons salt
- 1/4 teaspoon ground nutmeg
- 2 slices white bread, toasted
- 1/3 cup mashed potato flakes, optional

Melted butter and toasted bread crumbs, optional

Cook potatoes in salted water just until tender; drain. Refrigerate for 2 hours or overnight. Peel and grate potatoes. In a bowl, combine the flour, egg, salt and nutmeg. Add potatoes and mix until a stiff batter is formed, adding additional flour if necessary.

Slice toasted bread into 24 squares, 1/2 in. each; shape 2 tablespoons of the potato mixture around two bread squares, forming a 2-in. ball.

In a large kettle, bring salted water to a boil; add the test dumpling. Reduce heat; cover and simmer for 15-20 minutes or until dumpling is no longer sticky in the center. If test dumpling falls apart during cooking, add the mashed potato flakes to the batter.

Let batter sit for 5 minutes; form the remaining dumplings. Add to boiling water; return to a boil and follow same cooking procedure. Remove dumplings with a slotted spoon to a serving bowl. If desired, drizzle with butter and sprinkle with crumbs. **Yield:** 6-8 servings.

Beef Rouladen

Our family was poor when I was growing up in Germany, so we ate garden vegetables for many weekday meals. When Mother made meat for a Sunday dinner, it was a terrific treat. My favorite is this tender beef dish, which gets great flavor from Dijon mustard.

- 1/4 cup Dijon mustard
- 8 slices top round steak, 1/4 inch thick (about 2 pounds)

Salt and pepper to taste
- 8 bacon strips
- 1 large onion, cut into thin wedges
- 3 tablespoons vegetable oil
- 3 cups beef broth
- 1/3 cup all-purpose flour
- 1/2 cup water

Chopped fresh parsley, optional

Lightly spread mustard on each slice of steak; sprinkle with salt and pepper. Place 1 bacon strip and a few onion wedges on each slice; roll up and secure with wooden picks. Brown in a skillet in oil; drain.

Add broth; bring to a boil. Reduce heat; cover and simmer for 1-1/2 hours or until meat is tender. Remove meat and keep warm. Combine flour and water until smooth; stir into broth. Bring to a boil, stirring constantly until thickened and bubbly. Remove wooden picks from meat and return to gravy; heat through. Sprinkle with parsley if desired. **Yield:** 8 servings.

Apple Date Crisp

My mother loves to make this old-fashioned dessert, and my family and I love to eat it. Each serving is chock-full of apple slices, nuts and chewy dates. When the weather is cold, I love to warm up with this dessert.

8   cups sliced peeled tart apples
2   cups chopped dates
2/3 cup packed brown sugar
1/2 cup all-purpose flour
1   teaspoon ground cinnamon
1/3 cup butter
1   cup chopped nuts
Additional apple slices, optional

Combine the apples and dates in an ungreased 13-in. x 9-in. x 2-in. baking dish. In a small bowl, combine sugar, flour and cinnamon; cut in butter until the mixture becomes crumbly.

Add nuts; sprinkle over apples and dates. Bake at 375° for 35-40 minutes or until the apples are tender. Serve warm. Garnish with apple slices if desired. **Yield:** 6-8 servings.

Spiced Red Cabbage

When it comes to vegetable dishes, this one is at the top of my list. The wonderful sweet-sour aroma and taste remind me of home. Plus, it looks so pretty on the table.

✓ Uses less fat, sugar or salt. Includes Nutritional Analysis and Diabetic Exchanges.

1/2 medium head red cabbage, diced
1   tablespoon vegetable oil
1/2 cup chopped onion
1   medium tart apple, quartered
3   tablespoons tarragon *or* red wine vinegar
1   tablespoon sugar
1   bay leaf
1   teaspoon salt, optional
1/4 teaspoon pepper
1/8 teaspoon ground cloves

Place cabbage in a large kettle of boiling salted water; boil for 1 minute. Drain. Return to kettle; stir in remaining ingredients. Cover and simmer for 1 hour or until cabbage is tender. Remove bay leaf. **Yield:** 6 servings.

Nutritional Analysis: One 1/2-cup serving (prepared without salt) equals 78 calories, 23 mg sodium, 0 cholesterol, 14 g carbohydrate, 2 g protein, 3 g fat.
Diabetic Exchanges: 2 vegetable, 1/2 fat.

Soup Chases Away the Chills

By Cookie Curci-Wright, San Jose, California

When I look back on growing up in my family's house during the 1940s, one room comes most quickly to mind—Mom's kitchen.

Despite its size, this tiny room is where my mother, Sarah Curci (left), spent most of her time. That made it the heart of our home, especially during the cooler winter months.

One of the meals I remember best features Mom's Special Chicken Soup. The aroma of it simmering on the stove gave us a feeling of love that still remains.

Whenever I caught a cold, Mom always reached for this recipe, not the medicine cabinet. This soup was the perfect remedy. Even today, all I have to do is sip a steaming bowl of this soup and my cares melt away. My husband enjoys each spoonful as much as I do.

Mom is also known for her Cheesy Italian Bread. The crispy slices have a nice cheese taste and a heavenly aroma. This bread accompanied many meals while I was growing up.

A pretty side dish is Sweet Red Pepper Salad. Garlic, olive oil and oregano give this salad a bold flavor to match its bright color. It also tastes great on top of toasted bread slices.

A traditional cookie for us and many other Italian families, Memorable Biscotti have a toasty texture and delicate flavor that make them perfect for dunking.

I still fondly recall the mouth-watering food and the warmth and comfort of Mom's cozy kitchen. Hopefully this old-fashioned meal will help you create some memories of your own!

Mom's Special Chicken Soup, Cheesy Italian Bread, Sweet Red Pepper Salad and Memorable Biscotti (recipes are on pp. 48-49).

Mom's Special Chicken Soup

*Nothing is more comforting than this chicken soup.
I am convinced a single bowl can soothe anything from
the common cold to a stressful day. My mother made
it often for our family when I was growing up.
Now I fix it for my husband, Dan, and me.*

✓ Uses less fat, sugar or salt. Includes Nutritional Analysis and
Diabetic Exchanges.

    1   broiler-fryer chicken (3-1/2 to 4 pounds)
    3   quarts water
    1   medium onion, quartered
    4   celery ribs
    2   chicken bouillon cubes
    2   parsley sprigs
    1   garlic clove
2-1/2   teaspoons salt, optional
  1/2   cup thinly sliced carrots
  1/2   cup chopped fresh parsley
    3   cups cooked rice

Place chicken and water in a large kettle or Dutch oven;
bring to a boil. Reduce heat; add onion, celery, bouillon, parsley sprigs, garlic and salt if desired. Cover and
simmer until the chicken is tender, about 1 hour.

Remove chicken; allow to cool. Strain and reserve
broth; discard vegetables. Add carrots to broth and simmer until tender, about 15 minutes. Debone chicken
and cut into cubes. Add chicken and chopped parsley
to the broth; heat through. Ladle into bowls; add rice
to each bowl. **Yield:** 14 servings (3-1/2 quarts).

Nutritional Analysis: One 1-cup serving (prepared
with reduced-sodium bouillon and without salt) equals
184 calories, 41 mg sodium, 44 mg cholesterol, 13 g carbohydrate, 15 g protein, 7 g fat. **Diabetic Exchanges:**
1-1/2 meat, 1 starch.

Cheesy Italian Bread

*This crusty bread is as big a treat today as it was when
Mom made it back when I was growing up. It goes so
well with an Italian meal or alongside a big bowl of soup.*

✓ Uses less fat, sugar or salt. Includes Nutritional Analysis and
Diabetic Exchanges.

    1   package (1/4 ounce) active dry yeast
1-1/4   cups warm water (110° to 115°)
    2   tablespoons sugar
    1   teaspoon salt
    1   teaspoon garlic salt
  1/2   cup grated Romano cheese
    3   to 3-1/2 cups all-purpose flour
Cornmeal

In a mixing bowl, dissolve yeast in water. Add sugar,
salt, garlic salt, cheese and 2 cups of flour; beat until
smooth. Add enough remaining flour to form a soft
dough. Turn onto a floured surface; knead until smooth
and elastic, about 6-8 minutes.

Place in a greased bowl, turning once to grease
top. Cover and let rise in a warm place until doubled,
about 1 hour. Punch dough down; divide in half. Shape
each half into a 14-in. loaf. Place on an ungreased baking sheet that has been sprinkled with cornmeal. Cover
and let rise until doubled, about 45 minutes.

Brush loaves with water. Make three diagonal
slashes about 1/2 in. deep with a very sharp knife in

each loaf. Fill a 13-in. x 9-in. x 2-in. baking pan with 1 in. of hot water and place on the bottom oven rack. Preheat to 400°. Bake loaves for 20-25 minutes. Remove to wire racks. **Yield:** 2 loaves (16 slices each).

Nutritional Analysis: One slice equals 60 calories, 102 mg sodium, 2 mg cholesterol, 11 g carbohydrate, 2 g protein, 1 g fat. **Diabetic Exchange:** 1 starch.

Sweet Red Pepper Salad

The garlic, oregano and olive oil give this salad a true Italian taste that just can't be beat. We've eaten it as a side dish or piled high on garlic toast as an appetizer or snack.

- 6 medium sweet red peppers
- 1/2 cup olive oil
- 1/4 cup chopped fresh parsley
- 2 to 3 garlic cloves, minced
- 1/2 teaspoon dried oregano
- 1/4 teaspoon salt

Lettuce leaves, optional

Place whole peppers on a broiler pan; broil 4 in. from the heat until skins blister, about 2-3 minutes. With tongs, rotate the peppers slightly. Continue broiling and rotating until all sides are blistered and blackened.

Immediately place peppers in a brown paper bag. Close bag and let stand for 15-20 minutes. Peel off the charred skin and discard. Remove the stem and seeds.

Cut peppers into 1/4-in.-wide strips. In a shallow container, combine the oil, parsley, garlic, oregano and salt. Add peppers and toss. Cover and chill for 3-4 hours. Serve on lettuce if desired. **Yield:** 6 servings.

Memorable Biscotti

The enticing aroma of anise filled the kitchen and wafted through the house as Mom baked these traditional cookies when I was a girl. Mom always kept a big glass jar filled so we had a supply of these crisp cookies on hand.

- 1 cup butter, softened
- 1 cup sugar
- 3 eggs
- 1 teaspoon vanilla extract
- 1 teaspoon anise extract
- 3 cups all-purpose flour
- 1 tablespoon baking powder
- 1/2 teaspoon salt
- 1 cup chopped almonds

In a mixing bowl, cream butter and sugar. Beat in the eggs, one at a time. Stir in extracts. Combine flour, baking powder and salt; add to creamed mixture. Stir in almonds.

Line a baking sheet with foil and grease the foil. Divide dough in half. On the foil, form dough into two 11-in. x 3-in. rectangles. Bake at 300° for 35 minutes or until golden brown and firm to the touch. Remove from the oven; increase temperature to 325°. Using the foil, lift the rectangles onto wire racks; cool completely. Place on a cutting board; cut diagonally with a serrated knife into 3/4-in. slices.

Place with cut side down on ungreased baking sheets. Bake for 10 minutes. Turn over; bake 10 minutes longer. Cool completely on wire racks. Store in an airtight container. **Yield:** about 2-1/2 dozen.

Birthday Meal Is Mouth-Watering

By Lisa Andis, Morristown, Indiana

My mother, Sue Wortman (left), always prepared our favorite foods on our birthdays and invited our grandparents to celebrate with us.

On my birthday, I would request her Broiled Pork Chops. These juicy tender chops are made with a tangy barbecue sauce that's more zippy than sweet. Chili powder gives it a nice kick that makes these chops deliciously unique.

A comforting side dish that's perfect with the pork chops is Creamed Beans and Potatoes. I'd help myself to several servings.

Hawaiian Salad makes a cool, crisp addition to this meal. With just a few ingredients, it's simple to make. I love the refreshing tropical flavor.

The best part, of course, is the German Chocolate Birthday Cake. As a girl, I preferred the coconut-pecan frosting—partly because I like coconut and partly because my brother doesn't care for it. That assured he wouldn't be eating much of "my" cake!

Even though Mom helped Dad with the family business, she still found time to cook from scratch. She learned from her mother and encouraged me in the kitchen.

These days, Mom still makes dinner on our birthdays. But now she's cooking for a crowd with Dad, my brother and me and our spouses, all the grandkids and my two grandmothers.

We've agreed to compromise on the cake. Mom frosts half in plain frosting and half with the coconut-pecan. The whole meal tastes just as good today as I remember!

Broiled Pork Chops, Creamed Beans and Potatoes, Hawaiian Salad and German Chocolate Birthday Cake (recipes are on pp. 52-53).

Creamed Beans and Potatoes

This soothing side dish is so much nicer than plain potatoes. Mom relied on hearty, down-home recipes such as this one. Now I make it for my own family.

- 4 medium red potatoes, cut into wedges
- 1 package (10 ounces) frozen beans
- 2 tablespoons butter
- 2 tablespoons all-purpose flour
- 1/2 teaspoon salt
- 1/8 teaspoon pepper
- 1 cup milk

Place the potatoes in a saucepan; cover with water and cook until tender, about 10 minutes. Cook the beans according to package directions.

Meanwhile, melt the butter in a saucepan; stir in flour, salt and pepper until smooth. Gradually add milk. Bring to a boil; boil for 1 minute. Drain potatoes and beans; place in a serving bowl. Add sauce and stir to coat. **Yield:** 6 servings.

Broiled Pork Chops

These zippy, tender chops are one of my mother's specialties. She's been making them for years. I still request this delightful main dish when our family gets together to celebrate birthdays and other occasions.

- 3/4 cup ketchup
- 3/4 cup water
- 2 tablespoons vinegar
- 1 tablespoon Worcestershire sauce
- 2 teaspoons brown sugar
- 1 teaspoon salt
- 1/2 teaspoon paprika
- 1/2 teaspoon chili powder
- 1/8 teaspoon pepper
- 6 pork loin chops (3/4 inch thick)

In a saucepan, combine the first nine ingredients; bring to a boil. Reduce heat; simmer for 5 minutes, stirring occasionally. Set aside half of the sauce.

Place the pork chops on broiling pan rack. Broil about 4 in. from the heat for 4 minutes on each side. Brush with remaining sauce. Continue broiling, turning and basting occasionally, for 3-4 minutes or until juices run clear. Serve with reserved sauce. **Yield:** 6 servings.

Hawaiian Salad

To add a refreshing spark to any meal, try this tempting salad with tropical flair. A few simple ingredients are easily combined for a memorable salad. We always empty the bowl.

- 1 can (8 ounces) pineapple tidbits
- 6 to 8 cups torn salad greens
- 1 cup (4 ounces) shredded cheddar cheese
- 1/2 cup mayonnaise
- 1 tablespoon sugar

Drain pineapple, reserving 1 tablespoon juice. In a large bowl, combine greens, pineapple and cheese. In a small bowl, combine the mayonnaise, sugar and reserved pineapple juice; mix well. Pour over salad; toss to coat. Serve immediately. **Yield:** 6 servings.

German Chocolate Birthday Cake

This moist, flavorful cake was the traditional birthday cake at our house when I was growing up. Everyone requested it. I especially like it topped with sweet coconut-pecan frosting.

    1 package (4 ounces) German sweet
       chocolate
  1/2 cup water
    1 cup butter, softened
    2 cups sugar
    4 eggs, *separated*
    1 teaspoon vanilla extract
2-1/2 cups cake flour
    1 teaspoon baking soda
  1/2 teaspoon salt
    1 cup buttermilk

Reusable Wrappers

Save the paper wrapping from sticks of butter or margarine and store them in the freezer. When a recipe calls for a greased pan, rub the pan with one of the wrappings.

COCONUT-PECAN FROSTING:
    1 cup evaporated milk
    1 cup sugar
    3 egg yolks, lightly beaten
  1/2 cup butter
    1 teaspoon vanilla extract
1-1/3 cups flaked coconut
    1 cup chopped pecans

In a saucepan over low heat, stir chocolate and water until chocolate is melted. Cool. In a mixing bowl, cream butter and sugar. Add egg yolks, one at a time, beating well after each addition. Add chocolate mixture and vanilla; mix well.

Combine flour, baking soda and salt; add alternately with buttermilk to creamed mixture. In another mixing bowl, beat egg whites until stiff peaks form; fold into batter.

Line a greased 13-in. x 9-in. x 2-in. baking pan with waxed paper. Grease and flour the paper. Spread batter evenly in pan. Bake at 350° for 50-55 minutes or until a toothpick inserted near the center comes out clean. Cool in pan for 10 minutes; invert onto a wire rack to cool completely. Remove waxed paper.

For frosting, combine milk, sugar, egg yolks, butter and vanilla in a saucepan; cook and stir over medium heat until thickened. Remove from the heat; stir in coconut and pecans. Beat until frosting is cool and reaches desired spreading consistency. Place cake on a serving platter; spread frosting over the top and sides. **Yield:** 12-15 servings.

Old-Fashioned Family Fare

By Gloria Grant, Sterling, Illinois

Even in her 80s, my mother, Berneda Grant (left) of Pekin, Illinois, works wonders in the kitchen! When we kids were growing up, she always made delicious, hearty meals with many special touches.

For example, Mom freezes sweet corn in the summer so we can enjoy that fresh taste at the holidays. She also makes pickles to round out many of her menus.

My two sisters, brother and I unanimously agree that our mom's Chuck Roast with Homemade Noodles is still our all-time favorite. Even her five grandchildren request this memorable main dish to celebrate their birthdays.

Simmered in beef broth, the noodles taste wonderfully old-fashioned. Sometimes she has to triple or quadruple the noodles to satisfy all of us.

My mom loves to cook and share recipes. She picked up the one for Carrot Casserole from a dear friend. It's a comforting and colorful side dish.

And Molded Strawberry Salad is a tasty recipe Mom makes year-round with berries she picks and freezes. For years, Mom has included this salad in meals she prepares for our family.

We typically like ice cream for dessert, but Mom often whips up Surprise Meringues (pictured on page 57). She knows these sweet light cookies are a fitting finale to a big meal.

Some of us kids live close to Mom and Dad, and some are far away. So, going home for one of Mom's meals means a lot and sustains us when we're apart. We're pleased to honor Mom by sharing this meal. We know your family will enjoy it, too.

Chuck Roast with Homemade Noodles, Mom's Carrot Casserole and Molded Strawberry Salad (recipes are on pp. 56-57).

Chuck Roast with Homemade Noodles

The whole family loves Mom's tender beef and hearty noodles. Mom has to make a huge batch since even the grandchildren gobble them up.

- 1 boneless chuck roast (3 to 4 pounds)
- 1/2 cup chopped onion
- 2 tablespoons vegetable oil
- 2-1/2 cups water, *divided*
- 1 cup all-purpose flour
- 1/2 teaspoon salt
- 1 egg
- 2 tablespoons milk
- 1 can (14 ounces) beef broth

Pepper to taste

In a Dutch oven, brown roast and onion in oil. Add 1/2 cup of water. Cover and bake at 325° for 2-1/2 to 3 hours or until the meat is tender. Meanwhile, for noodles, combine flour and salt in a bowl; make a well in the center. Beat egg and milk; pour into well. Stir to form a stiff dough. Turn onto a well-floured surface; roll into a 15-in. x 12-in. rectangle. Cut into 1/8-in. strips. Cover and refrigerate until ready to cook.

Remove roast and keep warm; add broth and remaining water to pan. Bring to a boil; add noodles. Cook for 8-10 minutes or until tender. Drain; season with pepper. Serve with the roast. **Yield:** 8 servings.

Editor's Note: Uncooked noodles may be stored in the refrigerator for 2-3 days or frozen for up to 1 month.

Mom's Carrot Casserole

Rich and cheesy, this casserole is the very best way to eat carrots. Pretty orange slices peek out from under a topping of buttery cracker crumbs.

- 2 pounds carrots, sliced
- 1/2 cup butter, *divided*
- 6 ounces process cheese (Velveeta), cubed
- 1/4 teaspoon dill weed
- 1/2 cup crushed saltines (about 15 crackers)

Place carrots in a saucepan and cover with water; bring to a boil. Reduce heat; cover and simmer until tender, about 10 minutes. Drain and place in a greased 1-1/2-qt. baking dish.

In a small saucepan, melt 1/4 cup butter and cheese, stirring often. Stir in dill. Pour over the carrots. Melt remaining butter; toss with saltines. Sprinkle over carrots. Bake, uncovered, at 350° for 25-30 minutes or until lightly browned and bubbly. **Yield:** 8 servings.

Molded Strawberry Salad

This refreshing salad has two layers—a pretty pink bottom that includes sour cream and a ruby red top with strawberries and pineapple.

1 package (6 ounces) strawberry gelatin
1-1/2 cups boiling water
1 package (10 ounces) frozen sweetened strawberries, thawed
1 can (8-1/4 ounces) crushed pineapple, undrained
1 cup (8 ounces) sour cream
Leaf lettuce and fresh strawberries, optional

In a bowl, dissolve gelatin in water. Add strawberries and pineapple. Strain, reserving liquid and fruit. Set aside 1 cup of the liquid at room temperature. Pour fruit and remaining liquid into a 5-cup mold or 9-in. square pan that has been coated with nonstick cooking spray. Cover and refrigerate until set, about 1 hour.

Whisk sour cream and reserved liquid; pour over top. Cover and refrigerate until set. Cut into squares and place on individual plates or unmold onto a serving platter. Garnish with lettuce and strawberries if desired. **Yield:** 8 servings.

✳ ✳ ✳

Surprise Meringues

These crisp, delicate cookies are light as a feather. Mini chocolate chips and chopped nuts are a delightful and yummy surprise in every bite.

3 egg whites
1/8 teaspoon cream of tartar
3/4 cup sugar

1/8 teaspoon salt
1 teaspoon vanilla extract
1 cup (6 ounces) miniature semisweet chocolate chips
1/4 cup chopped pecans *or* walnuts

In a mixing bowl, beat egg whites and cream of tartar until soft peaks form. Gradually add sugar, salt and vanilla, beating until stiff peaks form and sugar is dissolved, about 5-8 minutes.

Fold in the chocolate chips and nuts. Drop by rounded teaspoonfuls onto greased baking sheets.

Bake at 300° for 30 minutes or until lightly browned. Cool on baking sheets. Store in an airtight container. **Yield:** 4 dozen.

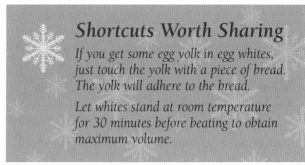

Shortcuts Worth Sharing

If you get some egg yolk in egg whites, just touch the yolk with a piece of bread. The yolk will adhere to the bread.

Let whites stand at room temperature for 30 minutes before beating to obtain maximum volume.

Tried-and-True Christmas Menu

By Chere Bell, Colorado Springs, Colorado

When I was growing up, my great-grandma, Bertha Morgan, was like a mother to me. My mom was ill, so I was raised for many years by both Grandma and Great-Grandma.

Grandma worked outside the home, so I spent a lot of time with Great-Grandma, who took care of the house and did most of the cooking.

Whenever anyone visited, she'd say, "Sit down—you look hungry." Then she'd get busy fixing them something to eat.

For the holidays, Great-Grandma cooked up a storm. At Christmas, the house smelled heavenly. She was raised on a farm and cooked everything from scratch—I don't remember ever seeing her use a written recipe.

Over the years, I've re-created those memorable Christmas dinners based on what I learned working in the kitchen with my grandmas.

Cranberry-Stuffed Chicken is a mouth-watering main dish. The tart cranberries make the stuffing extra-special. Everyone relishes the moist meat and tempting stuffing.

For wonderful old-fashioned flavor, we enjoy Wilted Curly Endive. Vinegar and bacon make it a savory warm salad.

Christmas Rice has a wonderful flavor. And it looks festive with red and green pepper mixed in. It's the perfect light side dish for the big holiday meal.

To top off this delicious dinner, we have Honey Baked Apples. They're sweet and tender—a real treat topped with ice cream. The wonderful aroma as they bake beckons people to the kitchen.

I always think of Great-Grandma when I fix this meal for my husband, our four children and their families during the holidays.

Cranberry-Stuffed Chicken, Wilted Curly Endive, Christmas Rice and Honey Baked Apples (recipes are on pp. 60-61).

sprinkle over inside and outside of chicken. Loosely stuff with cranberry mixture. Melt remaining butter; brush over chicken. Bake, uncovered, at 350° for 2-1/2 to 3 hours or until juices run clear and a meat thermometer reads 180° for the chicken and 165° for the stuffing, basting occasionally. **Yield:** 6-8 servings.

Editor's Note: Stuffing may be baked separately in a greased 1-1/2-qt. baking dish. Cover and bake at 350° for 40 minutes.

✳ ✳ ✳

Wilted Curly Endive

This warm salad is a deliciously different way to serve lettuce. Unlike other wilted versions, this one is not sweet. Vinegar and bacon give it old-fashioned, savory goodness.

- 12   bacon strips, diced
- 3   medium bunches curly endive
- 4   quarts water
- 2-1/4   teaspoons salt, *divided*
- 2 to 3   tablespoons cider vinegar
- 3   tablespoons finely chopped onion
- 1/4   teaspoon pepper

Cook the bacon until crisp; remove with a slotted spoon to paper towels to drain. Reserve 3 tablespoons drippings. Cut or tear endive from center stalk; discard the stalks.

In a large saucepan or Dutch oven, bring water and 1-1/2 teaspoons salt to a boil. Add endive; cover and cook for 3 minutes. Drain. Stir in bacon, reserved

Cranberry-Stuffed Chicken

For the holidays or any Sunday dinner, I suggest this delightful main dish. My great-grandma used to roast this chicken for our family, and now I do the same for our nine grandchildren.

- 1   cup chopped celery
- 1   cup chopped onion
- 2/3   cup dried cranberries
- 1/2   cup plus 2 tablespoons butter, *divided*
- 1   garlic clove, minced
- 3   cups herb-seasoned stuffing croutons
- 1   cup corn bread stuffing *or* crumbled corn bread
- 1-1/2 to 2   cups chicken broth
- 1   roasting chicken (5 to 7 pounds)
- 1/2   teaspoon salt
- 1/2   teaspoon pepper
- 1/4   teaspoon poultry seasoning
- 1/4   teaspoon rubbed sage

In a skillet, saute celery, onion and cranberries in 1/2 cup of butter until tender. Stir in garlic, stuffing and enough broth to moisten; set aside. Place chicken with breast side up on a rack in a roasting pan.

Combine salt, pepper, poultry seasoning and sage;

drippings, vinegar, onion, pepper and remaining salt; mix well. Serve immediately. **Yield:** 6 servings.

Christmas Rice

My family has enjoyed this delicious rice dish for many years. With chopped red and green peppers, it's both fresh-tasting and festive-looking.

✓ Uses less fat, sugar or salt. Includes Nutritional Analysis and Diabetic Exchanges.

1/2	cup finely chopped onion
3	celery ribs, finely chopped
1/2	medium sweet red pepper, chopped
1/2	medium green pepper, chopped
1	tablespoon butter
2	cups chicken broth
2	cups uncooked instant rice
1/2	teaspoon salt, optional
1/4	teaspoon pepper

In a skillet, saute onion, celery and peppers in butter over medium heat for 2 minutes or until crisp-tender. Remove from the heat; set aside.

Stuffing Stretcher

Turn leftover stuffing into a succulent new side dish. To 1-1/2 cups stuffing, add 2 eggs, 1/4 cup milk and 1/2 cup flour to form a dough. Divide dough and shape into patties, then fry in a small amount of oil. They're delicious!

In a saucepan, bring broth to a full boil. Remove from the heat. Quickly stir in rice, celery mixture, salt if desired and pepper. Cover and let stand for 6-7 minutes. Stir before serving. **Yield:** 6 servings.

Nutritional Analysis: One 1/2-cup serving (prepared with margarine and reduced-sodium broth and without salt) equals 152 calories, 44 mg sodium, trace cholesterol, 30 g carbohydrate, 3 g protein, 2 g fat. **Diabetic Exchanges:** 1-1/2 starch, 1 vegetable, 1/2 fat.

Honey Baked Apples

These tender apples smell so good while they're in the oven—and taste even better. We enjoy the golden raisins inside and the soothing taste of honey. They're a yummy change from the cinnamon and sugar seasoning traditionally used with apples.

2-1/4	cups water
3/4	cup packed brown sugar
3	tablespoons honey
6	large tart apples
1	cup golden raisins
Vanilla ice cream, optional	

In a saucepan, bring water, brown sugar and honey to a boil. Remove from the heat. Core apples and peel the top third of each. Place in an ungreased 9-in. baking dish. Fill apples with raisins; sprinkle any remaining raisins into pan. Pour sugar syrup over apples.

Bake, uncovered, at 350° for 1 hour or until tender, basting occasionally. Serve with ice cream if desired. **Yield:** 6 servings.

Southern-Style Sunday Dinner

By Sandra Pichon, Slidell, Louisiana

When my brother and I were growing up, my mother, Maxine Haynes (left), and my father both loved to cook. Even though there were only four of us, they cooked like they were feeding an army.

We regularly enjoyed full-course meals with lots of vegetables, homemade biscuits, bread or corn bread and dessert. Even breakfast was not a simple meal. It commonly consisted of pork chops, milk gravy, sliced tomatoes, biscuits and eggs!

Over the years, Mom and Dad owned and operated three restaurants. One meal was on the menu every time since it's Mom's favorite: Sunday Pork Roast, Mom's Sweet Potato Bake, Country Turnip Greens and Dixie Pie.

Flavorful Sunday Pork Roast was often Sunday dinner at our house. Mom made it countless times for our family and guests, not to mention all of those restaurant customers. I think the pork drippings make the absolute best gravy.

Even our small family could polish off a pan of Mom's Sweet Potato Bake. It's so rich and creamy, you'd almost think it was a dessert!

Country Turnip Greens are a Southern staple that round out any meal.

The recipe for Dixie Pie actually came from my brother, who is also a good cook. Mom quickly adopted it as one of her signature desserts. When she baked this old-fashioned sugar pie, family members would clamor for second servings.

After I married and moved away, I often called Mom long-distance for step-by-step instructions on the delicious foods I enjoyed while growing up.

Now Mom lives with me and my husband, Stanley. Together we continue her long tradition of preparing good, down-home food.

Sunday Pork Roast, Mom's Sweet Potato Bake, Country Turnip Greens and Dixie Pie (recipes are on pp. 64-65).

Sunday Pork Roast

Mom has prepared this delectable main dish numerous times over the years for our family, friends and customers at the restaurants she and Dad owned. Using a simple herb rub and roasting with vegetables give this lovely golden roast remarkable flavor.

- 4 tablespoons all-purpose flour, *divided*
- 1 teaspoon salt
- 1 teaspoon pepper
- 1 bay leaf, finely crushed
- 1/2 teaspoon dried thyme
- 1 bone-in pork loin roast (4 to 5 pounds)
- 2 medium onions, chopped
- 2 medium carrots, chopped
- 1 celery rib, chopped
- 2-1/3 cups cold water, *divided*
- 1/3 cup packed brown sugar

Combine 2 tablespoons flour, salt, pepper, bay leaf and thyme; rub over entire roast. Place roast with fat side up in a shallow roasting pan. Arrange vegetables around the roast. Pour 2 cups cold water into pan.

Bake, uncovered, at 325° for 1-1/2 hours, basting with pan juices every 30 minutes. Sprinkle with brown sugar. Bake 30 minutes longer or until a meat thermometer reads 160°. Remove roast to a serving platter; keep warm. Strain pan drippings, reserving the broth; discard vegetables.

Add water to the broth to measure 1-2/3 cups. Return to pan. Combine the remaining flour and cold water until smooth; stir into pan. Bring gravy to a boil; cook and stir for 2 minutes. Serve with the roast. **Yield:** 10-12 servings.

Mom's Sweet Potato Bake

Mom loves sweet potatoes and fixed them often in this creamy, comforting casserole. With its nutty topping, it's a yummy treat!

- 3 cups cold mashed sweet potatoes (prepared without milk or butter)
- 1 cup sugar
- 1/2 cup milk
- 1/4 cup butter, softened
- 3 eggs
- 1 teaspoon salt
- 1 teaspoon vanilla extract

TOPPING:
- 1/2 cup packed brown sugar
- 1/2 cup chopped pecans
- 1/4 cup all-purpose flour
- 2 tablespoons cold butter

In a mixing bowl, beat sweet potatoes, sugar, milk, butter, eggs, salt and vanilla until smooth. Transfer to a greased 2-qt. baking dish.

In a small bowl, combine brown sugar, pecans and flour; cut in butter until crumbly. Sprinkle over potato mixture. Bake, uncovered, at 325° for 45-50 minutes or until golden brown. **Yield:** 8-10 servings.

* * *

Country Turnip Greens

This easy recipe results in a delicious dish of cooked greens sure to please any palate. The key is the rich flavors of pork and onion simmered with the fresh greens.

3/4	pound lean salt pork *or* bacon, diced
4-1/2	pounds fresh turnip greens, trimmed
1-1/2	cups water
1	large onion, chopped
1	teaspoon sugar
1/4	to 1/2 teaspoon pepper

In a Dutch oven or soup kettle, fry salt pork just until cooked. Drain, reserving 2 tablespoons of drippings. Stir in the remaining ingredients. Bring to a boil. Reduce heat; cover and simmer for 45 minutes or until greens are tender. **Yield:** 8-10 servings.

Editor's Note: Fresh spinach can be substituted for the turnip greens. Reduce the cooking time to 10 minutes or until spinach is tender.

* * *

Dixie Pie

Everybody in our family loves the combination of cinnamon, coconut, nuts and raisins in this pie. Sometimes Mom would toss in a few chocolate chips for variety. Thanksgiving and Christmas dinner were not complete without this memorable dessert.

Pastry for two single-crust pies (9 inches)

1-1/2	cups raisins
1	cup butter, softened
1	cup sugar
1	cup packed brown sugar
6	eggs
2	teaspoons vanilla extract
2	to 4 teaspoons ground cinnamon
1	cup chopped nuts
1	cup flaked coconut

Whipped topping and additional chopped nuts, optional

Line two 9-in. pie plates with pastry. Trim pastry to 1/2 in. beyond edge of plate; flute edges. Line crusts with a double thickness of heavy-duty foil. Bake at 450° for 10 minutes. Discard foil. Cool on wire racks.

Place raisins in a saucepan and cover with water; bring to a boil. Remove from the heat; set aside. In a mixing bowl, cream butter and sugars. Beat in eggs, vanilla and cinnamon until smooth. Drain raisins. Stir raisins, nuts and coconut into creamed mixture (mixture will appear curdled). Pour into the crusts.

Bake at 350° for 30-35 minutes or until set. Cool on wire racks. Garnish with whipped topping and nuts if desired. **Yield:** 2 pies (6-8 servings each).

Holiday Feast For the Family

By Sandy Jenkins, Elkhorn, Wisconsin

Every Sunday seemed like a holiday when I was growing up because Mom always fixed a feast.

My mom, Ruth Poritz Celia (left) of Pell Lake, Wisconsin, was raised on a dairy farm and regularly helped cook for crowds, whether it was for a family gathering or a gang of threshers.

She was in her element preparing a big meal for my father, sister, three brothers, me and any of our friends who just happened to be hanging around at dinnertime. Those who stayed always walked away from the table happy and full!

Since my parents had a farm, we raised all of our own meat and vegetables. Mom even made homemade bread and butter weekly. Between the fresh ingredients and the care she put into her cooking and baking, everything tasted delicious.

My favorite meal is one that Mom made frequently since it was also one my father requested often. She used recipes handed down from her mother.

Mom's Duck with Cherry Sauce is a mouth-watering main dish. The thick cherry sauce complements the tender duck so nicely.

Alongside, she served Scalloped Corn, a hearty side dish with garden-fresh flavor. There was no need to tell us to eat our vegetables—we did so gladly.

Lime Pear Gelatin added a light fruity touch to the meal. We kids, especially, considered it an ideal salad.

And for a festive finale, Mom prepared her scrumptious Cranberry Raisin Pie. Dotted with plump raisins and rosy red cranberries, this lovely pie is so good topped with a scoop of homemade ice cream.

These days, Mom enjoys cooking for her grandchildren. She continues to satisfy our appetites with wonderful food and nourish our spirits with her love.

Duck with Cherry Sauce, Scalloped Corn, Pear Lime Gelatin and Cranberry Raisin Pie (recipes are on pp. 68-69).

Scalloped Corn

This comforting casserole features sunny corn kernels tucked into a creamy custard. My mom got this recipe, and many other excellent ones, from her mother. By the time this dish got around the table, my father, sister, brothers and I would have almost scraped it clean.

- 4 cups fresh *or* frozen corn
- 3 eggs, beaten
- 1 cup milk
- 1 cup crushed saltines (about 30 crackers), *divided*
- 3 tablespoons butter, melted
- 1 tablespoon sugar
- 1 tablespoon finely chopped onion

Salt and pepper to taste

In a large bowl, combine the corn, eggs, milk, 3/4 cup cracker crumbs, butter, sugar, onion, salt and pepper. Transfer to a greased 1-1/2-qt. baking dish. Sprinkle with remaining cracker crumbs. Bake, uncovered, at 325° for 1 hour or until a knife inserted near the center comes out clean. **Yield:** 6 servings.

Pear Lime Gelatin

This jolly gelatin salad is a light and refreshing treat. My mom knew that fruit served in this form would get gobbled right up. The bowl looked like a sparkling jewel on our holiday dinner table.

✓ Uses less fat, sugar or salt. Includes Nutritional Analysis and Diabetic Exchanges.

- 1 can (29 ounces) pear halves in juice
- 1 package (3 ounces) lime gelatin
- 1 package (3 ounces) cream cheese, cubed
- 1 cup whipped topping

Duck with Cherry Sauce

My mom prepared this golden tender roast duck often for Sunday dinner when I was growing up. It was one of my dad's favorite meals. The cherry sauce stirs up easily and makes this dish doubly delightful.

- 1 domestic duckling (4 to 5 pounds)
- 1 jar (12 ounces) cherry preserves
- 1 to 2 tablespoons red wine vinegar

Bing cherries, star fruit and kale, optional

Prick skin of duckling well and place, breast side up, on a rack in a shallow roasting pan. Tie drumsticks together. Bake, uncovered, at 325° for 2 hours or until juices run clear and a meat thermometer reads 180°. (Drain fat from pan as it accumulates.)

Cover and let stand for 20 minutes before carving. Meanwhile, for sauce, combine preserves and vinegar in a small saucepan. Cook and stir over medium heat until heated through. Serve with duck. Garnish platter with fruit and kale if desired. **Yield:** 4-5 servings.

FILLING:
1-1/2 cups sugar
1/4 cup all-purpose flour
1/2 teaspoon ground cinnamon
1/4 teaspoon salt
1/4 teaspoon ground nutmeg
1 cup orange juice
2-2/3 cups fresh *or* frozen cranberries
1 cup raisins
Milk, optional

In a bowl, combine flour and salt. In another bowl, combine oil and water. Gradually add to flour mixture, stirring with a fork until blended. Shape into a ball; divide dough in half so one ball is slightly larger than the other. Roll out larger ball between two sheets of waxed paper to fit a 9-in. pie plate. Transfer pastry to pie plate; trim pastry even with edge. Set aside.

For filling, combine sugar, flour, cinnamon, salt and nutmeg in a saucepan; gradually stir in orange juice until smooth. Stir in cranberries and raisins; bring to a boil. Reduce heat; cook and stir over medium heat until thickened, about 5 minutes. Pour into crust. Roll out remaining dough between two sheets of waxed paper. Cut slits in pastry or use a 1-1/2-in. holly leaf cutter to make a design. Place over filling. Trim, seal and flute edges. Brush pastry with milk if desired.

Bake at 400° for 35-40 minutes or until golden brown and filling is bubbly. Cool on a wire rack. Refrigerate leftovers. **Yield:** 6-8 servings.

Drain pears, reserving juice; set pears aside. Measure the juice; add water if needed to equal 1-1/2 cups. Pour into a saucepan; bring to a boil. Add gelatin; stir until dissolved. Gradually add cream cheese, whisking until smooth. Cover and refrigerate until cool.

Mash reserved pears; fold into gelatin mixture. Fold in whipped topping. Pour into a 6-cup serving bowl. Refrigerate until set. **Yield:** 6 servings.

Nutritional Analysis: One serving (prepared with sugar-free gelatin and reduced-fat cream cheese and whipped topping) equals 172 calories, 3 g fat (2 g saturated fat), 5 mg cholesterol, 398 mg sodium, 21 g carbohydrate, 2 g fiber, 8 g protein. **Diabetic Exchanges:** 2 fruit, 1 fat.

Cranberry Raisin Pie

Even though it was difficult, we saved room for dessert when my mom made this festive pie.

2 cups all-purpose flour
1 teaspoon salt
1/2 cup vegetable oil
5 tablespoons cold water

Keeping Corn Fresh

Fresh sweet corn is best if used the day you buy it. It can be stored for no more than 1 day in a plastic bag in the refrigerator.

For Meat and Potato Lovers

By Linda Gaido, New Brighton, Pennsylvania

For years, my mother has had a reputation among family and friends for making the very best roast beef. And that honor still stands today.

Mom is one of those people who was born to be a good cook. She rarely measures anything, and everything she makes tastes wonderful.

When my two older sisters and I were growing up, the house smelled simply heavenly on those chilly winter days when Mom's Roast Beef was cooking on the stovetop.

People always ask Mom what her secret ingredients are. And they're surprised to hear that the rich flavor comes from brewed coffee! Hard as I try to follow Mom's recipe step-by-step, I can never make it taste just like hers.

To make Country Green Beans, Mom added garlic, chopped ham and onion. These additions blend so well with the beans and really complement the beef.

Mom's melt-in-your-mouth Oven-Roasted Potatoes round out this meat-and-potatoes meal. They're also convenient because they can share the oven with the Baked Apples Slices.

Mom enjoyed serving this updated version of baked apples over cool, creamy vanilla ice cream. But you could also top individual servings with whipped cream. It's an easy recipe to double when cooking for more people.

Mom and I are happy to pass on the treasured family recipes for this warm, satisfying meal to you and your family.

Why not give these dishes a try when cold weather has you craving hearty, old-fashioned foods?

Mom's Roast Beef, Oven-Roasted Potatoes, Country Green Beans and Baked Apple Slices (recipes are on pp. 72-73).

Mom's Roast Beef

Everyone loves slices of this fork-tender roast beef and its savory gravy. This well-seasoned roast is Mom's specialty. People always ask what her magic ingredients are. Now you know the secret of what makes this our favorite meat dish!

- 1 tablespoon vegetable oil
- 1 eye of round beef roast (about 2-1/2 pounds)
- 1 medium onion, chopped
- 1 cup brewed coffee
- 1 cup water, *divided*
- 1 beef bouillon cube
- 2 teaspoons dried basil
- 1 teaspoon dried rosemary, crushed
- 1 garlic clove, minced
- 1 teaspoon salt
- 1/2 teaspoon pepper
- 1/4 cup all-purpose flour

Heat oil in a Dutch oven; brown roast on all sides. Add onion and cook until transparent. Add coffee, 3/4 cup water, bouillon, basil, rosemary, garlic, salt and pepper.

Cover and simmer for 2-1/2 hours or until meat is tender. Combine flour and the remaining water until

smooth; stir into pan juices. Cook and stir until thickened and bubbly. Remove roast and slice. Serve with the gravy. **Yield:** 8 servings.

Oven-Roasted Potatoes

These golden, melt-in-your-mouth potatoes go perfectly with roast beef. They make a homey side dish that's also convenient because they can share the oven with the baked apple slices Mom serves for dessert.

- 4 baking potatoes (about 2 pounds)
- 2 tablespoons butter, melted
- 2 teaspoons paprika
- 1 teaspoon salt
- 1/2 teaspoon pepper

Peel potatoes and cut into large chunks; place in a shallow 2-qt. baking pan. Pour butter over and toss until well coated. Sprinkle with paprika, salt and pepper.

Bake, uncovered, at 350° for 45-60 minutes or until potatoes are tender. **Yield:** 4 servings.

Country Green Beans

This deliciously different way to dress up green beans is sure to become a family favorite at your house, too. The garlic, chopped ham and onion blend so well with the beans. It's a beautiful and tasty side dish that has real country appeal.

- 1 **pound fresh green beans, trimmed**
- 1/4 **cup chopped onion**
- 1/4 **cup chopped fully cooked ham**
- 1/4 **cup butter**
- 1/4 **cup water**
- 1 **garlic clove, minced**
- 1/2 **teaspoon salt**
- 1/4 **teaspoon pepper**

In a saucepan, combine all ingredients. Cover and simmer for 15-20 minutes or until beans are tender. **Yield:** 4 servings.

Baked Apple Slices

Nothing beats these warm tender apple slices over ice cream for satisfying flavor. This old-fashioned treat gives a new twist to traditional baked apples. They are also excellent served over waffles or with ham. I make sure to save room for dessert when this is the finale!

- 3 **large baking apples, peeled and sliced**
- 3/4 **cup sugar**
- 1 **tablespoon ground cinnamon**

- 1/4 **teaspoon ground nutmeg**
- 1/4 **teaspoon ground ginger**
- 1/4 **cup apple cider**
- 1/2 **cup butter**
- 1/2 **cup walnuts *or* raisins**

Vanilla ice cream

Place the sliced apples in a greased 1-qt. baking dish. Combine sugar, cinnamon, nutmeg, ginger and apple cider; pour over apples. Dot with butter. Sprinkle with nuts or raisins.

Bake, uncovered, at 350° for 45-60 minutes or until the apples are tender. Serve warm over ice cream. **Yield:** 4 servings.

Good Gravy

To avoid lumps in your gravy, whisk the hot liquid rapidly as you gradually add the flour-based paste to the hot liquid.

For a little richer color and flavor, stir in a teaspoon or two of instant coffee powder or unsweetened cocoa powder.

When making a big family dinner, make your gravy as usual and then keep it warm on the low setting in a slow cooker. It's easy to refill the gravy boat with hot gravy throughout the meal.

A special ham dinner highlights a family holiday like Easter. Recipes are on pp. 98-99.

Delicious SPRING MEALS

Late-Afternoon Easter Dinner

By Lorrie Bailey, Pulaski, Iowa

Easter was a memorable day when I was growing up on our family farm. After coming home from church in the morning, my mom, June Mullins (left), would serve the most terrific Easter dinner later in the afternoon.

Mom was always happy to share a warm smile and some good advice along with her wonderful cooking and baking. She especially loved to make bread and rolls and did so almost weekly to the delight of my dad, us four kids, our spouses and her six grandchildren.

For a special main dish on Easter Sunday, Mom fixed Pineapple Mustard Ham. Juicy ham slices get mouth-watering zip from the tangy glaze made with ground mustard, pineapple topping and horseradish.

To simplify the day, Mom rounded out the meal with items she could make ahead, like a creamy potato casserole, the world's best deviled eggs and Colorful Vegetable Salad. That eye-catching combination of carrots, celery, tomatoes, broccoli and cauliflower is crisp and refreshing.

The mainstay of this holiday meal was her Hot Cross Buns. We all looked forward to them since Mom fixed these golden rolls only once a year. She used a recipe passed down from her own mother.

Mom's desserts were always spectacular. One of our favorites was Strawberry Satin Pie, made with the fresh-picked fruit of the season. This pie is as pretty as it is scrumptious.

Preparing delicious recipes like these was one of the many ways Mom showed her love for us on special occasions and every day of the year. We know she'd be thrilled to have you try them out on your family, too!

Pineapple Mustard Ham, Colorful Vegetable Salad, Hot Cross Buns and Strawberry Satin Pie (recipes are on pp. 78-79).

1 medium bunch broccoli, cut into florets (5 cups)
3 large tomatoes, chopped
1 medium onion, chopped
2 celery ribs, chopped
1 medium carrot, shredded

DRESSING:
3/4 cup vegetable oil
3 tablespoons lemon juice
1 teaspoon salt
1/2 teaspoon sugar
1/2 teaspoon pepper

In a large salad bowl, combine the cauliflower, broccoli, tomatoes, onion, celery and shredded carrot. In a jar with a tight-fitting lid, combine the dressing ingredients; shake well. Pour over vegetables and toss to coat. Serve immediately. **Yield:** 16-20 servings.

Hot Cross Buns

These golden buns, with a light seasoning from cinnamon and allspice, were a family Easter tradition. Icing crosses make a tasty topping and reflect the meaning of the holiday.

2 packages (1/4 ounce *each*) active dry yeast
1/4 cup warm water (110° to 115°)
1 cup warm milk (110° to 115°)
1/2 cup sugar
1/4 cup shortening
2 eggs
2 teaspoons salt
1 teaspoon ground cinnamon
1/4 teaspoon ground allspice

Pineapple Mustard Ham

Sweet and spicy ingredients combine in a fruity glaze to top this delightful ham, which was one of my mom's specialties.

1/2 spiral-sliced *or* semi-boneless fully cooked ham (8 to 10 pounds)
1 jar (12 ounces) apple jelly
1 jar (12 ounces) pineapple ice cream topping
1 container (1-3/4 ounces) ground mustard
2 tablespoons prepared horseradish
1 tablespoon pepper

Place ham on a rack in a shallow roasting pan. Cover and bake at 325° for 1-3/4 hours. In a small bowl, combine the remaining ingredients until blended. Pour mixture over the ham. Bake, uncovered, 30-45 minutes longer or until a meat thermometer reads 140°. **Yield:** 16-20 servings.

Colorful Vegetable Salad

Carrots, celery and tomatoes go so well with broccoli and cauliflower in this crisp, refreshing salad with a light vinaigrette dressing. My mom used this popular salad to round out a number of different meals.

1 medium head cauliflower, broken into florets (8 cups)

4-1/2 to 5 cups all-purpose flour
1 cup dried currants
1 egg white, lightly beaten
ICING:
1-3/4 cups confectioners' sugar
1/2 teaspoon vanilla extract
4 to 6 teaspoons milk

In a mixing bowl, dissolve yeast in warm water. Add the milk, sugar, shortening, eggs, salt, cinnamon, allspice and 3 cups flour. Beat until smooth. Stir in currants and enough remaining flour to form a soft dough. Turn onto a floured surface; knead until smooth and elastic, about 6-8 minutes. Place in a greased bowl, turning once to grease top. Cover and let rise in a warm place until doubled, about 1 hour.

Punch dough down. Cover and let rest for 10 minutes. On a lightly floured surface, roll out to 1/2-in. thickness. Cut with a floured 2-1/2-in. biscuit cutter. Place 2 in. apart on lightly greased baking sheets. Cover and let rise until doubled, about 30 minutes.

Brush with egg white. Bake at 350° for 12-15 minutes or until golden brown. Remove from pans to wire racks to cool. For icing, combine confectioners' sugar, vanilla and enough milk to achieve piping consistency. Pipe a cross on top of each bun. **Yield:** 2 dozen.

Strawberry Satin Pie

My mom loved to spoil us with tempting desserts like this ruby-red springtime treat.

1 pastry shell (9 inches), baked
1/2 cup sliced almonds, toasted
1/2 cup sugar
3 tablespoons all-purpose flour
3 tablespoons cornstarch
1/2 teaspoon salt
2 cups milk

1 egg, lightly beaten
1 teaspoon vanilla extract
1/2 cup heavy whipping cream, whipped
GLAZE:
3 cups fresh strawberries
1 cup water
1/3 cup sugar
2 tablespoons cornstarch
12 drops red food coloring, optional

Cover bottom of pie shell with almonds; set aside. In a saucepan, combine the sugar, flour, cornstarch and salt. Stir in milk until smooth. Bring to a boil; cook and stir for 2 minutes or until thickened. Remove from the heat.

Stir a small amount of hot filling into egg. Return all to the pan, stirring constantly. Bring to a gentle boil; cook and stir 2 minutes longer. Remove from the heat. Stir in the vanilla. Cool to room temperature. Whisk in whipped cream until blended. Pour into pie shell. Cover and refrigerate for at least 2 hours.

Crush 1 cup of strawberries; set remaining berries aside. In a saucepan, bring crushed berries and water to a boil; cook, uncovered, for 2 minutes. Strain through cheesecloth; discard fruit and set liquid aside to cool.

In another saucepan, combine sugar and cornstarch; gradually stir in berry liquid until blended. Bring to a boil; cook and stir for 2 minutes or until thickened. Stir in food coloring if desired. Cool for 20 minutes. Slice the reserved strawberries; arrange over chilled filling. Pour glaze evenly over berries. Refrigerate for at least 1 hour before serving. **Yield:** 6-8 servings.

A Timeless Chicken Dinner

By Peter Baumert, Jameson, Missouri

As the youngest of six children, I didn't have a lot of patience. I always rushed through the blessing because I was in a hurry to eat one of Mom's great home-cooked meals.

Afterward, my mother, Mary Lou Baumert, would finally pass the food. It seemed like an eternity. It always smelled so good, and I was so hungry. My brothers and I ate quickly so we'd be sure to get seconds. Of course, there wasn't any real danger. Mom always made plenty, but we weren't willing to take any chances.

Of all Mom's tasty meals, this has always been my favorite: Chicken and Rice Dinner, Carrot Raisin Salad, Homemade Bread and Lemon Bars. It reminds me of spring on our family homestead, 160 acres of fertile farmland in Nebraska. My folks still live there.

When I left home as a bachelor, Mom sent along that chicken recipe, knowing it was my favorite. For years, it was my only recipe card.

It's not a really difficult recipe, but it sure is good. The chicken browns up nicely, and it tastes so good with the fluffy and flavorful rice.

I passed the card along to my wife, Denise, and she's since gotten many more recipes from my mom's fabulous collection. Denise fixes this old-time dinner often for me and our family.

The carrot salad is one of Mom's favorites from many years ago. It hasn't lost its appeal, even after all this time.

I remember Mom's bread always tasted heavenly. You'd know how good it was going to be just by the aroma wafting through the kitchen.

Her Lemon Bars are a wonderful dessert. They're both tart and sweet at the same time. Boy, I could eat a handful of those back then. In fact, I still can today. I guess it's true the more things change, the more they stay the same.

Chicken and Rice Dinner, Carrot Raisin Salad, Homemade Bread and Lemon Bars (recipes are on pp. 82-83).

Chicken and Rice Dinner

My family always lines up for seconds of this hearty main dish when my wife, Denise, makes my mother's recipe. In this easy but tasty entree, the chicken bakes to a beautiful golden brown.

- 1 broiler/fryer chicken (2 to 3 pounds), cut up
- 1/4 to 1/3 cup all-purpose flour
- 2 tablespoons vegetable oil
- 1-1/2 cups uncooked long grain rice
- 1 teaspoon poultry seasoning
- 1 teaspoon salt
- 1/2 teaspoon pepper
- 1 cup milk
- 2-1/3 cups water

Chopped fresh parsley

Dredge the chicken pieces in flour. In a skillet, heat the oil on medium and brown the chicken on all sides. Meanwhile, combine the rice, poultry seasoning, salt, pepper, milk and water.

Pour into a greased 13-in. x 9-in. x 2-in. baking pan. Top with chicken. Cover tightly with foil and bake at 350° for 55 minutes or until the rice and chicken are tender. Sprinkle with parsley before serving. **Yield:** 4-6 servings.

Carrot Raisin Salad

This colorful traditional salad is one of my mother's favorites. It's fun to eat because of its crunchy texture, and the raisins give it a slightly sweet flavor. Plus, it's easy to prepare, which everyone appreciates.

 Uses less fat, sugar or salt. Includes Nutritional Analysis and Diabetic Exchanges.

- 4 cups shredded carrots (about 4 to 5 large)
- 3/4 to 1-1/2 cups raisins
- 1/4 cup mayonnaise
- 2 tablespoons sugar
- 2 to 3 tablespoons milk

Place carrots and raisins in a bowl. In another bowl, mix together mayonnaise, sugar and enough milk to reach a salad dressing consistency. Pour over carrot mixture and toss to coat. **Yield:** 8 servings.

Keeping Raisins

Store raisins in a tightly sealed plastic bag at room temperature for several months. Raisins stored in the refrigerator or freezer will keep up to 1 year.

If raisins clump together, put them in a strainer and spray hot, running water over them. Or pop them in the microwave on high for 15 seconds.

Nutritional Analysis: One serving (prepared with fat-free milk and 1 cup raisins) equals 110 calories, 80 mg sodium, 2 mg cholesterol, 24 g carbohydrate, 1 g protein, 2 g fat. **Diabetic Exchanges:** 1 fruit, 1 vegetable, 1/2 fat.

Homemade Bread

On more than one occasion while I was growing up, I stayed home sick from school, napped on the couch and woke to the aroma of my mother's freshly baked bread. That's enough to make anyone feel better!

2	**packages (1/4 ounce** *each***) active dry yeast**
2	**cups warm water (105° to 115°)**
2/3	**cup nonfat dry milk powder**
2	**tablespoons butter, melted**
2	**tablespoons sugar**
1	**tablespoon salt**
6	**to 7 cups all-purpose flour**

In a large bowl, dissolve yeast in warm water. Stir in milk, butter, sugar, salt and enough flour to form a stiff dough. Turn out onto a floured surface; knead until smooth and elastic, about 10-12 minutes.

Place in a greased bowl, turning once to grease top. Cover and let rise in a warm place until doubled, about 1 hour. Punch down and divide in half. Shape into two loaves and place in greased 8-in. x 4-in. x 2-in. pans. Cover and let rise until doubled, about 1 hour. Bake at 400° for 30 minutes or until golden brown. **Yield:** 2 loaves.

Lemon Bars

When I was a child, memorable family meals were complete once these tangy bars were served. That's still true today for my own family. The bars' sweetness rounds out the meal, but the lemony flavor keeps them light. Don't expect any leftovers!

CRUST:

1	**cup all-purpose flour**
1/3	**cup butter, softened**
1/4	**cup confectioners' sugar**

TOPPING:

1	**cup sugar**
2	**eggs**
2	**tablespoons all-purpose flour**
2	**tablespoons lemon juice**
1/2	**teaspoon lemon extract**
1/2	**teaspoon baking powder**
1/4	**teaspoon salt**

Confectioners' sugar

Combine the crust ingredients and pat into an 8-in. square baking pan. Bake at 375° for 15 minutes. Meanwhile, for the topping, combine the sugar, eggs, flour, lemon juice, extract, baking powder and salt in a mixing bowl. Mix until frothy; pour over crust.

Bake at 375° for 18-22 minutes or until light golden brown. Dust bars with confectioners' sugar. **Yield:** 9 servings.

A Very Special Birthday Dinner

By Deborah Amrine, Grand Haven, Michigan

When we were growing up, Mom let us kids choose our favorite meal on our birthday, and then she'd prepare it for us. Oh, how I'd count the days until it was my turn!

It might seem like it would be a tough decision, because Mom made lots of great meals, but it wasn't. My brother, two sisters and I each had our favorite.

I always picked Breaded Pork Chops, Cheese Potatoes, Chunky Applesauce and Chocolate Mayonnaise Cake. Today, that same meal is a favorite with our three sons. When I make it, I'm reminded of my childhood back in Columbus, Ohio.

We were always underfoot as Mom cooked. Using recipes she'd received from her mother, Mom made down-home food using simple ingredients—with extraordinary results.

The pork chops sizzling in the pan really teased your senses. Not only could you hear them, the aroma wafted through the whole house. It was nearly impossible to wait until dinner!

Mom's Cheese Potatoes, with melted cheddar cheese on top, are pure bliss. I can't think of another potato dish I enjoy as much.

Homemade Chunky Applesauce has so much more flavor than canned bought at the store. This recipe has just the right amount of sweetness and cinnamon.

The Chocolate Mayonnaise Cake was always light and tasty with its deliciously rich brown sugar frosting. Sometimes I could even talk Mom into giving "the birthday girl" an extra little piece.

Even today, whenever my husband, our boys and I visit Mom, I still request this meal. Absolutely nothing compares to Mom's home cooking made with her very own hands—and love.

Breaded Pork Chops, Cheese Potatoes, Chunky Applesauce and Chocolate Mayonnaise Cake (recipes are on pp. 86-87).

Cheese Potatoes

Don't let the basic ingredients fool you—this recipe has anything but ordinary taste. The hearty potatoes have a wonderful cheesy flavor and practically melt in your mouth. They're simple to prepare and impressive to serve.

- 3 **tablespoons butter**
- 6 **large potatoes, peeled and thinly sliced**
- 1 **teaspoon salt**
- 1/4 **teaspoon pepper**
- 1 **cup milk**
- 2 **cups (8 ounces) shredded cheddar cheese**

Chopped fresh parsley

Melt butter in a large nonstick skillet. Cook potatoes until almost tender and lightly browned. Sprinkle with salt and pepper.

Pour milk over potatoes; cook gently until milk is absorbed. Sprinkle with cheese and allow to melt. Stir; sprinkle with parsley and serve immediately. **Yield:** 6 servings.

Chunky Applesauce

There's just something extra special about homemade applesauce. This simple recipe is tart and not too sweet. It makes the perfect side dish, especially with pork chops or a pork roast.

Breaded Pork Chops

These traditional pork chops have a wonderful home-cooked flavor like the ones Mom used to make. The breading makes them crispy outside and tender inside. Why not treat your family to them tonight?

- 1/2 **cup milk**
- 1 **egg, lightly beaten**
- 6 **pork chops (1 inch thick)**
- 1-1/2 **cups crushed saltines (about 45 crackers)**
- 1/4 **cup vegetable oil**

In a shallow pan, combine the milk and beaten egg. Dip each pork chop in the mixture, then coat with cracker crumbs, patting to make a thick coating. Heat the oil in a large skillet.

Cook the pork chops, uncovered, for about 8-10 minutes per side or until outside is browned and no pink remains inside. **Yield:** 6 servings.

8 cups chopped peeled tart apples
(about 3-1/2 pounds)
1/2 cup packed brown sugar
2 teaspoons vanilla extract
1 teaspoon ground cinnamon

Place all ingredients in a large saucepan or Dutch oven. Cover and cook over medium-low heat for 30-40 minutes or until apples are tender.

Remove from the heat; mash apples (a potato masher works well) until the sauce reaches the desired consistency. Serve warm or cold. **Yield:** 6 servings (about 3-1/2 cups).

Chocolate Mayonnaise Cake

Mom always made this special cake for my birthday meal. It's very moist and has a nice, light chocolate taste. The flavorful frosting is the ideal topping. It was a perfect birthday if I could talk her into giving me a second piece.

Potato Primer

Low-moisture russet or Idaho potatoes are the best choice for baking or frying. Long, white taters can be boiled, baked or fried. Thin-skinned round red or white potatoes are best suited for boiling. New potatoes are great boiled or roasted.

2 cups all-purpose flour
1 cup sugar
3 tablespoons baking cocoa
2 teaspoons baking soda
1 cup water
1 cup mayonnaise
1 teaspoon vanilla extract
BROWN SUGAR FROSTING:
1/4 cup butter
1/2 cup packed brown sugar
2 tablespoons milk
1-3/4 cups sifted confectioners' sugar

In a large mixing bowl, combine flour, sugar, cocoa and baking soda. Add water, mayonnaise and vanilla; beat at medium speed until thoroughly combined.

Pour into a greased 9-in. square or 11-in. x 7-in. x 2-in. baking pan. Bake at 350° for 30-35 minutes or until a toothpick inserted near the center comes out clean. Cool completely.

For frosting, melt butter in a saucepan. Stir in brown sugar; cook and stir until bubbly. Remove from the heat and stir in milk. Gradually add confectioners' sugar; beat by hand until frosting is of spreading consistency. Immediately frost cake. **Yield:** 9-12 servings.

Editor's Note: Reduced-fat or fat-free mayonnaise should not be substituted for regular mayonnaise in this recipe.

Country-Style Cornish Hens

By Maria Costello, Monroe, North Carolina

My mother's cooking was always a treat, but now that I live far away, going home to a meal Mom has prepared is extra-special.

My mother, Delores Briggs (left) of Houlton, Maine, is sure to have my favorite meal waiting when we walk in the door. Herbed Cornish Hens come out of the oven golden and flavorful. The seasonings in this recipe also work great on a whole roasted chicken. Either way, the result is a mouth-watering feast.

Mom's Macaroni and Cheese is old-fashioned comfort food, yet it's so simple to prepare. I can make a whole meal out of it, but it's also a good side dish with any meat. It has tender noodles and a crowd-pleasing golden crumb topping.

Her Homemade Brown Bread recipe produces beautiful crusty loaves. The moist slices are great even without butter.

And I know I'll never outgrow a fun dessert like Old-Fashioned Whoopie Pies. With all the delicious food Mom prepares, it's not easy to save room, but we always do. They're a treat that never lasted very long with me and my two brothers around.

Helping Mom in the kitchen and savoring her culinary creations continue to give me lots of wonderful memories. She still sends my husband, Robbie, and me "care packages" of goodies throughout the year. Nothing compares to her cookies and pies.

I've picked up Mom's love of cooking, and I hope our son, Caleb, sees in me the same joy that comes from preparing foods for others.

Herbed Cornish Hens, Mom's Macaroni and Cheese, Homemade Brown Bread and Old-Fashioned Whoopie Pies (recipes are on pp. 90-91).

Herbed Cornish Hens

The refreshing basting sauce that Mom makes with thyme, lemon juice and butter gives these hens savory flavor throughout.

- **6** Cornish game hens (about 20 ounces *each*)
- **1** cup lemon juice
- **3/4** cup butter, melted
- **1/2** teaspoon paprika
- **1-1/2** teaspoons dried thyme, *divided*
- **1-1/4** teaspoons seasoned salt, *divided*
- **1-1/8** teaspoons garlic powder, *divided*
- **1/4** teaspoon salt
- **1/8** teaspoon pepper

Place the hens on a wire rack in a large roasting pan. In a small bowl, combine the lemon juice, butter, paprika and 1 teaspoon each of thyme, seasoned salt and garlic powder. Pour half over the hens; set the remaining mixture aside for basting.

Combine the salt, pepper and remaining thyme, seasoned salt and garlic powder; sprinkle evenly over the hens. Bake, uncovered, at 375° for 30 minutes. Baste with the reserved lemon juice mixture. Bake 30 minutes longer, basting occasionally, or until the meat is tender and juices run clear. **Yield:** 6 servings.

Mom's Macaroni and Cheese

The wonderful homemade goodness of this creamy macaroni and cheese makes it a staple side dish in my mother's kitchen and in mine as well.

- **1-1/2** cups uncooked elbow macaroni
- **5** tablespoons butter, *divided*
- **3** tablespoons all-purpose flour
- **1-1/2** cups milk
- **1** cup (4 ounces) shredded cheddar cheese
- **2** ounces process cheese (Velveeta), cubed
- **1/2** teaspoon salt
- **1/4** teaspoon pepper
- **2** tablespoons dry bread crumbs

Cook macaroni according to package directions; drain. Place in a greased 1-1/2-qt. baking dish; set aside. In a saucepan, melt 4 tablespoons of butter over medium heat. Stir in flour until smooth. Gradually add milk; bring to a boil. Cook and stir for 2 minutes; reduce heat.

Stir in cheeses, salt and pepper until the cheese is melted. Pour over macaroni; mix well. Melt the remaining butter; add the bread crumbs. Sprinkle over casserole. Bake, uncovered, at 375° for 30 minutes. **Yield:** 6 servings.

Homemade Brown Bread

This yummy bread has a light texture and includes richly flavored ingredients like molasses, brown sugar and oats. One slice absolutely calls for another!

1-1/2 cups boiling water
1 cup old-fashioned oats
2 tablespoons shortening
2 teaspoons salt
1 package (1/4 ounce) active dry yeast
3/4 cup warm water (110° to 115°)
1/2 teaspoon sugar
1/4 cup packed brown sugar
1/4 cup molasses
4-3/4 to 5-1/4 cups all-purpose flour
Melted butter

In a bowl, combine boiling water, oats, shortening and salt. Cool to 110°- 115°. In a mixing bowl, dissolve yeast in warm water. Sprinkle with sugar. Add oat mixture, brown sugar, molasses and 3 cups of flour; mix well. Add enough remaining flour to form a soft dough. Turn onto a floured surface and knead until smooth and elastic, about 6-8 minutes.

Place in a greased bowl, turning once to grease top. Cover and let rise in a warm place until doubled, about 1 hour. Punch dough down. Divide in half and shape into two loaves. Place in greased 9-in. x 5-in. x 3-in. loaf pans. Cover and let rise until doubled, about 30-45 minutes. Bake at 375° for 30-35 minutes or until golden brown. Remove from pans to cool on wire racks. Brush with melted butter. **Yield:** 2 loaves.

Old-Fashioned Whoopie Pies

Who can resist soft chocolate sandwich cookies filled with a layer of fluffy white frosting? Mom has made these tasty treats for years.

1/2 cup baking cocoa
1/2 cup hot water
1/2 cup shortening
1-1/2 cups sugar

2 eggs
1 teaspoon vanilla extract
2-2/3 cups all-purpose flour
1 teaspoon baking powder
1 teaspoon baking soda
1/4 teaspoon salt
1/2 cup buttermilk
FILLING:
3 tablespoons all-purpose flour
Dash salt
1 cup milk
3/4 cup shortening
1-1/2 cups confectioners' sugar
2 teaspoons vanilla extract

In a small bowl, combine cocoa and water; mix well. Cool for 5 minutes. In a mixing bowl, cream shortening and sugar. Add cocoa mixture, eggs and vanilla; mix well. Combine dry ingredients. Add to creamed mixture alternately with buttermilk; mix well.

Drop by rounded tablespoonfuls 2 in. apart onto greased baking sheets. Flatten slightly with a spoon. Bake at 350° for 10-12 minutes or until firm to the touch. Remove to wire racks to cool.

In a saucepan, combine flour and salt. Gradually whisk in milk until smooth; cook and stir over medium-high heat until thick, about 5-7 minutes. Remove from the heat. Cover and refrigerate until completely cool.

In a mixing bowl, cream shortening, confectioners' sugar and vanilla. Add chilled milk mixture; beat for 7 minutes or until fluffy. Spread filling on the bottom of half of the cookies; top with remaining cookies. Store in the refrigerator. **Yield:** 2 dozen.

A Dinner to Delight Dad

By Ruth Ann Stelfox, Raymond, Alberta

Whenever I prepare this mouth-watering meal for my own family these days, the wonderful aromas of the homemade foods remind me of my happy childhood and how our large family often gathered around the big kitchen table with Dad at the head.

He especially loved the Sweet-and-Sour Spareribs with their thick, tangy sauce. Mom liked them, too, because the sauce was no hassle to make.

Baking the ribs for hours keeps the meat tender and delicious. These ribs never lasted long around our house!

Confetti Rice is a classic dish that's stood the test of time. Much to our disappointment—and my mother's amazement—there never seemed to be any left over, no matter how much she made!

This colorful recipe combines rice and vegetables for a nutritious side dish that Mom was glad we gobbled up.

It seemed that Creamy Pineapple Salad made frequent appearances on our dinner table, but we kids didn't mind. Whenever we saw Mom preparing this cool, sweet salad, we couldn't wait to eat.

After all of these delicious dished were served up, we knew Raisin Custard Pie was sure to follow. Cutting the pie into seven equal pieces was tricky, though we didn't hear any complaints from Dad.

Mom felt it was important for us to eat together as a family, and that fostered a closeness we've tried to carry over to our homes today.

Now you, too, can make some happy memories with this meal!

Sweet-and-Sour Spareribs, Confetti Rice, Creamy Pineapple Salad and Raisin Custard Pie (recipes are on pp. 94-95).

Confetti Rice

I still enjoy the superb combination of bacon and rice in this dish. The peas add color and a bit of a crunch. It's so easy to make, and so good! It cooks on the stovetop, keeping the oven open for the ribs.

- 1/2 **pound sliced bacon, diced**
- 1 **cup long grain rice, cooked**
- 1 **cup diced carrots, parboiled**
- 1 **cup diced celery, parboiled**
- 1/2 **cup fresh *or* frozen peas**

Soy sauce, optional

In a large skillet, cook bacon until crisp. Remove to paper towels; drain all but 3 tablespoons of the drippings. Cook rice, carrots, celery and peas in drippings until heated through, about 5-7 minutes. Stir in bacon. Serve with soy sauce if desired. **Yield:** 6-8 servings.

Creamy Pineapple Salad

Mom made this slightly sweet, fruity salad often. It was a favorite because the cool and creamy texture tasted so good paired with her zesty spareribs. We kids couldn't wait to eat when we saw this salad appear on the table. As an added plus, it can be prepared the night before, so it's convenient, too.

Sweet-and-Sour Spareribs

Just the tempting aroma of these ribs reminds me of many simple but delicious meals my mom made. Dad especially loved these tender tasty ribs with their thick, tangy sauce. Mom liked them because the sauce was no fuss to make.

- 5 **to 6 pounds pork spareribs *or* pork loin back ribs**
- 1/2 **cup packed brown sugar**
- 1/2 **cup sugar**
- 2 **tablespoons cornstarch**
- 1 **cup ketchup**
- 2/3 **cup vinegar**
- 1/2 **cup cold water**

Place ribs on a rack in a large shallow roasting pan. Bake, uncovered, at 350° for 1-1/2 hours. Meanwhile, combine sugars and cornstarch in a medium saucepan. Stir in ketchup, vinegar and water; bring to a boil. Cook and stir until thickened and clear.

Remove ribs and rack from pan. Discard fat. Place ribs back in roasting pan; pour about 1-1/2 cups of the sauce over ribs. Bake 30 minutes longer. Cut ribs into serving-size pieces; brush with remaining sauce. **Yield:** 6-8 servings.

Pizza-Style Stuffed Potatoes kids can prepare

Mention the word pizza and you'll get kids excited. Kids can help microwave potatoes, scoop out the insides and mix the filling of this yummy recipe.

Ingredients:

baking potatoes (Russets), unpeeled, washed
oz. (50 g) pepperoni slices, cut in quarters
pizza toppings such as sliced olive, bell peppers, etc. (optional)

1   4 cup (50 mL) tomato sauce
1   tbsp (15 mL) Parmesan or
1   omano cheese
1/4   tsp (5 mL) soft margarine or
1   tter

Drain   cup (75 mL) grated Ched-
Set p r cheese
make   thod:
bowl   Cut potatoes in half length-
slight se. Prick each potato three
        es.
suga Place potatoes cut side
and wn on microwaveable plate.
serv rowave on high for four to
8-10 minutes, or until a fork
        rces potato easily. Remove
        te of potatoes from
        rowave and cover with
        n tea towel for five minutes
        et potatoes continue cook-

In a bowl, mix pepperoni,
and th

tomato sauce, Parmesan cheese and margarine or butter. Set aside.

Scoop out flesh in each potato half, leaving a thin shell of potato inside skins. Stir scooped potato into pepperoni mixture.

Fill potato shells with potato-pepperoni mixture. Sprinkle with grated cheese. Place on a baking sheet, Bake 15 to 20 minutes in a regular oven at 400 F (200 C), until cheese is lightly browned. Or heat in toaster oven until cheese is browned.

Makes four Pizza-Style Stuffed Potatoes. (NC)

Just cool the pie filling in the crust completely and then refrigerate. Just before serving, top with whipped cream instead of meringue. It's just as delicious.

- 1/2   **cup sugar**
- 3   **tablespoons cornstarch**
- 3   **egg yolks**
- 2   **cups milk**
- 2   **teaspoons lemon juice**
- 1/2   **cup raisins**
    ry shell (9 inches), baked

whites
sugar

m saucepan, combine sugar and cornstarch.
e egg yolks and milk until thoroughly com-
k over medium heat, stirring constantly, until
mes to a boil; boil for 1 minute. Remove
e heat. Add lemon juice and raisins. Pour into

meringue, beat egg whites in a small bowl
amy. Gradually add sugar, about 1 tablespoon at
beating until stiff and glossy. Spread over warm
king sure meringue covers all of the filling.
ake at 350° for 10-15 minutes or until light gold-
wn. Serve warm or cold. Store leftovers in the
rator. **Yield:** 8 servings.

gh water to juice
oil. Place gelatin in a
to dissolve. Cool until

eam; gradually beat in
xture. Stir in pineapple
l. Pour into a 1-1/2-qt.
urs or overnight. **Yield:**

tard Pie

dessert, this custard pie raisins are a nice surprise, makes it look so special. For a variation, you can skip the meringue.

Storing Vinegar

Store vinegar in a cool, dry place. Unopened, it will keep almost indefinitely. Once opened, store vinegar at room temperature for about 6 months.

Eastertime Ham And Egg Treats

By Ruth Seitz, Columbus Junction, Iowa

My sister and I well remember the Orange-Glazed Ham that our mom served for Easter dinner. She'd put it in the oven in the morning, and the sweet aroma filled the house even before we left for church.

My mother, Naomi King (left), basted the ham with the glaze when we returned home. It made a beautiful and tasty main dish.

Along with the festive ham, Mom's Parmesan Baked Potatoes were so delicious. And we even liked to eat broccoli and cauliflower when Mom served them in her Fresh Vegetable Salad.

For us girls, the end of the meal was most special. That's when we'd hunt for Mom's wonderful home-made Chocolate Easter Eggs! They're so creamy and delicious. Just knowing Mom made them herself made the holiday extra sweet.

Mom passed along her love of cooking to us, my two daughters and my four granddaughters. Even after she was living at a nursing home, Mom was always sharing her recipes, which she could recite by heart.

She would be thrilled if this meal were to become a holiday tradition at your house, too.

Orange-Glazed Ham, Parmesan Baked Potatoes, Fresh Vegetable Salad and Chocolate Easter Eggs (recipes are on pp. 98-99).

Orange-Glazed Ham

This delicious ham looked like a sparkling jewel on the table when my mom served it for Easter dinner. The flavor of the spice rub penetrates through every tender slice. Even its enticing aroma while baking can't match the wonderful taste.

1   **fully cooked bone-in ham (6 to 8 pounds)**
1   **tablespoon ground mustard**
1   **teaspoon ground allspice**
3/4 **cup orange marmalade**
Kumquats and kale, optional

Score the ham. Combine mustard and allspice; rub over ham. Place on a rack in a shallow baking pan. Bake, uncovered, at 325° for 2 to 2-1/2 hours or until a meat thermometer reads 140°.

Spread top of ham with marmalade during the last hour of baking. Baste occasionally. Garnish ham with kumquats and kale if desired. **Yield:** 12-16 servings.

Parmesan Baked Potatoes

It always amazed me that this simple recipe could make potatoes that taste so good. Mom liked to make them for Easter and other holidays since they were more special than ordinary baked potatoes.

6   **tablespoons butter, melted**
3   **tablespoons grated Parmesan cheese**
8   **medium unpeeled red potatoes (about 2-3/4 pounds), halved lengthwise**

Pour melted butter into a 13-in. x 9-in. x 2-in. baking pan. Sprinkle Parmesan cheese over butter. Place the potatoes with cut side down over cheese. Bake, uncovered, at 400° for 40-45 minutes or until tender. **Yield:** 8 servings.

Tater Tip

When purchasing potatoes, don't pick ones that are soft or have excessive cuts, cracks, bruises or discoloration. If you have to use green potatoes, peel away the green. When a potato is more than half green, throw it out.

Fresh Vegetable Salad

It was such a treat to have a crisp, garden-fresh salad back when Mom didn't have much room in our little icebox to keep produce chilled. This salad is as colorful and festive as it is refreshing.

- 2 cups broccoli florets
- 2 cups cauliflowerets
- 1/2 cup chopped celery
- 1/2 cup chopped green pepper
- 1/2 cup chopped onion
- 1/4 cup grated carrot
- 1 cup mayonnaise
- 1/4 cup sugar
- 3 tablespoons grated Parmesan cheese
- 2 bacon strips, cooked and crumbled

Toss the first six ingredients in a large salad bowl. In a small bowl, combine mayonnaise, sugar and Parmesan cheese; pour over vegetables and toss to coat. Cover and chill. Sprinkle with the crumbled bacon just before serving. **Yield:** 8 servings.

Chocolate Easter Eggs

No store-bought Easter candy can compare to Mom's homemade chocolate-covered eggs. The heavenly centers have peanut butter, coconut and walnuts. These rich candies just melt in your mouth.

- 3/4 cup chunky peanut butter
- 1/4 cup butter, softened
- 1 cup flaked coconut

- 1/2 cup finely chopped walnuts
- 1-1/2 to 2 cups confectioners' sugar, *divided*
- 2 cups (12 ounces) semisweet chocolate chips
- 2 tablespoons shortening

In a mixing bowl, cream peanut butter and butter until well mixed. Fold in coconut, nuts and 1 cup sugar; mix well. Sprinkle some of the remaining sugar on a board.

Turn peanut butter mixture onto board; knead in enough of the remaining sugar until mixture holds its shape when formed. Shape into small egg-shaped pieces. Cover and chill for 1 hour.

In a double boiler over hot water, melt chocolate chips and shortening, stirring until smooth. Dip eggs; place on waxed paper to harden. Chill. **Yield:** 2 dozen.

Melting Chocolate

Because chocolate scorches easily—which ruins its flavor—it should be melted slowly over low heat.

One melting method is to place chocolate in the top of a double boiler over simmering water. Remove the top of the pan from the heat when the chocolate is a little more than halfway melted and stir until it's completely smooth.

Chocolate can also be melted in a microwave oven.

A Sunday Feast Fit for a King

By Willa Govoro, St. Clair, Missouri

I'm in my 80s, but I still remember so clearly the delicious meals my mother prepared on her old wood-burning stove.

Sunday dinner was always special at our house. My mom, Ellen Gibson (left), set out her good dishes and flatware on the big oak table.

My brother and sister and I couldn't wait to dig into her comforting Chicken and Dumplings, which filled the house with a wonderful aroma while simmering on the back of the stove.

Tender chicken and succulent dumplings are covered with a creamy gravy, while carrots and celery add a little bit of color.

A big bowl of her Old-Fashioned Green Beans got passed around until it was scraped clean. Bacon adds a little zip and brown sugar adds a touch of sweetness. You'll appreciate the short list of ingredients in this reliable recipe.

To round out the meal, Mother's Dinner Rolls were set on the table fresh from the oven. With their wonderfully light texture and slightly sweet dough, we could never eat just one.

For dessert, Mom would present a lovely Orange Dream Cake featuring citrus and coconut. Even full from the hearty meal, we'd still manage to devour thick slices of this refreshing sweet delight.

Although our family didn't have much money back then, Mom always made satisfying and balanced meals. And she instilled in me the joy of cooking for others, which I never lost.

Chicken and Dumplings, Old-Fashioned Green Beans, Mother's Dinner Rolls and Orange Dream Cake (recipes are on pp. 102-103).

Add celery, carrots, parsley and seasonings. Add enough water to cover chicken; bring to a boil. Reduce heat; cover and simmer until chicken is almost tender, about 45-50 minutes.

Remove 1 cup of broth to use for dumplings; cool, then add flour, baking powder and eggs. Mix well to form a stiff batter; drop by tablespoonfuls into simmering broth. Cover and simmer for 15-20 minutes. Remove chicken and dumplings to a serving dish and keep warm.

For gravy, remove 4 cups broth and vegetables to a large saucepan; bring to a boil. Combine flour and water; mix well. Stir into vegetable mixture. Cook over medium heat, stirring constantly, until thickened and bubbly. Pour over chicken and dumplings. Serve immediately. **Yield:** 6-8 servings.

Editor's Note: Any remaining chicken broth can be frozen for future use.

Old-Fashioned Green Beans

Mom would prepare homegrown green beans using this recipe, and did they ever taste good. The bacon provides rich flavor and the brown sugar a touch of sweetness. This is one irresistible side dish.

- **6   bacon strips, cut into 1/2-inch pieces**
- **2   pounds fresh green beans**
- **3   tablespoons brown sugar**
- **1/2 cup water**

In a large skillet, cook bacon over medium heat until crisp-tender, about 5 minutes. Add beans, brown sugar and water. Stir gently; bring to a boil. Reduce heat; cover and simmer for 15 minutes or until beans are crisp-tender. Remove to a serving bowl with a slotted spoon. **Yield:** 6-8 servings.

Chicken and Dumplings

On Sundays, Mom set our big round oak table with a snowy white cloth and her fine dishes and tableware. On the old woodstove, pushed way back to simmer slowly, was a big pot of chicken and dumplings in a thick gravy. I can still taste it.

- **1   cup all-purpose flour**
- **2   broiler-fryer chickens (2-1/2 to 3 pounds each), cut up**
- **2   tablespoons vegetable oil**
- **3   celery ribs, cut into 1-inch pieces**
- **3   medium carrots, cut into 1-inch pieces**
- **1/4 cup chopped fresh parsley**
- **2   teaspoons salt**
- **1   teaspoon garlic powder**
- **1   teaspoon dried thyme**
- **1/2 teaspoon pepper**
- **8   to 12 cups water**

DUMPLINGS:
- **2   cups all-purpose flour**
- **2   teaspoons baking powder**
- **2   eggs, beaten**

GRAVY:
- **1/4 cup all-purpose flour**
- **1/2 cup water**

Place flour in a bowl or bag; add the chicken pieces and dredge or shake to coat. In a large skillet, brown chicken in oil; drain. Place in an 8-qt. Dutch oven.

Mother's Dinner Rolls

These tender rolls will melt in your mouth. Mom would set out her big square-footed honey bowl with them— some sweet butter and a drizzle of honey make these rolls a special treat.

       2   **packages (1/4 ounce *each*) active dry yeast**
       1   **cup warm water (110° to 115°)**
       1   **cup boiling water**
       1   **cup shortening**
    3/4   **cup sugar**
       1   **teaspoon salt**
       2   **eggs, beaten**
7-1/2   **to 8 cups all-purpose flour**

In a small bowl, dissolve yeast in warm water. Meanwhile, in a large mixing bowl, combine boiling water, shortening, sugar and salt. Allow to stand 3-4 minutes or until shortening is melted and sugar is dissolved. Add the yeast mixture and eggs; mix well. Add 2 cups of flour; beat until smooth. Add enough remaining flour to form a soft dough (do not knead).

Place in a greased bowl, turning once to grease top. Cover and refrigerate overnight. Turn dough onto a floured surface. Pinch off a piece and form a 2-1/2-in. ball. Roll into a 5-in. rope; shape into a knot. Repeat with remaining dough. Place on a greased baking sheet. Cover and let rise in a warm place until doubled, about 30 minutes. Bake at 350° for 20-25 minutes or until golden brown. **Yield:** 2-1/2 dozen.

Orange Dream Cake

We tried to save room for a big slice of this pretty cake. The flavor of orange and lemon really comes through. With a heavenly whipped cream frosting, this cake is a delightful end to a terrific meal.

    2/3   **cup butter, softened**
1-1/3   **cups sugar**

    2/3   **cup fresh orange juice**
       3   **tablespoons fresh lemon juice**
       1   **teaspoon grated orange peel**
       1   **teaspoon grated lemon peel**
       2   **eggs**
       2   **cups cake flour**
       2   **teaspoons baking powder**
       1   **teaspoon salt**
FROSTING:
       1   **cup flaked coconut**
    1/4   **cup sugar**
       2   **tablespoons fresh orange juice**
       1   **tablespoon fresh lemon juice**
       4   **teaspoons grated orange peel, *divided***
       1   **cup heavy whipping cream, whipped**

In a large mixing bowl, cream butter and sugar. Add juices and peels; mix well (mixture may appear curdled). Add eggs, one at a time, beating well after each addition. Sift flour with baking powder and salt; add to creamed mixture and mix well.

Pour into two greased and floured 8-in. baking pans. Bake at 375° for 25-30 minutes or until a toothpick inserted near the center comes out clean. Cool in pans for 10 minutes before removing to a wire rack to cool completely.

For frosting, combine coconut, sugar, juices and 3 teaspoons peel; mix well. Let stand for 10-15 minutes or until sugar is dissolved. Fold in whipped cream. Spread between cake layers and over the top. Sprinkle with remaining orange peel. Chill for at least 1 hour. Store in the refrigerator. **Yield:** 10-12 servings.

Great Food on a Tight Budget

By Lucile Proctor, Panguitch, Utah

Mother had a special knack for making delicious, satisfying meals on a budget—a very important skill with 13 hungry children to feed!

My mom, Augusta Wilcox Hunt (left), used lots of venison since our family had some avid hunters. Beef and homegrown vegetables and fruits were other favorite ingredients.

Mom's Beef Stew (often made with venison) was a favorite main dish on bread-baking day. Mom would simmer her mouth-watering stew on the back of the woodstove all day while preparing four loaves of bread and two pans of crusty Yeast Biscuits.

We kids rode the school bus for 15 miles. On cool days, nothing tasted better or warmed us up faster than a steaming bowl of Mom's stew.

Mom's Yeast Biscuits were great for sandwiches, but they were especially yummy with the stew. They were perfect for sopping up the beefy gravy!

Using cabbage and apples from our root cellar, Mom would whip up a big batch of flavorful, crunchy Apple Cabbage Slaw. Since the ingredients were always on hand, she fixed this often to feed our big family.

Even after all that stew and slaw, we kids could always find room for Mom's Marshmallow Graham Dessert. It made a sweet, light and refreshing end to a great family meal.

Mom, who especially enjoyed fishing and quilting, passed away a few years ago at age 93. Her family, which now includes 82 grandchildren, 205 great-grandchildren and five great-great-grandkids, will long remember and carry on her legacy. She taught us that good eating starts with good cooking.

Mom's Beef Stew, Apple Cabbage Slaw, Yeast Biscuits and Marshmallow Graham Dessert (recipes are on pp. 106-107).

Mom's Beef Stew

This warming, stick-to-your-ribs main dish was one Mom relied on often to feed us 13 kids. Mildly seasoned with lots of satisfying ingredients like barley, potatoes and carrots in a tomato-beef broth, it still hits the spot on cool days.

- 2 pounds meaty beef soup bones, beef shanks *or* short ribs
- 6 cups water
- 5 medium potatoes, peeled and cubed
- 5 medium carrots, chopped
- 1 medium onion, chopped
- 1/2 cup medium pearl barley
- 1 can (28 ounces) plum tomatoes, undrained
- 1 to 1-1/2 teaspoons salt
- 1/2 teaspoon pepper
- 2 garlic cloves, minced, optional
- 1 bay leaf, optional
- 3 tablespoons cornstarch
- 1/2 cup cold water

Place soup bones and water in a soup kettle or Dutch oven. Slowly bring to a boil. Reduce heat; cover and simmer for 2 hours.

Set beef bones aside until cool enough to handle. Remove meat from bones; discard bones and return meat to broth. Add the potatoes, carrots, onion, barley, tomatoes, salt, pepper, garlic and bay leaf if desired.

Cover and simmer for 50-60 minutes or until the vegetables and barley are tender. Discard bay leaf. Combine cornstarch and cold water until smooth; stir into stew. Bring to a boil; cook and stir for 2 minutes or until thickened. **Yield:** 10 servings.

Apple Cabbage Slaw

Chopped apple adds fruity sweetness, crunch and color to the tangy cabbage in this flavorful slaw. It's a refreshing side dish any time of the year.

✓ Uses less fat, sugar or salt. Includes Nutritional Analysis and Diabetic Exchanges.

- 6 cups shredded cabbage
- 3 medium red apples, chopped
- 1 can (5 ounces) evaporated milk
- 1/4 cup lemon juice
- 2 tablespoons sugar
- 2 teaspoons grated onion
- 1 teaspoon celery seed
- 1/2 teaspoon salt, optional

Dash pepper

In a large bowl, toss the cabbage and apples. In a small bowl, combine the remaining ingredients. Pour over cabbage mixture and toss to coat. Refrigerate until serving. **Yield:** 10 servings.

Nutritional Analysis: One 3/4-cup serving (prepared with fat-free evaporated milk and sugar substitute equivalent to 2 tablespoons sugar and without salt) equals 53 calories, 26 mg sodium, 1 mg cholesterol, 12 g carbohydrate, 2 g protein, trace fat, 2 g fiber. **Diabetic Exchanges:** 1 vegetable, 1/2 fruit.

Yeast Biscuits

Wonderful from-scratch yeast biscuits—golden and crusty outside and moist inside—were a staple Mom prepared regularly when I was growing up. They are just right for scooping up the gravy from bowls of beef stew and are also great for sandwiches.

- 3-1/4 teaspoons active dry yeast
- 1/2 cup warm water (110° to 115°)
- 1/2 cup sugar
- 1/2 cup butter, softened
- 1 can (5 ounces) evaporated milk
- 2 eggs, lightly beaten
- 1-1/2 teaspoons salt
- 2 cups whole wheat flour
- 2 cups all-purpose flour

In a large mixing bowl, dissolve yeast in water. Add sugar, butter, milk, eggs, salt and whole wheat flour; beat until smooth. Add enough all-purpose flour to form a soft dough. Turn onto a floured surface; knead until smooth and elastic, about 10 minutes.

Place in a greased bowl, turning once to grease top. Cover and let rise in a warm place until doubled, about 1-1/2 hours. Punch dough down; divide into thirds. Let rest for 5 minutes. On a floured surface, roll out each portion to 1/2-in. thickness.

Cut with a 2-1/2-in. biscuit cutter. Place on lightly greased baking sheets. Cover and let rise until doubled, about 30 minutes. Bake at 375° for 10-12 minutes or until golden brown. Remove from pans and cool on wire racks. **Yield:** about 2-1/2 dozen.

Marshmallow Graham Dessert

For a light, fluffy treat, this sweet and creamy dessert with bits of pineapple mixed in just can't be beat!

- 1 package (16 ounces) large marshmallows
- 2 cups milk
- 1-1/2 teaspoons lemon extract
- 1 can (20 ounces) crushed pineapple, drained
- 2 cups heavy whipping cream, whipped
- 2 cups graham cracker crumbs (about 32 squares)
- 1/2 cup butter, melted

In a heavy saucepan over low heat, melt marshmallows and milk. Remove from the heat. Cool, stirring occasionally. Stir in extract. Fold in pineapple and whipped cream. Combine cracker crumbs and butter.

Press 1-1/2 cups into a greased 13-in. x 9-in. x 2-in. pan. Spread with the pineapple mixture. Sprinkle with the remaining crumb mixture. Refrigerate for 2-3 hours before serving. **Yield:** 12-16 servings.

Shear Pleasure

Use kitchen shears to make quick work of many projects. They are great for cubing raw stew meat, cutting bread cubes for bread pudding or chopping up canned whole tomatoes. They also easily make bite-size pieces out of canned fruit and cooked meat for young children.

Fine Fare from The Southwest

By Jerri Moror, Rio Rancho, New Mexico

My mother, Lupe Mirabal (left), had the daily challenge of preparing economical foods that could feed a family of 10 *and* that would appeal to all of our different palates.

She managed to make every meal terrific, even though she also had to meet the needs of our father, who's diabetic.

Being a nutritionist and fixing foods suitable for Father's diet, Mom was a very careful cook and measured everything she added.

Since she has lived her whole life in New Mexico, Mom relies on Southwestern-style recipes. Her Chicken Tortilla Bake has been my favorite for years. She made this casserole often when I was growing up.

Using ingredients she had on hand, Mom developed her more mild version of Spanish Rice. It's a colorful side dish that pairs perfectly with the chicken or any other meat.

Lots of hearty and refreshing ingredients go into the Southwestern Salad. After our family said grace, we kids would quickly reach for this fun salad.

Even if Mom made a big batch of her special Anise Cutout Cookies for dessert, they'd be gone before she knew it.

There was plenty of work to be done in the kitchen to keep us all well-fed. I'm grateful for the cooking skills I learned from her.

We still love going home for Mom's meals. And now I use her recipes for my husband and three children. I look forward to the day when I can pass these recipes on to our own children and grandchildren!

Chicken Tortilla Bake, Spanish Rice, Southwestern Salad and Anise Cutout Cookies (recipes are on pp. 110-111).

Spanish Rice

We were always glad to see a big bowl of this festive rice on the table. The carrots, peas and tomatoes make it so pretty. This versatile side dish goes great with any meat or Mexican meal.

 Uses less fat, sugar or salt. Includes Nutritional Analysis and Diabetic Exchanges.

- 1 **cup uncooked long grain rice**
- 2 **tablespoons vegetable oil**
- 1 **small onion, chopped**
- 1 **garlic clove, minced**
- 1/2 **teaspoon salt, optional**
- 2 **large tomatoes, peeled and chopped**
- 1 **cup water**
- 1 **cup chicken broth**
- 1/3 **cup frozen peas, thawed**
- 1/3 **cup diced cooked carrots**

In a large skillet over medium heat, saute rice in hot oil until lightly browned. Add the onion, garlic and salt if desired; cook over low heat until onion is tender. Add tomatoes; cook over medium heat until softened. Add water; cover and simmer until water is absorbed.

Stir in broth, peas and carrots; cover and simmer until liquid is absorbed and rice is tender, about 10 minutes. **Yield:** 6 servings.

Nutritional Analysis: One 3/4-cup serving (prepared with reduced-sodium broth and without salt) equals 185 calories, 40 mg sodium, 1 mg cholesterol, 31 g carbohydrate, 4 g protein, 5 g fat. **Diabetic Exchanges:** 2 starch, 1 fat.

Chicken Tortilla Bake

Mother frequently made this comforting casserole when I was growing up. Our family would scrape the pan clean. Chicken, cheese and zippy green chilies are a mouth-watering mix.

- 3 **cups shredded cooked chicken**
- 2 **cans (4 ounces *each*) chopped green chilies**
- 1 **cup chicken broth**
- 1 **can (10-3/4 ounces) condensed cream of mushroom soup, undiluted**
- 1 **can (10-3/4 ounces) condensed cream of chicken soup, undiluted**
- 1 **small onion, finely chopped**
- 12 **corn tortillas**
- 2 **cups (8 ounces) shredded cheddar cheese, *divided***

In a bowl, combine the chicken, chilies, broth, soups and onion; set aside. Warm tortillas according to package directions.

Layer half of the tortillas on the bottom of a greased 13-in. x 9-in. x 2-in. baking pan, cutting to fit pan if desired. Top with half of the chicken mixture and half of the cheese. Repeat layers. Bake, uncovered, at 350° for 30 minutes. **Yield:** 6-8 servings.

Anise Cutout Cookies

Mother prepared these soft cookies for holidays and special-occasion meals. My seven siblings and I gobbled them up as fast as she made them. I still can't resist the cinnamon-sugar coating.

2 cups shortening
1 cup sugar
2 eggs
2 teaspoons aniseed
6 cups all-purpose flour
1 tablespoon baking powder
1 teaspoon salt
1/4 cup apple juice
1/2 cup sugar
1 teaspoon ground cinnamon

In a mixing bowl, cream shortening and sugar until fluffy; add eggs and aniseed. Combine flour, baking powder and salt; add to the creamed mixture. Add apple juice and mix well.

On a floured surface, knead until well blended, about 4-5 minutes. Roll dough to 1/2-in. thickness; cut into 2-in. shapes. Place on greased baking sheets. Bake at 375° for 12-16 minutes or until lightly browned. Combine sugar and cinnamon; roll cookies in the mixture while still warm. Cool on wire racks. **Yield:** about 5 dozen.

Southwestern Salad

You get an explosion of Southwestern flavor in every bite of this deliciously different salad. It's a favorite for kids of all ages since it mixes beans and cheese, tasty vegetables and crisp corn chips.

2-1/2 cups corn chips
1/2 head iceberg lettuce, torn
1 cup (4 ounces) shredded Mexican cheese blend
1 can (15 ounces) pinto beans, rinsed and drained
1 small tomato, seeded and diced
1/4 to 1/2 cup salad dressing of your choice
2 tablespoons sliced green onions
1 to 2 tablespoons chopped green chilies
1 small avocado, peeled and sliced

In a serving bowl or platter, toss chips, lettuce, cheese, beans, tomato, salad dressing, onions and chilies. Top with avocado. Serve immediately. **Yield:** 6-8 servings.

About Avocados

Perfectly ripe avocados are the easiest to peel. The skin is hard to remove from under-ripe fruit, whereas the flesh of those that are over-ripe often gets mashed and bruised during peeling.

To stop peeled avocado from browning, brush the cut surfaces with lemon juice.

Special Spring Family Dinner

By Helen Vail, Glenside, Pennsylvania

When I was growing up, my family's farm was complete with livestock, a garden, a fruit orchard, raspberry bushes and a strawberry patch.

In spring, my mother, Dorothy Wanamaker (left), would fire up the old stove and fix a hearty meal—no small task with 10 people in our family. This meal is one of my favorites.

It was always an occasion when my mother made this gorgeous golden Apple-Mustard Glazed Ham. I was thrilled to help her by inserting the cloves. It looked beautiful as it came out of the oven and tasted so good.

The perfect side dish was her Peppery Scalloped Potatoes. Once the first of us eight kids picked up this dish, it didn't hit the table again until we all helped ourselves to big servings.

We also couldn't wait to dig into the special Candied Carrots. They often looked too good to eat—but that didn't stop us!

Mother's Walnut Cake had a wonderful aroma while it baked, and each tall slice was a joy to eat. She often made it with black walnuts since we had three black walnut trees on the farm.

I can still picture how my dear mother stood in front of the hot stove, humming to herself as she cooked. Maybe that was her way of staying on track with us rambunctious children running in and out of the kitchen.

And maybe that's why I have such a love of cooking—Mother always made it look like such fun!

Apple-Mustard Glazed Ham, Peppery Scalloped Potatoes, Candied Carrots and Mother's Walnut Cake (recipes are on pp. 114-115).

Apple-Mustard Glazed Ham

The sweet and tangy glaze is so simple to mix up, but it turns an ordinary baked ham into a special feast.

- 1 cup apple jelly
- 1 tablespoon prepared mustard
- 1 tablespoon lemon juice
- 1/4 teaspoon ground nutmeg
- 1 fully cooked bone-in ham (5 to 7 pounds)

Whole cloves
Spiced apple rings, optional

In a small saucepan, combine jelly, mustard, lemon juice and nutmeg; bring to a boil, stirring constantly. Remove from the heat; set aside. Score the surface of the ham, making diamond shapes 1/2 in. deep; insert a clove in each diamond.

Place ham on a rack in a shallow roasting pan. Bake, uncovered, at 325° for 20 minutes per pound or until a meat thermometer reads 140°. During the last 30 minutes of baking, brush with glaze twice. Garnish with apple rings if desired. **Yield:** 8-10 servings.

Peppery Scalloped Potatoes

Mother knew these rich, hearty potatoes are good on a cold day since the cayenne pepper warms you up.

- 1 can (10-3/4 ounces) condensed cream of mushroom soup, undiluted
- 1-1/2 cups milk
- 1/2 to 1 teaspoon salt
- 1/8 teaspoon cayenne pepper
- 5 cups thinly sliced peeled potatoes
- 1/4 cup butter, melted
- 1/4 cup all-purpose flour

In a small bowl, combine the soup, milk, salt and cayenne; set aside. Place a third of the potatoes in a greased 13-in. x 9-in. x 2-in. baking dish; layer with a third of the butter, flour and soup mixture.

Repeat layers twice. Bake, uncovered, at 350° for 1 hour and 20 minutes or until the potatoes are tender. **Yield:** 6-8 servings.

Candied Carrots

When I was a girl, Mother made carrots taste more like candy than a vegetable with this recipe. She'd serve them, garnished with parsley, in a pretty bowl.

 Uses less fat, sugar or salt. Includes Nutritional Analysis and Diabetic Exchanges.

- 1-1/2 cups water
- 2 pounds carrots, sliced 1/2 inch thick

- 2 cinnamon sticks (3 inches)
- 1 teaspoon ground cumin
- 1 teaspoon ground ginger
- 6 tablespoons honey
- 4 teaspoons lemon juice

Bring water to a boil in a large skillet; add carrots, cinnamon sticks, cumin and ginger. Reduce heat; cover and simmer for 10 minutes.

Add honey and lemon juice. Bring to a boil. Boil, uncovered, for 4 minutes or until the liquid evaporates and the carrots are tender. **Yield:** 6-8 servings.

Nutritional Analysis: One 1/2-cup serving equals 78 calories, 56 mg sodium, 0 cholesterol, 20 g carbohydrate, 1 g protein, trace fat. **Diabetic Exchange:** 1 starch.

Mother's Walnut Cake

Even though Mother baked this tall, beautiful cake often when I was growing up, it was a real treat every time. I like the walnuts in the cake and the frosting.

- 1/2 cup butter, softened
- 1/2 cup shortening
- 2 cups sugar
- 4 eggs
- 3-1/2 cups all-purpose flour
- 2 teaspoons baking soda

- 1/2 teaspoon salt
- 1-1/2 cups buttermilk
- 2 teaspoons vanilla extract
- 1-1/2 cups ground walnuts

FROSTING:
- 2 packages (one 8 ounces, one 3 ounces) cream cheese, softened
- 3/4 cup butter, softened
- 5 to 5-1/2 cups confectioners' sugar
- 1-1/2 teaspoons vanilla extract
- 1/3 cup finely chopped walnuts

In a large mixing bowl, cream butter, shortening and sugar. Add eggs, one at a time, beating well after each addition.

Combine the flour, baking soda and salt; add to the creamed mixture alternately with buttermilk and vanilla. Beat on low speed just until combined. Stir in walnuts.

Pour into three greased and floured 9-in. x 1-1/2-in. round baking pans. Bake at 350° for 20-25 minutes or until a toothpick inserted near the center comes out clean. Cool for 5 minutes; remove from pans to a wire rack to cool completely.

For frosting, beat cream cheese and butter in a mixing bowl. Add confectioners' sugar; mix well. Add vanilla; beat until smooth. Spread between layers and over top and sides of cake. Sprinkle with walnuts. Store in the refrigerator. **Yield:** 12-16 servings.

Birthday Meal Takes the Cake

By Kim Orr, Louisville, Kentucky

I remember my mother, Cindy Robbins (left) of Waynesville, Ohio, always making sure we had a home-cooked meal when we were growing up, no matter how busy the day.

Mom is a self-taught cook who enjoys preparing foods for family, friends and church dinners. Everyone loves to gather at my parents' home, since she fixes delicious meals and always makes them extra-special with a festively set table.

When my sister and I were younger, Mom would make us our favorite dinner on our birthdays. I always chose lasagna. I loved to watch her assemble this dish layer by layer. The aroma while it was baking in the oven was mouth-watering! Her recipe card is yellow and worn now, but it doesn't matter. Mom can practically make this lasagna in her sleep!

To go with this hearty main course, she would fix a crusty loaf of Chive Garlic Bread. Those savory slices were ideal with an Italian meal.

We all looked forward to a crispy lettuce salad draped with her chunky and flavorful Thousand Island Salad Dressing.

Each year, I requested Old-Fashioned Carrot Cake for my birthday dessert. Since it was my special day, I always asked for seconds of this yummy layer cake. Lucky for me, Mom never said "no" to the birthday girl. The moist cake was chock-full of sweet carrots and topped with a rich cream cheese frosting.

I could not have been blessed with a more wonderful role model both in and out of the kitchen. Mom has taught me that bringing a family together for a meal is one of the most wonderful opportunities we have for sharing. Both of us are pleased to share this meal with you. Don't wait for a birthday to try it!

Mom's Lasagna, Chive Garlic Bread, Thousand Island Salad Dressing and Old-Fashioned Carrot Cake (recipes are on pp. 118-119).

Spoon 1/2 cup meat sauce into a greased 13-in. x 9-in. x 2-in. baking dish. Layer with three noodles and a third of the cottage cheese, mozzarella, meat sauce and Parmesan cheese. Repeat layers twice.

Cover and bake at 350° for 40 minutes or until bubbly and heated through. Uncover; bake 5-10 minutes longer. Let stand for 10 minutes before cutting. **Yield:** 12 servings.

Chive Garlic Bread

A purchased loaf of French bread gets a real boost with a few simple ingredients. Garlic and chives make the savory slices irresistible. Along with lasagna or another Italian meal, we munch them until the last crumbs have vanished!

1/4 cup butter, softened
1/4 cup grated Parmesan cheese
2 tablespoons snipped chives
1 garlic clove, minced
1 loaf (1 pound) French bread, cut into 1-inch slices

In a bowl, combine the butter, Parmesan cheese, chives and garlic. Spread on one side of each slice of bread; wrap in a large piece of heavy-duty foil. Seal the edges. Place on a baking sheet. Bake at 350° for 25-30 minutes or until heated through. **Yield:** 12 servings.

Mom's Lasagna

This recipe is one of my mom's specialties. It's a hearty main dish that gets requested time and time again. The from-scratch sauce makes it more flavorful and softer-textured than other versions.

1 pound ground beef
2 garlic cloves, minced
1-1/2 cups water
1 can (15 ounces) tomato sauce
1 can (6 ounces) tomato paste
1/2 to 1 envelope onion soup mix
1 teaspoon dried oregano
1/2 teaspoon sugar
1/4 teaspoon pepper
9 lasagna noodles, cooked and drained
2 cups (16 ounces) small-curd cottage cheese
4 cups (16 ounces) shredded mozzarella cheese
2 cups grated Parmesan cheese

In a large saucepan, cook beef and garlic over medium heat until meat is no longer pink; drain. Stir in the water, tomato sauce and paste, soup mix, oregano, sugar and pepper. Bring to a boil. Reduce heat; cover and simmer for 30 minutes.

Thousand Island Salad Dressing

This comforting homemade dressing is chock-full of tasty ingredients, including chopped onion, celery and hard-cooked eggs. It's a delightful topping for any crisp green salad.

- 1 cup mayonnaise
- 1/4 cup chili sauce
- 2 hard-cooked eggs, chopped
- 2 tablespoons chopped green onion
- 2 tablespoons chopped celery
- 4-1/2 teaspoons finely chopped onion
- 1 teaspoon paprika
- 1/2 teaspoon salt

In a bowl, combine all ingredients; mix well. Cover and refrigerate until serving. Serve over salad greens. **Yield:** 1-1/2 cups.

Old-Fashioned Carrot Cake

A pleasingly moist cake, this treat is the one I requested that my mom make each year for my birthday. It's dotted with sweet carrots and a hint of cinnamon. The fluffy, buttery cream cheese frosting is scrumptious with chopped walnuts stirred in. One piece of this cake is never enough!

- 4 eggs
- 2 cups sugar
- 1-1/2 cups vegetable oil
- 2 cups all-purpose flour
- 2 to 3 teaspoons ground cinnamon
- 1 teaspoon baking powder
- 1 teaspoon baking soda
- 1/4 teaspoon salt
- 1/4 teaspoon ground nutmeg
- 2 cups grated carrots

FROSTING:
- 1/2 cup butter, softened
- 1 package (3 ounces) cream cheese, softened
- 3-3/4 cups confectioners' sugar
- 1 teaspoon vanilla extract
- 2 to 3 tablespoons milk
- 1 cup chopped walnuts

Carrot curls and additional walnuts, optional

In a mixing bowl, combine the eggs, sugar and oil; mix well. Combine the flour, cinnamon, baking powder, baking soda, salt and nutmeg; beat into egg mixture. Stir in carrots.

Pour into two greased and floured 9-in. round baking pans. Bake at 350° for 35-40 minutes or until a toothpick inserted near the center comes out clean. Cool for 10 minutes before removing from pans to wire racks to cool completely.

For frosting, in a mixing bowl, cream butter and cream cheese. Gradually beat in confectioners' sugar and vanilla. Add enough milk to achieve desired consistency. Stir in walnuts. Spread frosting between layers and over top and sides of cake. Garnish with carrot curls and walnuts if desired. Refrigerate any leftovers. **Yield:** 12 servings.

Tender, Tasty Baked Chicken

By Barbara Wheeler, Sparks Glencoe, Maryland

When we were growing up, my sister, Sandy, my brother, Ed, and I were lucky enough to have a mom who was a full-time homemaker. My mother, Barbara "Be Be" Mead (left) of Avalon, New Jersey, has always been devoted to her family.

Mom delights in creating flavorful meals...and even leftovers become a fun smorgasbord when she assembles them. The kitchen is still her favorite room of the house, and the tempting aromas of dishes she's cooking or baking from scratch tend to draw in friends and family. You can tell she enjoys what she's doing and takes pride in serving a tasty supper.

Trying to identify just one meal as Mom's best is really hard, but we all especially enjoy her Baked Chicken. It's so tender and flavorful. A sauce made of ketchup, lemon juice, brown sugar and spices coats every piece with wonderful flavor.

Scored Potatoes make an excellent side dish. They're simple to prepare yet look like extra care went into them. In Mom's case that's true, of course.

Mom's Caesar Salad is a real classic. The homemade dressing makes it extra fresh-tasting.

We all try to save room for dessert, especially when Mom makes her famous Picnic Chocolate Cake. It's moist and chocolaty, and it tastes great alone or with a big scoop of vanilla ice cream plopped on top.

Mom learned most of her kitchen skills from her aunt and grandmother, and I'm happy to say she passed along many of her secrets to us kids. She and Dad have been married more than 50 years.

My husband, our son and I love to be invited to share a meal at my parents' house. We always feel welcome. The only trouble is it's hard to decide what's better—the food or the company!

Baked Chicken, Scored Potatoes, Caesar Salad and Chocolate Picnic Cake (recipes are on pp. 122-123).

Baked Chicken

A tangy from-scratch sauce makes this tender chicken extra flavorful. My mom is an excellent cook who has fixed delicious dishes like this one for years. If you're in a hurry, prepare it ahead and pop it in the oven when you get home.

- 1 broiler/fryer chicken (3 pounds), cut up
- 1 tablespoon all-purpose flour
- 1/4 cup water
- 1/4 cup packed brown sugar
- 1/4 cup ketchup
- 2 tablespoons white vinegar
- 2 tablespoons lemon juice
- 2 tablespoons Worcestershire sauce
- 1 small onion, chopped
- 1 teaspoon ground mustard
- 1 teaspoon paprika
- 1 teaspoon chili powder
- 1/2 teaspoon salt
- 1/8 teaspoon pepper

Place chicken in a greased 13-in. x 9-in. x 2-in. baking dish. In a saucepan, whisk the flour and water until smooth. Stir in brown sugar, ketchup, vinegar, lemon juice and Worcestershire sauce. Bring to a boil; cook and stir for 2 minutes or until thickened. Cool.

Stir in the remaining ingredients. Pour over chicken. Cover and refrigerate for 2-4 hours. Remove from the refrigerator 30 minutes before baking. Bake, uncovered, at 350° for 35-45 minutes or until chicken juices run clear. **Yield:** 4 servings.

Scored Potatoes

These well-seasoned baked potatoes are a fun alternative to plain baked potatoes. It's easy to help yourself to just the amount you want, too, since the potato halves are scored into sections. My mom serves them alongside many different kinds of meat.

- 4 large baking potatoes
- 2 tablespoons butter, melted, *divided*
- 1/8 teaspoon paprika
- 1 tablespoon minced fresh parsley
- Salt and pepper to taste

With a sharp knife, cut the potatoes in half lengthwise. Slice each half widthwise six times, but not all the way through; fan potatoes slightly. Place in a shallow baking dish. Brush the potatoes with 1 tablespoon melted butter. Sprinkle with paprika, parsley, salt and pepper.

Bake, uncovered, at 350° for 50 minutes or until the potatoes are tender. Drizzle with the remaining butter. **Yield:** 4 servings.

Caesar Salad

This classic recipe can't be beat! When Mom's cooking, our whole family looks forward to this refreshing salad that's tossed with a tangy homemade dressing.

- 3 tablespoons olive oil
- 4-1/2 teaspoons lemon juice
- 1 teaspoon prepared mustard
- 1 garlic clove, minced

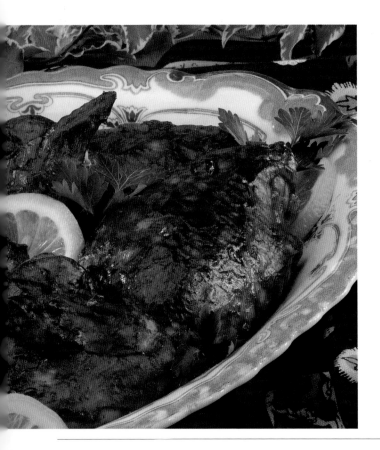

  6 cups torn romaine
2/3 cup Caesar salad croutons
1/2 cup shredded Parmesan cheese
Coarsely ground pepper to taste

In a jar with a tight-fitting lid, combine the oil, lemon juice, mustard and garlic; shake well. In a salad bowl, combine the romaine, croutons, Parmesan cheese and pepper. Drizzle with dressing and toss to coat. **Yield:** 4 servings.

Chocolate Picnic Cake

Rich, moist and chocolaty, this scrumptious cake is very versatile. It freezes well…and the chocolate chip topping makes it easy to pack in lunches and carry along to picnics. At home, we like it topped with vanilla ice cream.

  2 squares (1 ounce *each*) unsweetened chocolate
1-1/4 cups all-purpose flour
1/2 teaspoon baking soda
1/2 teaspoon salt
  1 egg
  1 cup sugar
3/4 cup cold water
1/3 cup vegetable oil
  1 cup (6 ounces) semisweet chocolate chips

In a microwave, melt chocolate; cool for 10 minutes. Combine the flour, baking soda and salt; set aside. In a mixing bowl, beat the egg and sugar. Beat in the water and oil.

Stir in melted chocolate and dry ingredients; mix until blended. Pour batter into a greased 8-in. square baking pan. Sprinkle with chocolate chips. Bake at 350° for 32-38 minutes or until a toothpick inserted near the center comes out clean. Cool on a wire rack. **Yield:** 9 servings.

Salad Solutions

When buying lettuce or other salad greens, look for those that are crisp and blemish-free.

Greens will last longer if you wash them as soon as you get them home.

An easy way to clean most greens is to cut off the bottom to separate the leaves, then put them in a large container of water. Swish the greens around with your hands, then let them sit for a few minutes so any dirt can sink to the bottom.

To clean iceberg lettuce, first remove the core. To do so, hit the core against the countertop, then twist and remove the core. Pour cold water into the hole and swish around. Turn the head of lettuce over to drain the water.

Dry greens before eating or storing.

A Fork-Tender Swiss Specialty

By Linda McGinty, Parma, Ohio

For my mother, Edythe Wagy (left) of Winter Haven, Florida, preparing an evening meal for our family was not a chore, but a labor of love.

In those days, she was a real home-maker. She not only loved to sew, cook and bake, she also strived to make our home a warm, inviting place.

Sunday mornings were extra nice since Mom would make a batch of homemade fritters or pecan rolls. All of my friends would beg to sleep overnight on Saturday so they could indulge in the scrumptious breakfast pastries.

Mom also hosted many large gatherings when my two brothers and I were growing up. Everyone looked forward to a satisfying main dish like her flavorful So-Tender Swiss Steak.

Fork-tender pieces of beef topped with a rich, thick gravy over hot cooked noodles made everyone's mouth water.

Side dishes, like her Cauliflower Casserole and Strawberry Pear Gelatin, were both comforting and extra-special at the same time.

A blend of cheeses, crushed cornflakes and garden-fresh peppers dress up plain cauliflower, while the addition of cream cheese makes the gelatin salad smooth and creamy.

But the thing family and friends most eagerly anticipated was dessert, which Mom always made from scratch. Mom's Chocolate Cake, with its delicate chocolate flavor and fluffy frosting, is a wonderful end to any special-occasion or weekday meal.

Although Mom and Dad are not as active as they used to be, Mom still prepares one of our favorites whenever we visit. After all, the kitchen is still her favorite room in the house.

So-Tender Swiss Steak, Cauliflower Casserole, Strawberry Pear Gelatin and Mom's Chocolate Cake (recipes are on pp. 126-127).

bake at 325° for 2 to 2-1/2 hours or until meat is very tender. Remove to a serving platter and keep warm.

In a small bowl, combine flour, salt, pepper and broth until smooth; stir into the pan juices. Bring to a boil over medium heat; cook and stir for 2 minutes. Serve steak and gravy over noodles or mashed potatoes if desired. **Yield:** 8 servings.

Cauliflower Casserole

To dress up cauliflower, Mom used a delightful mixture of a cheesy sauce, bright red and green pepper pieces and crushed cornflakes. We enjoyed this casserole so much that leftovers were rare.

1   **medium head cauliflower, broken into florets**
1   **cup (8 ounces) sour cream**
1   **cup (4 ounces) shredded cheddar cheese**
1/2   **cup crushed cornflakes**
1/4   **cup chopped green pepper**
1/4   **cup chopped sweet red pepper**
1   **teaspoon salt**
1/4   **cup grated Parmesan cheese**
Paprika

Place cauliflower and a small amount of water in a saucepan; cover and cook for 5 minutes or until crisp-tender. Drain.

Combine cauliflower, sour cream, cheddar cheese, cornflakes, peppers and salt; transfer to a greased 2-qt. baking dish. Sprinkle with Parmesan cheese and paprika. Bake, uncovered, at 325° for 30-35 minutes or until heated through. **Yield:** 6-8 servings.

So-Tender Swiss Steak

This Swiss steak with rich, meaty gravy was an often-requested main dish around our house when I was growing up. Mom took pride in preparing scrumptious, hearty meals like this for our family and guests.

1/4   **cup all-purpose flour**
1/2   **teaspoon salt**
1/4   **teaspoon pepper**
2   **pounds round steak, cut into serving-size pieces**
2   **tablespoons vegetable oil**
1   **medium onion, thinly sliced**
2   **cups water**
2   **tablespoons Worcestershire sauce**
GRAVY:
1/4   **cup all-purpose flour**
1/4   **teaspoon salt**
1/8   **teaspoon pepper**
1-1/4   **cups beef broth *or* water**
Hot cooked noodles *or* mashed potatoes, optional

In a shallow bowl, combine flour, salt and pepper. Dredge steak, a few pieces at a time. Pound with a mallet to tenderize. In a Dutch oven, brown steak in oil on all sides. Arrange onion slices between layers of meat.

Add water and Worcestershire sauce. Cover and

Strawberry Pear Gelatin

Mom had a way of making every dish she served just a little more special. A good example is this fluffy salad. It's both fruity and refreshing.

- 1 **can (29 ounces) pears**
- 1 **package (6 ounces) strawberry gelatin**
- 1 **package (8 ounces) cream cheese, cubed**
- 1 **carton (8 ounces) frozen whipped topping, thawed**

Mandarin oranges, optional

Drain pears, reserving juice. Chop pears and set aside. Add water to the juice to measure 3 cups. Place in a saucepan; bring to a boil. Transfer to a large bowl. Add gelatin and stir until dissolved.

Whisk in cream cheese until smooth. Refrigerate until slightly thickened. Whisk in whipped topping until smooth. Add chopped pears. Transfer to a 13-in. x 9-in. x 2-in. dish coated with nonstick cooking spray. Cover; refrigerate until firm. Cut into squares. Garnish with mandarin oranges if desired. **Yield:** 12-16 servings.

Mom's Chocolate Cake

Over the years, Mom has become known for wonderful from-scratch desserts like this old-fashioned chocolate cake. It was difficult, but my brothers and I would always manage to save room for dessert.

- 2 **squares (1 ounce *each*) unsweetened chocolate, broken into pieces**
- 1/2 **cup boiling water**
- 1/2 **cup shortening**
- 2 **cups packed brown sugar**
- 2 **eggs, *separated***
- 2 **cups sifted cake flour**
- 2 **teaspoons baking powder**
- 1/2 **teaspoon baking soda**
- 1/2 **teaspoon salt**
- 1/2 **cup buttermilk *or* sour milk**
- 1/2 **cup water**
- 1/2 **cup chopped walnuts**
- 1 **teaspoon vanilla extract**

COCOA FROSTING:
- 6 **tablespoons butter, softened**
- 3-1/2 **cups confectioners' sugar**
- 1/2 **cup baking cocoa**
- 1-1/2 **teaspoons vanilla extract**

Pinch salt
- 4 **to 6 tablespoons milk**

In a small bowl, stir chocolate in boiling water until melted; set aside to cool, about 10 minutes. In a mixing bowl, cream shortening and brown sugar. Beat in egg yolks and chocolate mixture. Combine flour, baking powder, baking soda and salt; add to creamed mixture alternately with buttermilk. Gradually beat in water, nuts and vanilla.

In a small mixing bowl, beat egg whites until soft peaks form; fold into batter. Pour into a greased 13-in. x 9-in. x 2-in. baking pan. Bake at 350° for 35-40 minutes or until a toothpick inserted near the center comes out clean. Cool on a wire rack.

In a mixing bowl, cream butter. Combine confectioners' sugar and cocoa; gradually add to butter with vanilla, salt and enough milk to achieve desired spreading consistency. Frost cake. **Yield:** 12-15 servings.

Editor's Note: To sour milk, place 1-1/2 teaspoons white vinegar in a measuring cup. Add milk to equal 1/2 cup.

Family-Favorite Pork Chops

By Cris O'Brien, Virginia Beach, Virginia

Over the years, my mother has spent more time in her kitchen than any other room in the house.

When my two brothers and I were growing up, my mom, Louanne Davis (left) of Jackson, Michigan, made everything from scratch. And she canned the harvest from Dad's garden, so her meals were filled with fruits and vegetables. Because she refused to cater to picky eaters, we learned to enjoy a variety of foods.

In addition to feeding her family, Mom prepared meals for church dinners and, as a Girl Scout leader, taught many young girls how to bake. She went all out when relatives came to visit, lining the counter with yummy treats.

Mom's such an excellent cook that it's difficult to select one "best" meal, but there's a reason Favorite Pork Chops have that name. The tender chops are marinated for several hours, then baked and draped in a zippy red sauce. The whole family loves them.

For her comforting Au Gratin Potatoes, she coats thin potato slices with a rich, creamy sauce.

My grandma taught Mom to make meals as colorful as possible. Mom's Bean Medley gets a rainbow of color from green pepper, tomato and four kinds of beans.

Chocolate Cake Roll was reserved for special occasions. No one was allowed to sample this delicious dessert until it was served, but it was definitely worth the wait!

Mom is in her 70s now and still cooks for my dad and herself. I enjoy preparing her recipes for my husband and two teenage sons. My sisters-in-law use Mom's recipes, too. I hope you'll find them just as appetizing as we do.

Favorite Pork Chops, Au Gratin Potatoes, Mom's Bean Medley and Chocolate Cake Roll (recipes are on pp. 130-131).

Favorite Pork Chops

My mom often served this dish when relatives were visiting. The night before, I'd watch her prepare the soy sauce marinade. As the pork chops baked the next day, the tantalizing aroma would fill the kitchen. It was always a hit!

- 2 cups soy sauce
- 1 cup water
- 1/2 cup packed brown sugar
- 1 tablespoon molasses
- 6 bone-in pork loin chops (1-1/2 inches thick)

SAUCE:
- 3/4 cup ketchup
- 2/3 cup chili sauce
- 1/4 cup packed brown sugar
- 2 tablespoons water
- 1-1/2 teaspoons ground mustard

In a saucepan over medium heat, bring the soy sauce, water, brown sugar and molasses to a boil. Remove from the heat; cool to room temperature. Pour into a large resealable plastic bag; add pork chops. Seal bag and refrigerate for 3-6 hours.

Drain and discard marinade. Place pork chops in a greased 13-in. x 9-in. x 2-in. baking dish. Cover and bake at 350° for 30 minutes. Combine the sauce ingredients; pour over chops. Bake, uncovered, 30 minutes longer or until meat juices run clear. **Yield:** 6 servings.

Au Gratin Potatoes

These cheesy potatoes are always welcome at our dinner table, and they're so simple to make. A perfect complement to ham, this homey side dish also goes well with pork, chicken and other entrees.

- 3 tablespoons butter
- 3 tablespoons all-purpose flour
- 1-1/2 teaspoons salt
- 1/8 teaspoon pepper
- 2 cups milk
- 1 cup (4 ounces) shredded cheddar cheese
- 5 cups thinly sliced peeled potatoes (about 6 medium)
- 1/2 cup chopped onion

In a large saucepan, melt butter over low heat. Stir in the flour, salt and pepper until smooth. Gradually add milk. Bring to a boil; cook and stir for 2 minutes or until thickened. Remove from the heat; stir in cheese until melted. Add potatoes and onion; stir well.

Transfer to a greased 2-qt. baking dish. Cover; bake at 350° for 1 hour. Uncover; bake 30-40 minutes longer or until the potatoes are tender. **Yield:** 6-8 servings.

Mom's Bean Medley

Pinto, garbanzo, green and wax beans star in this snappy marinated salad. For a taste twist, Mom added tomatoes and mayonnaise to the colorful combination.

- 1 can (15 ounces) pinto beans, rinsed and drained
- 1 can (15 ounces) garbanzo beans, rinsed and drained
- 1 can (8 ounces) cut green beans, drained

 1 can (8 ounces) yellow wax beans, drained
1/2 cup thinly sliced green pepper
1/4 cup thinly sliced red onion
 6 tablespoons vegetable oil
 3 tablespoons cider vinegar
 1 tablespoon sugar
1/4 teaspoon dried oregano
1/8 teaspoon garlic powder
 3 tablespoons mayonnaise
 1 medium tomato, chopped

In a large bowl, combine the beans, green pepper and onion. In a jar with a tight-fitting lid, combine the oil, vinegar, sugar, oregano and garlic powder; shake well. Pour over vegetables and toss to coat. Cover and refrigerate for 8 hours or overnight. Stir in mayonnaise. Add tomato; toss gently. **Yield:** 6-8 servings.

Chocolate Cake Roll

This delectable dessert features sweet whipped cream and moist chocolate cake rolled up and dusted with confectioners' sugar. A family favorite, it winds up any special meal in festive fashion.

 6 eggs, *separated*
 1 cup sugar, *divided*
 1 teaspoon vanilla extract
1/4 cup all-purpose flour
1/4 cup baking cocoa
1/4 teaspoon salt
1/2 teaspoon cream of tartar

1-1/2 cups heavy whipping cream
 2 tablespoons confectioners' sugar
Additional confectioners' sugar

Place egg whites in a small mixing bowl; let stand at room temperature for 30 minutes. In a large mixing bowl, beat egg yolks on high speed until light and fluffy. Gradually add 1/2 cup sugar, beating until thick and lemon-colored. Stir in vanilla. Combine the flour, cocoa and salt; add to egg yolk mixture until blended.

Beat egg whites on medium until foamy. Add cream of tartar; beat until soft peaks form. Gradually add remaining sugar, 1 tablespoon at a time, beating on high until stiff peaks form. Stir a fourth of the egg white mixture into chocolate mixture. Fold in remaining egg white mixture until no egg white streaks remain.

Line a greased 15-in. x 10-in. x 1-in. baking pan with parchment paper; grease the paper. Spread batter evenly in pan. Bake at 350° for 12-15 minutes or until cake springs back when lightly touched in center (do not overbake). Cool for 5 minutes; invert onto a kitchen towel dusted with confectioners' sugar. Gently peel off parchment paper. Roll up cake in the towel jelly-roll style, starting with a short side. Cool completely on a wire rack.

In a mixing bowl, beat cream and confectioners' sugar until stiff peaks form; chill. Unroll cake; spread with whipped cream to within 1/2 in. of edges. Roll up again. Place seam side down on serving platter; chill. Dust with additional confectioners' sugar before serving. **Yield:** 12 servings.

Entertaining takes on an international flair with this kabob dinner. Recipes are on pp. 152-153.

Refreshing SUMMER MEALS

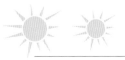

A Farm-Style Chicken Dinner

By Vera Reid, Laramie, Wyoming

As a true farm wife, my mom has always been a great cook. She worked hard to prepare delicious meals for Dad, my two sisters and me that would satisfy our hungry appetites after doing a variety of chores.

Of all the terrific foods Mom prepared, I remember her crispy summertime Buttermilk Fried Chicken the most. Served with a wonderful savory gravy, it was one of her many main meals guaranteed to make our mouths water.

As the plate of chicken was passed, we girls knew not to take a piece until Dad and Mom had each selected their favorites. We could hardly resist snatching a piece as the plate passed us by, but there was always plenty of chicken to go around.

With crisp radishes and smoky bacon bits, Wilted Lettuce Salad looked and tasted so tempting. It was the only salad we wanted her to make, and she was happy to watch us devour the nutritious greens.

I can still see Mom pulling the fluffy Buttermilk Biscuits out of the oven. They always seemed to disappear too quickly, especially when we slathered each delectable bite with sweet, creamy butter.

We couldn't wait for Mom to bring dessert to the table. Her Hot Fudge Cake was a rich, satisfying end to a perfect meal. Mom served it with a scoop of ice cream or cream poured over the top.

Living on a farm is not easy. But growing up there with all the cool green grass, the endless blue sky and Mom's home cooking, we knew we were safe and loved.

That's something I wish every child was able to experience. This memorable meal helps capture the comforting flavor of farm life!

Buttermilk Fried Chicken with Gravy, Wilted Lettuce Salad, Mom's Buttermilk Biscuits and Hot Fudge Cake (recipes are on pp. 136-137).

chicken is tender. Uncover and cook 5 minutes longer.

Remove chicken and keep warm. Drain all but 1/4 cup drippings in skillet; stir in flour until bubbly. Add milk and 1-1/2 cups water; cook and stir until thickened and bubbly. Cook 1 minute more. Add remaining water if needed. Season with salt and pepper. Serve with chicken. **Yield:** 4-6 servings.

Wilted Lettuce Salad

Fresh, colorful and lightly coated with a delectable dressing, this salad is perfect for a special meal or Sunday dinner. Mom made it look so tempting with the crisp radishes and crumbled bacon.

  1 **bunch leaf lettuce, torn**
  6 **to 8 radishes, thinly sliced**
  4 **to 6 green onions with tops, thinly sliced**
DRESSING:
  4 **to 5 bacon strips**
  2 **tablespoons red wine vinegar**
  1 **tablespoon lemon juice**
  1 **teaspoon sugar**
1/2 **teaspoon pepper**

Toss lettuce, radishes and onions in a large salad bowl; set aside. In a skillet, cook bacon until crisp. Remove to paper towels to drain.

To the hot drippings, add vinegar, lemon juice, sugar and pepper; stir well. Immediately pour dressing over salad; toss gently. Crumble the bacon and sprinkle on top. Serve immediately. **Yield:** 6-8 servings.

Buttermilk Fried Chicken with Gravy

We raised our own meat and vegetables when I was a girl. This golden chicken reminds me of Mom and home. There's nothing quite like a crispy piece smothered in creamy gravy.

  1 **broiler/fryer chicken (2-1/2 to 3 pounds), cut up**
  1 **cup buttermilk**
  1 **cup all-purpose flour**
1-1/2 **teaspoons salt**
1/2 **teaspoon pepper**
Vegetable oil for frying
GRAVY:
  3 **tablespoons all-purpose flour**
  1 **cup milk**
1-1/2 **to 2 cups water**
Salt and pepper to taste

Place chicken in a large flat dish. Pour buttermilk over; cover and refrigerate for 1 hour. Combine flour, salt and pepper in a double-strength paper bag. Drain chicken pieces; toss, one at a time, in flour mixture. Shake off excess; place on waxed paper for 15 minutes to dry.

Heat 1/8 to 1/4 in. of oil in a large skillet; brown chicken on all sides. Cover and simmer, turning occasionally, for 40-45 minutes, or until juices run clear and

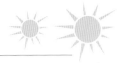

Hot Fudge Cake

Here's a wonderful way to top off a great meal—a rich, chocolaty cake that's not overly sweet. Mom served it with a scoop of ice cream or cream poured over. I'd always have room for a serving of this dessert.

1 **cup all-purpose flour**
3/4 **cup sugar**
6 **tablespoons baking cocoa,** *divided*
2 **teaspoons baking powder**
1/4 **teaspoon salt**
1/2 **cup milk**
2 **tablespoons vegetable oil**
1 **teaspoon vanilla extract**
1 **cup packed brown sugar**
1-3/4 **cups hot water**
Whipped cream *or* ice cream, optional

In a medium bowl, combine flour, sugar, 2 tablespoons cocoa, baking powder and salt. Stir in the milk, oil and vanilla until smooth.

Spread mixture in an ungreased 9-in. square baking pan. Combine brown sugar and remaining cocoa; sprinkle over batter. Pour hot water over all; do not stir. Bake at 350° for 35-40 minutes. Serve warm. Top with whipped cream or ice cream if desired. **Yield:** 9 servings.

Mom's Buttermilk Biscuits

These fluffy biscuits are so tasty served warm, slathered with butter or used to mop up every last drop of gravy off the plate. I can still see Mom pulling these tender biscuits out of the oven.

2 **cups all-purpose flour**
2 **teaspoons baking powder**
1/2 **teaspoon baking soda**
1/2 **teaspoon salt**
1/4 **cup shortening**
3/4 **cup buttermilk**

In a bowl, combine the flour, baking powder, baking soda and salt; cut in shortening until the mixture resembles coarse crumbs. Stir in buttermilk; knead dough gently. Roll out to 1/2-in. thickness.

Cut with a 2-1/2-in. biscuit cutter and place on a lightly greased baking sheet. Bake at 450° for 10-15 minutes or until golden brown. **Yield:** 10 biscuits.

Leftover Biscuits?

If you have leftover biscuits, wrap them in foil and store at room temperature for up to 3 days. To reheat, place the foil packet in a 300° oven for about 10 minutes or until warm.

Casual Cuisine For Summer Days

By Sally Holbrook, Pasadena, California*

I have many fond memories of my years growing up in a household where the kitchen was the center of activity.

Ours was a large, sunny kitchen with a work table in the center. It was a wonderful place where my mother and grandmother would spend hours lovingly preparing delicious meals, from simple family fare to delectable party dishes, filling the house with appealing aromas.

My parents and grandparents often entertained their friends on the patio overlooking the bay. A long wooden table, spread with a blue and white tablecloth, was topped with a treasure of flavorful foods that friends and family couldn't wait to dig into.

Hungry guests enjoyed a hearty casserole Mom called Sausage Pie, featuring pork sausage links and produce found in her own garden.

Mom dressed up thick slices of Buttery French Bread with simple seasonings and real butter.

As a special treat, Mom would give salad greens an added punch by preparing zippy Creamy Garlic Dressing. To save time, you can prepare this dressing and wash, cut and dry all salad ingredients the night before. You'll appreciate the extra time you have to spend visiting with guests.

For a fantastic finale, Mom's Peach Pie would overflow with fresh peach flavor, making it a delightful treat.

Now when my brother, sisters and I get together with friends and family in our homes, we still use all these wonderful recipes from Mom's delicious menu!

Sausage Pie, Buttery French Bread, Creamy Garlic Dressing and Mom's Peach Pie (recipes are on pp. 140-141).

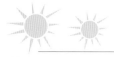

Sausage Pie

When I was growing up, Mom made this tasty casserole often in summer for our family and guests. People would comment on the pretty color. This recipe is a great way to use garden vegetables, and the sausage adds comforting flavor. I'm sure you'll enjoy it as much as we do. With rice, it truly is a meal-in-one, but Mom was sure to pair it with her other favorite foods.

- 16 small fresh pork sausage links (about 1 pound)
- 1/2 medium green pepper, chopped
- 1/2 medium sweet red pepper, chopped
- 1 tablespoon vegetable oil
- 3 cups cooked long grain rice
- 4 to 5 medium tomatoes, peeled and chopped
- 1 package (10 ounces) frozen corn, thawed
- 1 cup (4 ounces) shredded cheddar cheese
- 1 tablespoon Worcestershire sauce
- 1 teaspoon salt
- 2 tablespoons chopped fresh parsley
- 1 teaspoon dried basil
- 1 cup soft bread crumbs
- 2 tablespoons butter, melted

Place sausages on a rack in a baking pan; bake at 350° for 15 minutes or until lightly browned. Cut into 1-in. pieces; set aside.

In a skillet, saute peppers in oil for 3 minutes. Place in a 3-qt. casserole; add the sausages and the next eight ingredients. Combine bread crumbs and butter; sprinkle on top of the casserole. Bake, uncovered, at 350° for 30-40 minutes or until heated through. **Yield:** 6-8 servings.

Buttery French Bread

Instead of always having to make bread from scratch, Mom would frequently dress up plain purchased French bread with this interesting, delicious recipe. The combination of paprika, celery seed and butter makes for a full-flavored bread. Wrapping the bread in foil before baking keeps the crust nice and tender. Then bake it uncovered for just a few minutes to give it a lovely golden brown color.

- 1/2 cup butter, softened
- 1/4 teaspoon paprika
- 1/4 teaspoon celery seed
- 1 loaf French bread (about 20 inches), sliced

In a small bowl, combine butter, paprika and celery seed; spread between bread slices and over top. Wrap bread tightly in foil. Bake at 375° for 15 minutes. Open the foil and bake 5 minutes longer. **Yield:** 6-8 servings.

Creamy Garlic Dressing

This zippy dressing gives a refreshing warm-weather salad added punch. The wonderful garlic taste comes through as this creamy mixture coats just about any kind of salad greens beautifully.

- **1 cup vegetable oil**
- **1/2 cup sour cream**
- **1/4 cup heavy whipping cream**
- **1/4 cup cider vinegar**
- **1 teaspoon salt**
- **1 large garlic clove, minced**
- **Salad greens**

In a small bowl, combine the oil, sour cream, whipping cream, vinegar, salt and garlic; stir until smooth. Chill. Serve over salad greens. Refrigerate leftovers. **Yield:** 1-2/3 cups.

Mom's Peach Pie

A delightful summertime pie, this special dessert is overflowing with fresh peach flavor. Each sweet slice is packed with old-fashioned appeal. The streusel topping makes this pie a little different than the ordinary and adds homemade flair. For a change of pace, top with a scoop of vanilla ice cream.

- **1 egg white**
- **1 unbaked pastry shell (9 inches)**
- **3/4 cup all-purpose flour**
- **1/2 cup packed brown sugar**
- **1/3 cup sugar**
- **1/4 cup chilled butter, cut into 6 pieces**
- **6 cups sliced peeled fresh peaches**

Beat egg white until foamy; brush over the bottom and sides of the pastry. In a small bowl, combine the flour and sugars; cut in the cold butter until the mixture resembles fine crumbs.

Sprinkle two-thirds into the bottom of the pastry; top with peaches. Sprinkle with remaining crumb mixture. Bake at 375° for 40-45 minutes or until filling is bubbly and peaches are tender. **Yield:** 6-8 servings.

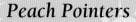

Peach Pointers

Purchase very fragrant peaches that give slightly to pressure; avoid those with soft spots. A pound (about 4 peaches) yields 2-3/4 cups sliced.

To easily remove the skin from a peach, dip the peach into boiling water for 20 to 30 seconds; remove with a slotted spoon and immediately plunge into a bowl of ice water. Remove the skin with a paring knife.

Finger-Licking Ribs 'n' Fixin's

By Judy Clark, Elkhart, Indiana

A cherished memory of growing up, shared by my two sisters, my brother and me, is coming home from church on Sunday to the wonderful aroma of Tangy Spareribs baking in the oven.

Mom's recipe for the nicely seasoned sauce always turns out finger-licking-good!

Along with the ribs, my mother, Thelma Arnold (above left), served tender baked potatoes topped with creamy butter and extra rib sauce, garden peas and golden Icebox Butterhorns.

Mom had just the right touch when mixing up the dough for these rich, buttery rolls. The result was a melt-in-your-mouth wonder!

This recipe is especially appealing because the dough is made the night before. The next day, just shape the rolls, let rise and bake. There were usually no rolls left over to enjoy at another meal.

We were always too full for dessert at the end of the meal. But by mid-afternoon, we were ready for one of our favorite dessert combinations—Cheery Cherry Cookies and Homemade Frozen Custard.

Mom's creamy custard is better than any other I've tried. And generous scoops of it were perfectly paired with the eye-catching cherry cookies.

Mom taught us girls that cooking is an adventure, not a chore. To her, a high compliment from family or guests was a look of delight at a first mouthful.

Eating delicious meals like this, all four of us kids would tell you we grew up enjoying a privileged childhood filled with happy memories.

Tangy Spareribs, Icebox Butterhorns, Cheery Cherry Cookies and Homemade Frozen Custard (recipes are on pp. 144-145).

Tangy Spareribs

I'll never forget the wonderful aroma of these spareribs when I was growing up. They have a real old-fashioned flavor. Who can resist when that mouth-watering homemade barbecue sauce clings to every morsel?

4   to 5 pounds pork spareribs
1   medium onion, finely chopped
1/2   cup finely chopped celery
2   tablespoons butter
1   cup ketchup
1   cup water
1/4   cup lemon juice
2   tablespoons vinegar
2   tablespoons brown sugar
1   tablespoon Worcestershire sauce
1/2   teaspoon ground mustard
1/8   teaspoon pepper
1/8   teaspoon chili powder

Cut ribs into serving-size pieces; place on a rack in a shallow roasting pan. Bake, uncovered, at 350° for 1 hour. Meanwhile, in a medium saucepan, saute onion and celery in butter for 4-5 minutes or until tender.

Add remaining ingredients; mix well. Bring to a boil; reduce heat. Cook and stir until slightly thickened, about 10 minutes. Remove from the heat. Drain fat from roasting pan. Pour sauce over ribs. Bake 1-1/2 hours longer or until meat is tender. **Yield:** 6-8 servings.

Icebox Butterhorns

If you'd like a roll that melts in your mouth, you have to try Mom's recipe. She has just the right touch when she's mixing up this dough. The rolls smell absolutely heavenly as they bake to a golden brown.

1   package (1/4 ounce) active dry yeast
2   tablespoons warm water (110° to 115°)
2   cups warm milk (110° to 115°)
1/2   cup sugar
1   egg, beaten
1   teaspoon salt
6   cups all-purpose flour
3/4   cup butter, melted
Additional melted butter

In a large mixing bowl, dissolve yeast in water. Add the milk, sugar, egg, salt and 3 cups flour; beat until smooth. Beat in butter and remaining flour (dough will be slightly sticky). Do not knead. Place in a greased bowl, turning once to grease top. Cover and refrigerate overnight.

Punch dough down and divide in half. On a floured surface, roll each half into a 12-in. circle. Cut each circle into 12 pie-shaped wedges. Beginning at the wide end, roll up each wedge. Place rolls, point side down, 2 in. apart on greased baking sheets. Cover and let rise in a warm place until doubled, about 1 hour.

Bake at 350° for 15-20 minutes or until golden brown. Immediately brush tops with melted butter. **Yield:** 2 dozen.

In a mixing bowl, cream butter and brown sugar; beat in the egg, milk and vanilla. Combine flour, salt and baking soda; gradually add to creamed mixture. Fold in cherries, pecans and coconut.

Drop by teaspoonfuls 3 in. apart onto ungreased baking sheets. Bake at 375° for 10-12 minutes or until golden brown. Cool on wire racks. **Yield:** 4 dozen.

Homemade Frozen Custard

My siblings and I had a hard time finding room for dessert after Mom's meals, but when we were ready, we could count on a creamy bowl of frozen custard.

- 4 **cups milk**
- 4 **eggs**
- 1-1/4 **cups sugar**
- 1/3 **cup cornstarch**
- 1/8 **teaspoon salt**
- 1 **can (14 ounces) sweetened condensed milk**
- 2 **tablespoons vanilla extract**

In a large heavy saucepan, bring the milk to a boil. Meanwhile, beat eggs; add sugar, cornstarch and salt. Mix well.

Gradually add a small amount of hot milk to the egg mixture; return all to the saucepan. Cook and stir constantly for 6-8 minutes or until mixture thickens and coats a spoon. Gradually stir in condensed milk and vanilla; mix well. Chill for 3-4 hours.

Pour into the cylinder of an ice cream freezer and freeze according to manufacturer's directions. **Yield:** about 1-1/2 quarts.

Cheery Cherry Cookies

With a tall glass of ice-cold milk, a couple of these cherry cookies really hit the spot for dessert or as a snack. The coconut, pecans and bits of cherries provide a fun look and texture.

- 3/4 **cup butter, softened**
- 1 **cup packed brown sugar**
- 1 **egg**
- 2 **tablespoons milk**
- 1 **teaspoon vanilla extract**
- 2 **cups all-purpose flour**
- 1/2 **teaspoon salt**
- 1/2 **teaspoon baking soda**
- 1/2 **cup maraschino cherries, well drained and chopped**
- 1/2 **cup chopped pecans**
- 1/2 **cup flaked coconut**

Avoid Drop Disasters

To help keep drop cookie dough from flattening too much during baking, always cool baking sheets completely between batches.

Grandma's Special Day

By Julianne Johnson, Grove City, Minnesota

Years ago, my grandmother invited family and friends over on her birthday, and then she made the meal herself! Grandma always served this hearty Chicken Macaroni Casserole and family-favorite Picnic Baked Beans. Everyone gobbled up every bite as we celebrated this special woman's day.

Eventually, my mom—also a wonderful cook—took over the tradition, adding her own special Garden Potato Salad. I consider this to be a key item on the menu. The crunchy radishes and creamy home-made dressing add an extra-special touch.

This tempting salad wasn't reserved for birthday parties, however. Mom would make it for summer picnics as well. No matter the gathering, this savory salad was always one of the first dishes to disappear.

Through the years, Mom also added Peanut Butter Pie to the menu. Everyone agrees that traditional birthday cake just can't hold a candle to this cool and creamy dessert. (And you'll be pleasantly surprised by its simple preparation!)

We loved a similar pie served at a local restaurant, but the cook wouldn't share the recipe with Mom. She was determined to come up with her own version. She did, and we all thought it was as good as or even better than the restaurant version. Of course, it required a few taste tests to be sure!

With some special additions to Grandma's original menu, this mouth-watering meal has become a tradition I now serve for all the birthdays in my family.

Chicken Macaroni Casserole, Garden Potato Salad, Picnic Baked Beans and Peanut Butter Pie (recipes are on pp. 148-149).

Chicken Macaroni Casserole

My favorite main-dish recipe passed on by Grandma and Mom, this casserole is considered "birthday food" because we often requested it for our birthdays. Hearty and flavorful, it's a real family pleaser.

- 2 tablespoons butter
- 1/4 cup all-purpose flour
- 2 cups half-and-half cream
- 1-1/2 to 2 cups chicken broth
- 3/4 pound process cheese (Velveeta), cubed
- 2 packages (7 ounces *each*) elbow macaroni, cooked and drained
- 3 cups cubed cooked chicken
- 1 jar (2 ounces) diced pimientos, drained
- 1 teaspoon salt
- 1/2 teaspoon pepper

Minced fresh parsley, optional

In a large saucepan, melt butter. Stir in flour until combined. Add cream and 1-1/2 cups of the broth all at once; stir until smooth. Cook and stir until thickened and bubbly; cook and stir 2 minutes more.

Remove from the heat; add the cheese and stir until melted. Stir in macaroni, chicken, pimientos, salt and pepper. Add additional broth if needed. Pour into a 3-qt. baking dish. Bake, uncovered, at 350° for 40 minutes or until heated through. Sprinkle with parsley if desired. **Yield:** 6-8 servings.

Garden Potato Salad

The tasty dressing on this potato salad makes it special. A great combination of flavors is a real treat and gives a traditional recipe a whole new twist. It's perfect for almost any occasion, and I consider it a key part of my "Mom's Best Meal."

- 6 large potatoes (about 3 pounds), cooked, peeled and cubed
- 4 hard-cooked eggs, sliced
- 2 celery ribs, diced
- 6 green onions with tops, sliced
- 6 radishes, sliced
- 1 teaspoon salt
- 1/2 teaspoon pepper

DRESSING:
- 3 eggs, beaten
- 1/4 cup vinegar
- 1/4 cup sugar
- 1/2 teaspoon ground mustard
- 1/2 teaspoon salt
- 1 cup mayonnaise

In a large bowl, combine potatoes, eggs, celery, green onions, radishes, salt and pepper; set aside.

For dressing, combine eggs, vinegar, sugar, ground mustard and salt in a saucepan. Cook and stir over medium heat until thickened. Cool. Stir in mayonnaise; mix well. Pour over the potato mixture; toss to coat. Refrigerate for several hours before serving. **Yield:** 8 servings.

Picnic Baked Beans

I loved it when my mom made these classic beans. Now I make them for my own family. They have great old-fashioned flavor and are a real crowd pleaser. I fix them for potlucks, picnics or as part of a summertime dinner.

3 cups dry navy beans (about 1-1/2 pounds)
4 quarts cold water, *divided*
1 medium onion, chopped
1 cup ketchup
1 cup packed brown sugar
2 tablespoons molasses
1 tablespoon salt
2 teaspoons ground mustard
1/4 pound bacon, cooked and crumbled

Rinse beans; place in a Dutch oven with 2 qts. water. Bring to a boil; reduce heat and simmer for 3 minutes. Remove from the heat and let stand for 1 hour. Drain and rinse.

Return beans to Dutch oven with remaining water; bring to a boil. Reduce heat; simmer for 1 hour or until beans are tender. Drain, reserving cooking liquid. In the Dutch oven or a 3-qt. baking dish, combine beans, 1 cup of the cooking liquid, onion, ketchup, brown sugar, molasses, salt, mustard and bacon; mix well.

Cover and bake at 300° for 2 to 2-1/2 hours or until beans are as thick as desired. Stir occasionally and add more of the reserved cooking liquid if needed. **Yield:** 16 servings.

Peanut Butter Pie

This smooth creamy pie with a big peanut butter taste reminds me of Mom. It's sure to be a hit around your house, too. I like to make it in the summer because it's simple to prepare and the kitchen stays cool.

4 cups milk
2 packages (3 ounces *each*) cook-and-serve vanilla *or* chocolate pudding
1/2 cup creamy peanut butter
3/4 cup confectioners' sugar
1 pie pastry (9 inches), baked
Whipped cream

In a saucepan, cook the milk and pudding over medium heat until thickened and bubbly. Remove from the heat and cool slightly. Meanwhile, in a bowl, cut peanut butter into confectioners' sugar until small crumbs form. (Peanut butter consistency may vary; add additional confectioners' sugar if necessary.)

Set aside about 2 tablespoons of crumbs; sprinkle remaining mixture into pie shell. Pour pudding over crumbs. Chill until set. Top with whipped cream; sprinkle reserved crumbs on top. **Yield:** 6-8 servings.

Portable Pie Pans

Lightweight foil pie pans are usually smaller than regular pans, so you may end up with extra filling. If so, pour in custard cups for snacks.

World-Class Cuisine

By Jennifer McQuillan, Jacksonville, Florida

My mom is an adventurous cook who loves to entertain. Since Dad was in the Air Force, they've both done a lot of traveling over the years. My mother Carol Stickney (left) of Sparta, New Jersey, picked up plenty of great recipes along the way.

This family-favorite meal combines some of those delicious recipes.

Curried Beef Kabobs is a colorful main dish that Mom came across while Dad was stationed in Turkey in the 1970s. She enrolled in a cooking class while living there, and she learned to fix many new dishes, including these zesty kabobs.

That's also where she got the recipe for Salsa Green Beans. Everyone who tries them agrees they're very fresh-tasting and nicely seasoned.

Years later, Mom discovered Mushroom Pasta Pilaf. She knew that savory dish featuring mushrooms, onions and pasta would pair perfectly with the kabobs.

Whenever she serves this menu, Mom usually includes light and fruity Frozen Hawaiian Pie. It's chock-full of tasty things like pineapple, maraschino cherries and walnuts.

Each summer, she and Dad like to host a barbecue that features this meal (the kabobs can be grilled rather than broiled). Family members and friends look forward to the party months in advance...Uncle Bob starts inquiring about it as early as April!

My brother, James, says he still lives at home because he loves Mom's cooking so much. My husband, Patrick, and I live far away from my parents, so we don't get to enjoy Mom's meals on a regular basis. But I try to duplicate terrific ones like this using her recipes.

Curried Beef Kabobs, Mushroom Pasta Pilaf, Salsa Green Beans and Frozen Hawaiian Pie (recipes are on pp. 152-153).

a broiler pan; broil 5 in. from the heat for 3 minutes on each side. Baste with reserved marinade.

Continue broiling, turning and basting for 8-10 minutes or until meat reaches desired doneness (for rare, a meat thermometer should read 140°; medium, 160°; well-done, 170°). **Yield:** 8 servings.

Mushroom Pasta Pilaf

This simmered side dish is an excellent complement to Mom's shish kabobs or any beef main dish. Tiny pieces of pasta pick up bold seasoning from mushrooms, onion and Worcestershire sauce.

  1 **small onion, chopped**
1/4 **cup butter**
1-1/3 **cups uncooked ring, orzo *or* other small pasta**
  1 **can (10-1/2 ounces) beef consomme, undiluted**
  1 **cup water**
  1 **can (7 ounces) mushroom stems and pieces, undrained**
  1 **tablespoon Worcestershire sauce**
  1 **teaspoon salt**
1/4 **teaspoon soy sauce**
Dash pepper

In a large skillet, saute onion in butter until tender. Add remaining ingredients; bring to a boil. Reduce heat; cover and simmer for 20 minutes or until the pasta is tender and the liquid is absorbed. **Yield:** 6-8 servings.

Curried Beef Kabobs

A tongue-tingling marinade gives delightful flavor to the tender chunks of beef in this main dish. My mother prepares these kabobs for guests often since they're so colorful and popular.

2/3 **cup olive oil**
1/2 **cup beef broth**
1/2 **cup lemon juice**
  2 **garlic cloves, minced**
  2 **teaspoons curry powder**
  2 **teaspoons salt**
  4 **bay leaves**
16 **whole peppercorns**
  2 **pounds beef tenderloin, cut into 1-1/4-inch cubes**
  2 **large green peppers, cut into 1-1/2-inch pieces**
  3 **medium tomatoes, cut into wedges**
  3 **medium onions, cut into wedges**

In a large resealable plastic bag or shallow glass dish, combine the first eight ingredients; mix well. Remove 2/3 cup for basting; refrigerate. Add beef to remaining marinade; turn to coat. Cover and refrigerate for 8 hours or overnight.

Drain and discard the marinade. On metal or soaked bamboo skewers, alternate beef, green peppers, tomatoes and onions. Place on a greased rack in

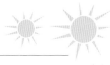

1 can (14 ounces) sweetened condensed milk
1 carton (12 ounces) frozen whipped topping, thawed
1 can (20 ounces) crushed pineapple, drained
1/2 cup chopped walnuts
1/2 cup chopped maraschino cherries
2 tablespoons lemon juice
2 graham cracker crusts (9 inches)
Fresh mint and additional walnuts and maraschino cherries

In a bowl, combine milk and whipped topping. Gently fold in pineapple, nuts, cherries and lemon juice. Pour into the crusts.

Freeze until firm, about 4 hours. Remove from the freezer 20 minutes before serving. Garnish with mint, nuts and cherries. **Yield:** 2 pies (6-8 servings each).

For a Nuttier Flavor

To add crunch and intensify the flavor of the walnuts that garnish Frozen Hawaiian Pie, spread the nuts in a single layer on a baking sheet. Bake at 350° for 6-10 minutes or until browned. Stir several times and watch closely so they don't get too dark.

Salsa Green Beans

This simple treatment is a wonderful way of dressing up plain green beans. Maybe the reason I really enjoy this vegetable is because Mom has been fixing it this way since I was a little girl. Onions, salsa and garlic add just the right amount of zip.

4 cups fresh *or* frozen cut green beans
2 small onions, chopped
1/4 cup butter
3 medium tomatoes, cut into wedges
2 tablespoons salsa
1 garlic clove, minced
1/4 to 1/2 teaspoon salt

In a saucepan, cover beans with water; bring to a boil. Cook, uncovered, for 8-10 minutes or until crisp-tender. Meanwhile, in a skillet, saute onions in butter until tender. Drain beans. Add the tomatoes, salsa, garlic, salt and onions; heat through. **Yield:** 6-8 servings.

Frozen Hawaiian Pie

Cool summer pies are one of Mom's specialties. This version offers pineapple, maraschino cherries and walnuts that are folded into a fluffy filling. It's an easy yet tempting no-bake dessert.

Casual Cuisine For Cookouts

By Sue Gronholz, Columbus, Wisconsin

When my sister and I were growing up, we eagerly awaited summer weekends. That's when my mother, Lila Koch (left) of Beaver Dam, Wisconsin, would fix one of her special suppers with the help of Dad at the grill.

My mouth waters just thinking about Mom's delicious Tangy Ham Steak. Dad still grills it to perfection while basting it with a glaze of mustard, honey and orange peel, keeping the meat really tender. He's even made this ham for Christmas dinner, much to everyone's delight!

Everyone raves over Mom's fluffy Whipped Potatoes. She got the recipe from her sister, and it's a standard dish at all of our family get-togethers. Mom appreciates the fact that she can make the potatoes ahead and bake them just before serving.

Mom has always loved to serve fresh foods she's grown herself (a passion I inherited). Mom's Vegetable Medley uses lots of colorful tasty garden veggies, simply seasoned with convenient onion soup mix.

For dessert, my sister and I would regularly request Chocolate Cherry Torte. The chocolate-covered graham cracker crust and fluffy white filling are extra-special. Mom could never make that rich creamy treat too often as far as we were concerned.

Our family has grown a bit since those summer weekends of my childhood. Since my husband and I and our two kids don't live far from my parents, Mom and Dad treat us to their wonderful weekend meals now and then.

Tangy Ham Steak, Whipped Potatoes, Mom's Vegetable Medley and Chocolate Cherry Torte (recipes are on pp. 156-157).

Tangy Ham Steak

This glazed ham steak is a yummy, quick-and-easy main dish. It tastes especially good heated on the grill but works well in the oven broiler, too. On summer weekends back home, Dad does the grilling while Mom prepares the rest of the meal.

- 1/3 **cup spicy brown mustard**
- 1/4 **cup honey**
- 1/2 **teaspoon grated orange peel**
- 1 **fully cooked ham steak (about 2 pounds)**

In a small bowl, combine mustard, honey and orange peel. Brush over one side of ham.

Broil or grill, uncovered, over medium-hot heat for 7 minutes. Turn; brush with mustard mixture. Cook until well glazed and heated through, about 7 minutes. **Yield:** 6-8 servings.

Whipped Potatoes

"More, please," is what you'll hear when you serve these light and creamy potatoes. Seasoned with just a hint of garlic, they go great with any meat.

- 2-1/2 **pounds potatoes, peeled, quartered and cooked**
- 1 **package (3 ounces) cream cheese, softened**

- 1/2 **to 3/4 cup sour cream**
- 1/4 **cup butter, softened**
- 1/2 **teaspoon garlic salt**
- **Salt and pepper to taste**
- **Paprika, optional**

In a large bowl, mash the potatoes. Add the cream cheese, sour cream, butter, garlic salt, salt and pepper; mix until smooth.

Transfer to a greased 1-1/2-qt. baking dish. Sprinkle with paprika if desired. Bake, uncovered, at 350° for 30 minutes or until heated through. **Yield:** 6-8 servings.

Mom's Vegetable Medley

A colorful mix of zucchini, onion, celery, green pepper and tomato is at its tasty best in this simple side dish. Mom came up with this recipe as a way to use up her garden vegetables. It has the taste of summer.

✓ Uses less fat, sugar or salt. Includes Nutritional Analysis and Diabetic Exchanges.

- 2 **celery ribs, chopped**
- 1 **medium green pepper, chopped**
- 2 **tablespoons chopped onion**
- 2 **tablespoons butter**

3   **small zucchini, quartered lengthwise and
    sliced**
1   **medium tomato, chopped**
1   **tablespoon onion soup mix**

In a skillet, saute the celery, green pepper and onion in butter for 6-8 minutes. Add the zucchini; cook and stir over medium heat until tender. Add tomato and soup mix; cook and stir until the tomato is tender. **Yield:** 8 servings.

   Nutritional Analysis: One 1/2-cup serving equals 42 calories, 127 mg sodium, 0 cholesterol, 4 g carbohydrate, 1 g protein, 3 g fat. **Diabetic Exchanges:** 1 vegetable, 1/2 fat.

Chocolate Cherry Torte

Mom has made this sweet treat for years. Since she knows how much my sister and I like it, she's still happy to serve this torte when we're home for a meal.

1   **pound chocolate-covered graham cracker
    cookies (56 cookies), crushed**
1   **cup butter, melted**
2   **envelopes whipped topping mix**
1   **cup cold milk**
1   **teaspoon vanilla extract**
1   **package (8 ounces) cream cheese,
    softened**
2   **cans (21 ounces *each*) cherry pie filling**

Set aside 1/4 cup of crushed cookies for topping. Combine the remaining cookies with butter; spread into a 13-in. x 9-in. x 2-in. dish. Set aside.

   In a mixing bowl, combine whipped topping mixes, milk and vanilla; beat on low speed until blended. Beat on high for 4 minutes or until thickened and stiff peaks form. Add cream cheese and beat until smooth.

   Spread over the crust; top with pie filling. Sprinkle with reserved cookies. Refrigerate for 12-24 hours before serving. **Yield:** 12-16 servings.

Buying and Cooking Potatoes

Look for firm potatoes that are free from cuts, decay, blemishes and green discoloration.

To cook potatoes for use in the Whipped Potatoes recipe, scrub them with a vegetable brush; remove all eyes and sprouts. Peel and quarter. Place in a saucepan; cover with water. Cover and cook for 15-30 minutes or until tender; drain well.

Flavorful Fish From the Grill

By Lisa Kivirist, Browntown, Wisconsin

When guests in our home compliment me on a great meal, I share some of the credit with my mom, Aelita Kivirist (left) of Glenview, Illinois. She's my inspiration in the kitchen.

I could put together a cookbook of all Mom's recipes we enjoy, but this savory and satisfying meal is my personal favorite.

When my husband, John Ivanko, and I visit my parents, Mom often prepares her light and flaky Lemon Grilled Salmon.

In the 1950s, Mom emigrated from Latvia, where dill is a very popular seasoning. It certainly tastes wonderful on this salmon. We savor every bite.

Cottage Cheese Spinach Salad is a unique take-off on a traditional spinach salad. Everyone who tries it comments on the unusual (and pleasing!) combination of ingredients.

Herbed Oven Potatoes have a delightful onion and herb flavor. These seasoned potatoes are easy to make since there's no peeling required. I'm always sure to help myself to a big serving.

We all save room for a big slice of Frozen Mocha Torte. It's surprisingly simple to make and never lasts long at gatherings.

Mom has a talent for making guests feel welcome. She's warm and cheerful as she dances around the kitchen putting the finishing touches on a meal.

She laughs when everyone crowds around the counter as she works instead of sitting in comfortable living room chairs just a few steps away.

They've discovered what I've known for many years—the best spot in the house is the kitchen when Mom's cooking.

Lemon Grilled Salmon, Cottage Cheese Spinach Salad, Herbed Oven Potatoes and Frozen Mocha Torte (recipes are on pp. 160-161).

onion slices over the top. Cover and cook for 15-20 minutes or until fish flakes easily with a fork. **Yield:** 6 servings.

Nutritional Analysis: One serving (prepared with salt-free lemon-pepper seasoning and reduced-sodium soy sauce and without salt) equals 199 calories, 181 mg sodium, 68 mg cholesterol, 7 g carbohydrate, 22 g protein, 9 g fat. **Diabetic Exchanges:** 3 lean meat, 1 vegetable.

Editor's Note: Salmon can be broiled instead of grilled. Place the fillet on a greased broiler pan. Broil 3-4 in. from the heat for 6-8 minutes or until fish flakes easily with a fork.

Cottage Cheese Spinach Salad

Even folks who don't care for spinach enjoy this distinctive salad. The creamy dressing is a bit sweet, and cottage cheese ensures that this dish is extra hearty and satisfying.

  1 **package (10 ounces) fresh spinach, torn**
  1 **carton (12 ounces) small-curd cottage cheese**
1/2 **cup chopped pecans, toasted**
1/2 **cup sugar**
  3 **tablespoons vinegar**
  2 **teaspoons prepared horseradish**
1/2 **teaspoon salt**
1/2 **teaspoon ground mustard**

Lemon Grilled Salmon

Mom proudly serves this tender, flaky fish to family and guests. A savory marinade that includes dill gives the salmon mouth-watering flavor. Since it can be grilled or broiled, we enjoy it year-round.

✓ Uses less fat, sugar or salt. Includes Nutritional Analysis and Diabetic Exchanges.

  2 **teaspoons snipped fresh dill *or* 3/4 teaspoon dill weed**
1/2 **teaspoon lemon-pepper seasoning**
1/2 **teaspoon salt, optional**
1/4 **teaspoon garlic powder**
  1 **salmon fillet (1-1/2 pounds)**
1/4 **cup packed brown sugar**
  3 **tablespoons chicken broth**
  3 **tablespoons vegetable oil**
  3 **tablespoons soy sauce**
  3 **tablespoons finely chopped green onions**
  1 **small lemon, thinly sliced**
  2 **onion slices, separated into rings**

Sprinkle dill, lemon-pepper, salt if desired and garlic powder over salmon. Place in a large resealable plastic bag or shallow glass container. Combine the brown sugar, broth, oil, soy sauce and green onions; pour over the salmon. Cover and refrigerate for 1 hour, turning once after 30 minutes.

Drain and discard marinade. Place salmon skin side down on grill over medium heat; arrange lemon and

Frozen Mocha Torte

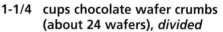

For an easy, make-ahead dessert that's elegant and luscious, try this recipe that Mom has used for years. The perfect blend of mocha and chocolate is in each cool refreshing slice. It never lasts long in the freezer.

1-1/4	cups chocolate wafer crumbs (about 24 wafers), *divided*
1/4	cup sugar
1/4	cup butter, melted
1	package (8 ounces) cream cheese, softened
1	can (14 ounces) sweetened condensed milk
2/3	cup chocolate syrup
2	tablespoons instant coffee granules
1	tablespoon hot water
1	cup heavy whipping cream, whipped

Chocolate-covered coffee beans, optional

Combine 1 cup wafer crumbs, sugar and butter. Press onto the bottom and 1 in. up the sides of a greased 9-in. springform pan; set aside.

In a mixing bowl, beat cream cheese, milk and chocolate syrup until smooth. Dissolve coffee granules in hot water; add to cream cheese mixture. Fold in whipped cream. Pour over the crust. Sprinkle with remaining crumbs.

Cover and freeze for 8 hours or overnight. Uncover and remove from the freezer 10-15 minutes before serving. Garnish with coffee beans if desired. **Yield:** 10-12 servings.

In a large serving bowl, layer half of the spinach, cottage cheese and pecans. Repeat layers. In a small bowl, combine the remaining ingredients. Drizzle over salad and toss to coat. Serve immediately. **Yield:** 10 servings.

Herbed Oven Potatoes

Mom loves to use the fresh new potatoes my husband and I share from our garden for this yummy recipe. The well-seasoned potato chunks are an excellent side dish for fish, poultry or meat. It's easy to make since there's no peeling required.

1/2	cup olive oil
1/4	cup butter, melted
1	envelope onion soup mix
1	teaspoon dried thyme
1	teaspoon dried marjoram
1/4	teaspoon pepper
2	pounds red potatoes, quartered

Minced fresh parsley

In a shallow bowl, combine the first six ingredients. Add potatoes, a few at a time; toss to coat. Place in a single layer in a greased 15-in. x 10-in. x 1-in. baking pan.

Drizzle with remaining oil mixture. Bake, uncovered, at 450° for 50-55 minutes or until tender, stirring occasionally. Sprinkle with parsley. **Yield:** 6 servings.

Pork Chops Are Just Peachy

By Brenda DuFresne, Midland, Michigan

Mom was a hard-working grade-school teacher when I lived at home, but she still took time to make wonderful meals for our family. She also made a point of sharing her kitchen skills with me and my sister.

Every summer, my mother, Susan Stancroff (left) of Ludington, Michigan, and I would put up lots of jams and jellies. One year we had so much peach jam that we needed to find creative new ways to use it.

Mom decided to experiment with pork chops. Her Peachy Pork Chops turned out deliciously. Sweet peaches dot the stuffing, and peach preserves make an appealing golden glaze. I've found that even the pickiest eaters love these tempting stuffed chops.

One of our favorite accompaniments to that main dish (and many others) was Cloverleaf Rolls. My sister and I ate more than our share of these versatile golden rolls.

In Mom's Green Beans Amandine, a few simple ingredients give new life to plain beans. I always thought the crunchy almonds were a super addition.

There's no better way to top off a meal than with Mom's incredible Dutch Apple Pie. The delightful crust cuts beautifully to reveal a filling with tiny pieces of diced apple. I still like mine a la mode. At harvest-time or any other time, you can't beat this delectable variety of apple pie.

Now I use many of Mom's recipes for my own family. She'll retire from teaching soon and will have more time to cook and spend with her grandchildren.

Peachy Pork Chops, Cloverleaf Rolls, Green Beans Amandine and Dutch Apple Pie (recipes are on pp. 164-165).

et in the side of each pork chop; spoon stuffing loosely into pockets. Tie with string to secure stuffing if necessary. Brush chops with oil. Sprinkle with garlic salt and pepper.

In a large skillet, brown chops on both sides. Place remaining stuffing in a greased 13-in. x 9-in. x 2-in. baking dish. Top with chops. Spread preserves over chops. Cover and bake at 350° for 45 minutes. Uncover and bake 15 minutes longer or until juices run clear. If string was used, remove before serving. **Yield:** 6 servings.

Cloverleaf Rolls

When I was a girl, it was a rare occasion when Mom made a gourmet meal. Most often, she relied on traditional recipes like this one.

1	package (1/4 ounce) active dry yeast
3	tablespoons sugar
1-1/4	cups warm milk (110° to 115°)
1/4	cup butter, softened
1	egg
1	teaspoon salt
4	to 4-1/2 cups all-purpose flour

Additional butter, melted

In a mixing bowl, combine yeast, sugar and milk; beat until smooth. Add butter, egg and salt; mix well. Add 3 cups flour; beat until smooth. Add enough remaining flour to form a soft dough. Turn onto a floured surface; knead until smooth and elastic, about 6-8 minutes.

Place in a greased bowl, turning once to grease top. Cover and let rise in a warm place until doubled,

Peachy Pork Chops

Pork and peaches are a palate-pleasing combination in this hearty main dish that Mom created.

1-1/2	cups finely chopped onion
1-1/2	cups finely chopped celery
1/3	cup butter
6	cups dry bread cubes
1/2	teaspoon poultry seasoning
1/2	teaspoon rubbed sage
1/8	teaspoon pepper
1	can (8 ounces) peaches, drained and diced
2	eggs
1	cup water
2	tablespoons minced fresh parsley
6	boneless pork chops (1-1/4 inches thick)
3	tablespoons olive oil

Garlic salt and additional pepper to taste

1/4	cup peach preserves

In a skillet, saute onion and celery in butter until tender; transfer to a large bowl. Add bread cubes, poultry seasoning, sage and pepper. Fold in peaches.

Combine eggs, water and parsley; add to bread mixture. Toss gently until well mixed. Cut a large pock-

Nutritional Analysis: One 1/2-cup serving (prepared with margarine and without seasoned salt) equals 92 calories, 50 mg sodium, 0 cholesterol, 7 g carbohydrate, 3 g protein, 7 g fat. **Diabetic Exchanges:** 1-1/2 fat, 1 vegetable.

Dutch Apple Pie

Everything about this dessert makes it the top request for family gatherings.

- 2 **cups all-purpose flour**
- 1 **cup packed brown sugar**
- 3/4 **cup butter, melted**
- 1/2 **cup quick-cooking oats**

FILLING:
- 2/3 **cup sugar**
- 3 **tablespoons cornstarch**
- 1-1/4 **cups water**
- 3 **cups diced peeled tart apples**
- 1 **teaspoon vanilla extract**

Combine the first four ingredients; set aside 1 cup for topping. Press remaining crumb mixture into an ungreased 9-in. pie plate; set aside.

For filling, combine sugar, cornstarch and water in a saucepan until smooth; bring to a boil. Cook and stir for 1 minute or until thickened. Remove from the heat; stir in apples and vanilla.

Pour into crust; top with reserved crumb mixture. Bake at 350° for 40-45 minutes or until crust is golden brown. **Yield:** 6-8 servings.

about 1 hour. Punch dough down and divide in half. Divide each half into 36 pieces and shape into balls. Place three balls each in greased muffin cups. Cover and let rise until doubled, about 30 minutes.

Brush with butter. Bake at 375° for 15-18 minutes or until lightly browned. Remove to wire racks. Serve warm. **Yield:** 2 dozen.

Green Beans Amandine

It's hard to improve on the taste Mother Nature gives to fresh green beans, but Mom has for years using this recipe.

✓ Uses less fat, sugar or salt. Includes Nutritional Analysis and Diabetic Exchanges.

- 1 **pound fresh *or* frozen green beans, cut into 2-inch pieces**
- 1/2 **cup water**
- 1/4 **cup slivered almonds**
- 2 **tablespoons butter**
- 1 **teaspoon lemon juice**
- 1/4 **teaspoon seasoned salt, optional**

In a saucepan, bring beans and water to a boil; reduce heat to medium. Cover and cook for 10-15 minutes or until beans are crisp-tender; drain and set aside.

In a large skillet, cook almonds in butter over low heat. Stir in lemon juice and seasoned salt if desired. Add beans and heat through. **Yield:** 6 servings.

City-Style Kabob Supper

By Barbara Hyatt, Folsom, California

I have warm, happy memories of growing up in Lorain, Ohio. Many of them include the hearty and comforting meals my mother, Ruth Toth (left), prepared for Dad, Grandfather and me.

Mom's best meal started with City Kabobs—a flavorful main dish made with cubes of pork on skewers, seasoned simply and served over mashed potatoes. I'm especially fond of the savory gravy.

In her Chunky Cinnamon Applesauce, red-hot candies give freshly cooked apples a rosy color and irresistible flavor. I'd always take a big helping. As a young girl, I was amazed when my mother transformed fresh apples into this delightful mixture.

Mom knew that a homemade salad topper like her Oil and Vinegar Dressing made even plain lettuce a super side dish.

In those days, Mom was an avid baker. It was nothing for her to bake 30 pies in two days for Dad's men's club dinner. Mom's Custard Pie was often requested for those gatherings and was a favorite dessert for our family meals as well.

Just as Mom did for many years, I love cooking for others. I've collected lots of recipes, but the best ones are those Mom passed on to me—now I'm sharing them with my daughter-in-law and granddaughter.

Mom, widowed in 1997 after 55 years of marriage, now lives nearby. She joins my husband, Bill, and me, our son, Scott, his wife, Lorna, and their two children for delicious meals like this one.

City Kabobs, Chunky Cinnamon Applesauce, Oil and Vinegar Dressing and Mom's Custard Pie (recipes are on pp. 168-169).

City Kabobs

This old-fashioned dish, which is made with perfectly seasoned pork, is one my mother relied on for years. The great gravy tastes so good over mashed potatoes.

- 2 pounds boneless pork, cut into cubes
- 1/2 cup all-purpose flour
- 1/2 teaspoon garlic salt
- 1/4 teaspoon pepper
- 1/4 cup butter
- 3 tablespoons vegetable oil
- 1 envelope onion soup mix
- 1 can (14-1/2 ounces) chicken broth
- 1 cup water

Hot mashed potatoes

Thread pork on small wooden skewers. Combine flour, garlic salt and pepper on a plate; roll kabobs in flour mixture until coated.

In a large skillet, heat butter and oil over medium heat. Brown the kabobs, turning frequently; drain. Sprinkle with soup mix. Add broth and water. Reduce heat; cover and simmer for 1 hour. Remove kabobs and keep warm. If desired, thicken pan juices and serve over mashed potatoes with the kabobs. **Yield:** 4-6 servings.

Chunky Cinnamon Applesauce

I'm not sure if I liked this so much because there were candies in it or because it tasted wonderful. Either way, Mom was delighted to see us gobble it up!

- 8 medium tart apples, peeled and quartered
- 1 cup water
- 1 cup sugar
- 1/4 cup red-hot candies

Place apples and water in a 5-qt. saucepan. Cover and cook over medium-low heat for 20 minutes or until tender.

Mash the apples. Add sugar and candies. Cook, uncovered, until sugar and candies are dissolved. Remove from the heat; cool. Refrigerate until serving. **Yield:** 6 cups.

Oil and Vinegar Dressing

The goodness of crisp salad ingredients comes through when topped with this simple homemade dressing. It tastes so fresh. My mother made it for us when I was growing up, and now I serve it to my family.

- 1-1/2 cups sugar
- 1 tablespoon ground mustard
- 1 teaspoon salt
- 1/2 teaspoon pepper

1/2 teaspoon paprika
1/2 cup hot water
1/4 cup vinegar
2 garlic cloves, halved
1/4 cup vegetable oil
Mixed salad greens and shredded red cabbage

In a 1-qt. jar with a tight-fitting lid, combine the first five ingredients. Add water, vinegar and garlic; shake until sugar is dissolved. Add oil; shake well. Store in the refrigerator.

Just before serving, remove garlic from the dressing. Drizzle over greens and cabbage. **Yield:** 2 cups

Mom's Custard Pie

Just a single bite of this old-fashioned treat takes me back to the days when my mom would fix this pie for my dad, my grandfather and me. Mom also regularly prepared this pie for one type of large gathering or another.

1 pastry shell (9 inches)
4 eggs
1/2 cup sugar
1/4 teaspoon salt
1 teaspoon vanilla extract
2-1/2 cups milk
1/4 teaspoon ground nutmeg

Line unpricked pastry shell with a double thickness of heavy-duty foil. Bake at 450° for 8 minutes. Remove foil; bake 5 minutes longer. Remove from the oven and set aside.

Separate one egg and set the white aside. In a mixing bowl, beat the yolk and remaining eggs just until combined. Blend in sugar, salt and vanilla. Stir in milk. Beat reserved egg white until stiff peaks form; fold into egg mixture. Carefully pour into crust.

Cover edges of pie with foil. Bake at 350° for 25 minutes. Remove foil; bake 15-20 minutes longer or until a knife inserted near the center comes out clean. Cool on a wire rack. Sprinkle with nutmeg. Store in the refrigerator. **Yield:** 6-8 servings.

Cool It with Custard

It's important not to overbake custard pies. Check for doneness a few minutes before the minimum baking time by inserting a knife near the center. If the knife comes out clean, the pie is done. The center will remain soft but will continue to cook while cooling. After the custard pie cools to room temperature, store it in the refrigerator.

Creative Fare Earns Praise

By Judi Messina, Coeur d'Alene, Idaho

Through the years, my mother, Lois Rafferty (left) of Palm Desert, California, has varied her cooking style.

When my older siblings were young, Mom prepared lots of traditional meals. By the time I came along, years later, Mom and Dad preferred more formal gourmet dinners.

Now she prepares an eclectic mix of favorite foods. The one common thread is Mom's flair for the creative—she has always been terrific at inventing delicious dishes.

Mom is one of the most cheerful, generous people I know. Although she's cooking for only two now, she still fixes big batches and shares food with neighbors and friends. When they see her coming with her arms full, they know they're in for a tasty treat.

One of her best main dishes is her Sirloin Sandwiches. They're so tasty, you'd never guess how easy they are to prepare.

And it's hard to resist a cheesy slice of her rich Swiss-Onion Bread Ring. We've tried it with many different kinds of meat—and it goes well with all of them.

When I was growing up, Mom loved to dress up vegetables with creamy sauces. Her Almond Celery Bake is a classic example.

In addition, Mom prepares delicious cookies and pies. Summer Berry Pie, which blends three luscious fruits, is both beautiful and refreshing.

I've learned a lot working with Mom in the kitchen, and I still call her periodically for favorite recipes or to get help making special dishes for my husband, Tom, and our young son.

Mom and I both hope her recipes here inspire some creativity in your kitchen.

Sirloin Sandwiches, Almond Celery Bake, Swiss-Onion Bread Ring and Summer Berry Pie (recipes are on pp. 172-173).

Almond Celery Bake

It takes a creative cook like Mom to find a way to make celery star in a satisfying side dish. She combines celery slices with a creamy sauce, cheddar cheese and crunchy almonds. It's deliciously different!

1 bunch celery, sliced (about 6 cups)
3/4 cup shredded cheddar cheese
1/2 teaspoon paprika
1/8 teaspoon pepper
1 can (10-3/4 ounces) condensed cream of celery soup, undiluted
1 cup soft bread crumbs
1/2 cup slivered almonds

Place the celery in a greased 2-qt. baking dish. Sprinkle with cheese, paprika and pepper. Top with the soup. Sprinkle with bread crumbs.

Cover and bake at 375° for 45 minutes. Uncover; sprinkle with the almonds. Bake 10-15 minutes longer or until golden brown. **Yield:** 10-12 servings.

Swiss-Onion Bread Ring

With the ease of prepared bread dough, this tempting cheesy bread has delicious down-home goodness. Its pleasant onion flavor goes great with any entree. You'll find it crisp and golden on the outside, rich and buttery on the inside.

Sirloin Sandwiches

Mom is always happy to share her cooking, and these tender, tasty beef sandwiches are a real crowd-pleaser. A simple three-ingredient marinade flavors the grilled beef wonderfully.

1 cup soy sauce
1/2 cup vegetable oil
1/2 cup cranberry *or* apple juice
1 boneless sirloin tip roast (3 to 4 pounds)
1 envelope beef au jus gravy mix
1 dozen French rolls, split

In a large resealable plastic bag or shallow glass container, combine the soy sauce, oil and juice; mix well. Remove 1/2 cup for basting; cover and refrigerate.

Add the roast to remaining marinade; turn to coat. Seal or cover and refrigerate for 8 hours or overnight, turning occasionally. Drain and discard the marinade.

Grill roast, covered, over indirect heat, basting and turning every 15 minutes, for 1 hour or until meat reaches desired doneness (for rare, a meat thermometer should read 140°; medium, 160°; well-done, 170°). Remove from the grill; let stand for 1 hour.

Cover and refrigerate overnight. Just before serving, prepare gravy mix according to package directions. Thinly slice roast; add to the gravy and heat through. Serve on rolls. **Yield:** 12 servings.

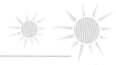

Summer Berry Pie

Mom puts luscious fresh blueberries, strawberries and raspberries to great use in this cool, refreshing pie. A super dessert on a hot day, it provides a nice light ending to a hearty meal.

1-1/2 **cups sugar**
   6 **tablespoons cornstarch**
   3 **cups cold water**
   1 **package (6 ounces) raspberry *or* strawberry gelatin**
   2 **cups fresh blueberries**
   2 **cups sliced fresh strawberries**
   2 **cups fresh raspberries**
   2 **graham cracker crusts (9 inches)**
1-1/2 **cups whipped topping**
Fresh mint and additional sliced strawberries

In a saucepan, combine sugar, cornstarch and water until smooth. Bring to a boil; cook and stir for 2 minutes or until thickened. Remove from the heat.

Stir in gelatin until dissolved. Refrigerate for 15-20 minutes or until mixture begins to thicken. Stir in the berries. Pour into crusts and chill until set. Garnish with whipped topping, mint and strawberries. **Yield:** 2 pies (6-8 servings each).

2-1/2 **teaspoons poppy seeds,** *divided*
   2 **tubes (11 ounces *each*) refrigerated French bread dough**
   1 **cup (4 ounces) shredded Swiss cheese**
 3/4 **cup sliced green onions**
 1/4 **cup butter, melted**

Sprinkle 1/2 teaspoon poppy seeds in a greased 10-in. fluted tube pan. Cut the dough into fourty 1-in. pieces; place half in prepared pan. Sprinkle with half of the cheese and onions.

Top with 1 teaspoon poppy seeds; drizzle with half of the butter. Repeat layers. Bake at 375° for 25 minutes or until golden brown. Immediately invert onto a wire rack. Serve warm. **Yield:** 1 loaf.

Caring for Berries

Heaping berries in a bowl will quickly crush the delicate fruit. It's best to refrigerate them, loosely covered, in a single layer and use them within a day or two. Also, don't wash berries until you're ready to use them.

Everyday Fare Is Extraordinary

By Debra Falkiner, St. Charles, Missouri

My mother is an excellent from-scratch cook who takes pride in every meal. Her everyday menus include dishes other cooks might reserve for Sundays or holidays.

Mom, Norma Falkiner (left), of Bevier, Missouri uses lots of fruits and vegetables, even in winter. She and Dad can the bounty from their immense garden, berry bushes and mini orchard.

When my brothers, sisters and I were young, our friends frequently asked to stay for dinner. Mom never said no. She would always make extra in case there was an additional person or two around the table.

These days, folks still stop by Mom's house just to see what's cooking (and to taste-test a dish or two, of course). They're never disappointed.

It's almost impossible to single out one of Mom's meals as my favorite. She always finds ways to make good foods taste even more special. Ham with Pineapple Sauce is a wonderful main dish that's enjoyable at any time of the year.

Her Creamy Spinach Bake was a sure way of getting us kids to eat our spinach. And everyone knows that kids and spinach don't usually mix well! This recipe has become a family tradition.

We're always thrilled to see a big basket of Mom's tasty golden Crescent Dinner Rolls. They're a delightful way to round out any meal.

The strawberries in her Upside-Down Strawberry Shortcake often come from her berry patch. It's a delightful summer treat.

Many of the recipes Mom cherishes have been passed down in her family over the years. In her honor, I compiled a five-generation cookbook. We're both very proud of it.

We hope you and your family enjoy the meal we've shared.

Ham with Pineapple Sauce, Creamy Spinach Bake, Crescent Dinner Rolls and Upside-Down Strawberry Shortcake (recipes are on pp. 176-177).

Ham with Pineapple Sauce

This ham is served with a sweet pineapple sauce.
A simple mixture of basic ingredients results
in a mouth-watering main dish.

- 1 boneless fully cooked ham (4 to 6 pounds)
- 3/4 cup water, *divided*
- 1 cup packed brown sugar
- 4-1/2 teaspoons soy sauce
- 4-1/2 teaspoons ketchup
- 1-1/2 teaspoons ground mustard
- 1-1/2 cups undrained crushed pineapple
- 2 tablespoons plus 1 teaspoon cornstarch

Place ham on a rack in a shallow roasting pan. Bake at 325° for 1-1/4 to 2 hours or until a meat thermometer reads 140° and ham is heated through.

Meanwhile, in a saucepan, combine 1/4 cup water, brown sugar, soy sauce, ketchup, mustard and pineapple. Bring to a boil. Reduce heat; cover and simmer for 10 minutes.

Combine cornstarch and remaining water until smooth; stir into pineapple sauce. Bring to a boil; cook and stir for 2 minutes or until thickened. Serve with the ham. **Yield:** 16-24 servings (3 cups sauce).

Creamy Spinach Bake

This casserole has a rich and creamy sauce,
french-fried onions and a cracker crumb topping.
Even as children, we couldn't resist it.

- 2 packages (8 ounces *each*) cream cheese, softened
- 2 cans (10-3/4 ounces *each*) condensed cream of mushroom soup, undiluted
- 4 packages (10 ounces *each*) frozen chopped spinach, thawed and well drained
- 2 cans (2.8 ounces *each*) french-fried onions
- 2/3 cup crushed saltines (about 16 crackers)
- 1/4 cup butter, melted

In a bowl, beat the cream cheese until smooth. Add soup; mix well. Stir in spinach and onions. Transfer to a greased 2-1/2-qt. baking dish.

Combine cracker crumbs and butter; sprinkle over spinach mixture. Bake, uncovered, at 325° for 30-35 minutes or until heated through. **Yield:** 10 servings.

Crescent Dinner Rolls

These light, golden rolls have a heavenly homemade
flavor and aroma. Mom never hesitates to whip up
a batch of these from-scratch rolls, since they're
a delightful way to round out a meal.

- 1 package (1/4 ounce) active dry yeast
- 1/4 cup warm water (110° to 115°)
- 1 tablespoon plus 1/2 cup sugar, *divided*
- 3/4 cup warm milk (110° to 115°)
- 3 eggs, lightly beaten
- 1/2 cup butter, softened
- 1 teaspoon salt
- 5 to 5-1/2 cups all-purpose flour

Melted butter

In a large mixing bowl, dissolve yeast in warm water. Add 1 tablespoon sugar; let stand for 5 minutes. Add the milk, eggs, butter, salt and remaining sugar. Stir in enough flour to form a stiff dough.

Turn onto a floured surface; knead until smooth and elastic, about 6-8 minutes. Place in a greased bowl, turning once to grease top. Cover and let rise in a warm place until doubled, about 1-1/2 hours.

Punch dough down. Divide into thirds. Roll each into a 12-in. circle; cut each circle into eight wedges. Brush with melted butter; roll up wedges from the wide end and place, pointed end down, 2 in. apart on greased baking sheets. Cover and let rise in a warm place until doubled, about 30 minutes.

Bake at 375° for 10-12 minutes or until golden brown. Remove from pans to wire racks. **Yield:** 2 dozen.

Upside-Down Strawberry Shortcake

For a tasty twist at dessert time, this special shortcake has a bountiful berry layer on the bottom. The moist and tempting cake is a treat our family has savored for many years.

- 1 **cup miniature marshmallows**
- 1 **package (16 ounces) frozen sweetened sliced strawberries, thawed**
- 1 **package (3 ounces) strawberry gelatin**
- 1/2 **cup shortening**
- 1-1/2 **cups sugar**
- 3 **eggs**
- 1 **teaspoon vanilla extract**

- 2-1/4 **cups all-purpose flour**
- 3 **teaspoons baking powder**
- 1/2 **teaspoon salt**
- 1 **cup milk**

Fresh strawberries and whipped cream

Sprinkle marshmallows evenly into a greased 13-in. x 9-in. x 2-in. baking dish; set aside. In a bowl, combine strawberries and gelatin powder; set aside.

In a mixing bowl, cream shortening and sugar. Add the eggs, one at a time, beating well after each addition. Beat in vanilla. Combine flour, baking powder and salt; add to creamed mixture alternately with milk. Pour batter over the marshmallows. Spoon strawberry mixture evenly over batter.

Bake at 350° for 45-50 minutes or until a toothpick inserted near the center comes out clean. Cool on a wire rack. Cut into squares. Garnish with fresh strawberries and whipped cream. **Yield:** 12-16 servings.

Satisfying Sandwiches

Mix ground leftover baked ham with chopped olives, green pepper, shredded cheddar cheese, Dijon mustard and mayonnaise. Stuff into hard rolls, wrap in foil and bake at 375° for 30 minutes.

Nothing Beats
A Barbecue

By Pat Cole, Polebridge, Montana

My mother is a person who loves to feed people. She is known for setting out trays of food as soon as someone enters her home.

When my older brothers, sister and I were growing up, my Mom, Betty Dillon (left) from Park Ridge, Illinois, worked full time in a factory, so she had to be creative with meal preparation. She set it up so that dinner could easily be completed by us kids.

On weekends, she fixed a big meal with lots of ethnic variety. Her mother was Polish and her mother-in-law was Irish, so she had plenty of influence.

Mom's also a great baker. Our friends loved to come to our house because there were always fresh, homemade cookies.

To commemorate Mom's 90th birthday, I put together a cookbook with her best recipes to share with family members and friends.

My favorite meal is one that is well-known throughout our extended family. Her beef and pork barbecue (fondly known as Betty's Barbecue) makes savory sandwiches that can't be beat.

Creamy Potato Salad and Tangy Coleslaw are two classic accompaniments to those sandwiches. She made big batches because we all went back for seconds—plus we'd gladly accept any leftovers she wanted to send home with us.

Mom's Frosted Shortbread, topped with a layer of chocolate and a sprinkling of walnuts, is a scrumptious, fitting finale for any meal.

Before my husband and I moved to a remote cabin in the woods, I was sure to get those recipes in writing from Mom (who usually cooks from memory).

Now a widow, grandma and great-grandma, Mom is still busy cooking and baking for those she loves. She and I are pleased to share these recipes with you and your family.

Betty's Barbecue, Creamy Potato Salad, Tangy Coleslaw and Frosted Shortbread (recipes are on pp. 180-181).

Creamy Potato Salad

Mildly seasoned with onion and dill, Mom's delightfully different potato salad is pretty, too, with the red potatoes left unpeeled. Of course, that also means it's quicker to make than traditional potato salad!

✓ Uses less fat, sugar or salt. Includes Nutritional Analysis and Diabetic Exchanges.

7-1/2	cups cubed red potatoes (about 2-1/2 pounds)
1	hard-cooked egg, chopped
3	celery ribs, chopped
3/4	cup chopped onion
2	tablespoons finely chopped green pepper
3/4	cup mayonnaise
1/4	cup sour cream
1	to 1-1/2 teaspoons salt
1/4	teaspoon pepper
1/8	to 1/4 teaspoon dill weed

Sliced hard-cooked egg, paprika and fresh dill sprigs, optional

Place potatoes in a large saucepan or Dutch oven; cover with water. Cover and bring to a boil. Reduce heat; cook for 20-30 minutes or until tender. Drain and cool.

Place potatoes in a large bowl. Add chopped egg, celery, onion and green pepper. In a small bowl, combine mayonnaise, sour cream, salt, pepper and dill. Pour over potato mixture and toss gently to coat. Cover and refrigerate until serving. Garnish with egg, paprika and dill if desired. **Yield:** 12 servings.

Betty's Barbecue

For a fun sandwich filling that's perfect for a picnic or potluck, try these sweetly spicy barbecue sandwiches. My 90-year-old mother came up with this outdoor specialty, which combines chunks of tender pork and beef. It's one of my family's favorites.

1	boneless beef rump roast (3 to 4 pounds)
1	pork tenderloin (1 pound)
2	cups water
1	envelope onion soup mix
1	garlic clove, minced
1/4	cup chopped celery with leaves
1/2	cup barbecue sauce
1/2	cup ketchup
1	tablespoon brown sugar
10	to 14 sandwich buns, split

Place beef and pork in a Dutch oven. Combine the water, soup mix and garlic; pour over meat. Cover and bake at 325° for 2-1/2 to 3 hours or until meat is very tender. Remove meat; cool.

Cut into small cubes. Skim fat from drippings. Saute celery in the drippings until tender. Add the barbecue sauce, ketchup and brown sugar; bring to a boil. Stir in cubed meat; heat through. Serve on buns. **Yield:** 10-14 servings.

In a large bowl, combine the cabbage, carrots, celery, green pepper and onion. In a small bowl, combine vinegar, oil, sugar, salt, pepper and paprika. Pour over cabbage mixture and toss to coat. Cover and refrigerate until serving. **Yield:** 10 servings.

Frosted Shortbread

My mom has always known that homemade cookies have a special appeal that can't be duplicated by the store-bought variety. Even today, she keeps us grown-up kids well stocked with fresh-from-the-oven treats such as this tender shortbread.

- 1 **cup butter, softened**
- 1 **cup packed brown sugar**
- 1 **egg yolk**
- 1 **teaspoon vanilla extract**
- 2 **cups all-purpose flour**
- 1/4 **teaspoon salt**
- 4 **milk chocolate candy bars (1.55 ounces** *each***), broken into rectangles**
- 1/2 **cup chopped walnuts**

In a mixing bowl, cream butter and brown sugar. Add egg yolk and vanilla; mix well. Combine flour and salt; add to creamed mixture. Press into a greased 15-in. x 10-in. x 1-in. baking pan.

Bake at 350° for 15-18 minutes or until golden brown. Immediately place candy bar pieces over crust. Let stand for 1 minute or until softened; spread the chocolate evenly. Sprinkle with walnuts. Cool. Cut into squares. **Yield:** 3 dozen.

Nutritional Analysis: One 1-cup serving (prepared with fat-free mayonnaise, reduced-fat sour cream and 1 teaspoon salt) equals 114 calories, 1 g fat (1 g saturated fat), 19 mg cholesterol, 320 mg sodium, 24 g carbohydrate, 2 g fiber, 3 g protein. **Diabetic Exchanges:** 1 starch, 1 vegetable.

Tangy Coleslaw

The fresh flavor and crunchy texture of garden vegetables star in this tart, colorful coleslaw. Lightly dressed with vinegar and oil, it's a refreshing salad. My mom fixed it often when I was growing up.

- 6 **cups shredded cabbage**
- 4 **medium carrots, shredded**
- 4 **celery ribs, chopped**
- 1/2 **cup finely chopped green pepper**
- 1/2 **cup finely chopped onion**
- 1/2 **cup cider vinegar**
- 1/4 **cup vegetable oil**
- 1/4 **cup sugar**
- 1-1/2 **teaspoons salt**
- 1/4 **teaspoon pepper**
- 1/4 **teaspoon paprika**

Customized Coleslaw

To make store-bought coleslaw taste homemade, add shredded cheese, apple, carrots or bell pepper.

In the Good Old Summertime

By Mared Metzgar Beling, Eagle River, Alaska

A close friend of my mother's once declared, "You don't meet Blanche, she meets you." And once Blanche Metzgar (left) meets you, you're likely to join the large circle of friends who relish dinner parties at my parents' home in Pennsylvania.

Mom absolutely loves to entertain, trying out new recipes on family and friends. She's always been just as creative cooking for my dad, sister and me. As kids, my sister and I were picky eaters, but Mom's mouth-watering meals exposed us to new dishes that helped us develop broader tastes.

My sister and I got to choose the entire menu for our summer birthday celebrations. My favorite meal still consists of Mom's Creamed Chicken in Patty Shells, Wild Rice Barley Salad, greens with Home-Style Salad Dressing and Zucchini Chip Snack Cake.

With its pretty presentation, Creamed Chicken in Patty Shells is the perfect entree for brunch or a special-occasion meal.

Mom's Wild Rice Barley Salad is a tangy accompaniment. I never thought I'd enjoy cold rice until I tasted this salad…now I serve it often. And people always request the recipe for Home-Style Salad Dressing with blue cheese to top a fresh tossed salad of mixed greens and vegetables.

Zucchini Chip Snack Cake is so moist, you don't even need a glass of milk to wash it down. When my dad harvests the overabundance of zucchini from his backyard garden, this scrumptious cake is the first thing everyone asks for.

Though my assignments as an Air Force nurse often take me far from my family, it's a comfort to have that little taste of home every time I make one of Mom's recipes. I hope you find them deliciously comforting as well.

Creamed Chicken in Patty Shells, Wild Rice Barley Salad, Home-Style Salad Dressing and Zucchini Chip Snack Cake (recipes are on pp. 184-185).

Creamed Chicken In Patty Shells

My mom's tasty creamed chicken makes a wonderful main dish, and when you add extra vegetables, it becomes an entire meal. The recipe might look long, but it's well worth the effort.

- 1 broiler/fryer chicken (3 to 4 pounds), cut up
- 2 quarts water
- 1-1/2 teaspoons salt, *divided*
- 1-1/2 teaspoons pepper, *divided*
- 2 packages (10 ounces *each*) frozen puff pastry shells
- 1 cup sliced fresh mushrooms
- 1 medium green pepper, chopped
- 1/2 cup small fresh broccoli florets
- 5 tablespoons butter
- 6 tablespoons all-purpose flour
- 2 cups milk
- 1 jar (2 ounces) diced pimientos, drained
- 1/4 teaspoon paprika

In a large kettle, bring the chicken, water, 1 teaspoon salt and 1 teaspoon pepper to a boil. Reduce heat; cover and simmer for 1-1/2 to 2 hours or until chicken is tender.

Remove chicken from broth; cool. Remove meat from bones; cut into cubes and set aside. Discard skin and bones. Strain broth and skim fat; set aside 1 cup broth (refrigerate remaining broth for another use).

Bake pastry shells according to package directions. Meanwhile, in a large saucepan, saute the mushrooms, green pepper and broccoli in butter until tender; sprinkle with flour. Gradually stir in milk and reserved broth until blended.

Bring to a boil; cook and stir for 2 minutes or until thickened. Add the pimientos, paprika, reserved chicken and remaining salt and pepper. Cook and stir until heated through. Spoon into pastry shells. **Yield:** 6 servings.

Wild Rice Barley Salad

I like this chilled salad because it's out of the ordinary. The rice is tossed with barley, green pepper, olives and cranberries, then coated with a tangy vinaigrette.

- 1 package (6 ounces) long grain and wild rice mix
- 1 cup cooked barley
- 1/2 cup chopped green pepper
- 1/2 cup sliced ripe olives
- 1/4 cup dried cranberries

DRESSING:
- 1/4 cup balsamic vinegar
- 2 tablespoons minced fresh basil
- 1 tablespoon chopped green onion
- 2 garlic cloves, minced
- 1/2 teaspoon pepper
- 1/3 cup olive oil

Cook the rice according to package directions. In a large serving bowl, combine the rice, barley, green pepper, olives and cranberries. In a blender, combine the vinegar, basil, green onion, garlic and pepper. While processing, gradually add the oil in a steady stream. Drizzle over salad and toss to coat. Cover; refrigerate until chilled. **Yield:** 4-6 servings.

Home-Style Salad Dressing

This pleasant-tasting salad dressing is delicious drizzled on a bed of greens with a sprinkling of crumbled blue cheese. Mom always gets requests for the recipe.

- 1 **cup mayonnaise**
- 1 **small onion, cut into wedges**
- 2 **tablespoons sugar**
- 2 **tablespoons white vinegar**
- 2 **tablespoons ketchup**
- 1 **teaspoon salt**
- 1/2 **teaspoon celery seed**
- 1/3 **cup vegetable oil**

Salad greens and vegetables of your choice
Crumbled blue cheese

Place the first seven ingredients in a blender; cover and process until smooth. While processing, gradually add oil in a steady stream.

In a salad bowl, combine greens and vegetables; sprinkle with blue cheese. Serve with dressing. Refrigerate any leftover dressing. **Yield:** 1-1/2 cups.

Zucchini Chip Snack Cake

Here's a mouth-watering dessert that is so rich, it doesn't need frosting to top it off. The shredded zucchini makes it especially moist. With a scoop of vanilla ice cream, this cake makes an unbeatable finale for any occasion. My mom especially likes to serve it in summer, when the zucchini is fresh from my dad's garden.

- 1/2 **cup butter, softened**
- 1-3/4 **cups sugar**
- 1/2 **cup vegetable oil**
- 2 **eggs**
- 1 **teaspoon vanilla extract**
- 2-1/2 **cups all-purpose flour**
- 2 **tablespoons baking cocoa**
- 1 **teaspoon baking soda**
- 1/2 **teaspoon baking powder**
- 1/2 **teaspoon ground cinnamon**
- 1/2 **teaspoon ground cloves**
- 1/2 **cup buttermilk**
- 2 **cups shredded peeled zucchini**
- 2 **cups (12 ounces) semisweet chocolate chips**

In a large mixing bowl, cream butter and sugar. Beat in oil, eggs and vanilla. Combine dry ingredients; add to creamed mixture alternately with the buttermilk. Stir in zucchini.

Pour into a greased 13-in. x 9-in. x 2-in. baking pan. Sprinkle with chocolate chips. Bake at 350° for 45-50 minutes or until a toothpick inserted near the center comes out clean. Cool on a wire rack. **Yield:** 12-15 servings.

A New Way To Do Burgers

By Nancy Holland, Morgan Hill, California

When I was growing up, I loved to watch my mom cook. She made fixing a hearty, mouth-watering meal from scratch appear so effortless.

My mom, LaVaun McMahon (left), made healthy, delicious dinners every night for my dad, younger brother, two older sisters and me. She served well-balanced meals, with something from every food group on the table.

Now when we visit my parents in Truckee, California, Mom asks what we'd like to eat...and that's a difficult decision! But no visit is complete without Cheeseburger Buns, Cauliflower Olive Salad, Dill Pickle Potato Salad and Custard Meringue Pie.

Mom came up with the Cheeseburger Buns recipe after my dad told her about the great meal they'd served in the school cafeteria (he's a teacher). So she made her yummy yeast rolls and stuffed them with meat and cheese.

Cauliflower Olive Salad, full of fresh veggies and tossed with a tangy dressing, is a recipe a neighbor shared with my mother.

Her Dill Pickle Potato Salad is legendary in our family. Mom flavors the salad with her homemade pickles. And, because she doesn't care for sweet dressings, she coats it with a mixture of mayonnaise, mustard and dill pickle juice.

Mom's Aunt Emily used to make Custard Meringue Pie at Christmastime. It's so scrumptious that we enjoy it year-round.

My mom's ease and skill in the kitchen taught me the joys of cooking, too. I like trying new things, and I think that's because I don't feel intimidated by a new recipe. I just picture my mom whipping up something wonderful, and I dig in!

Cheeseburger Buns, Cauliflower Olive Salad, Dill Pickle Potato Salad and Custard Meringue Pie (recipes are on pp. 188-189).

Cheeseburger Buns

My mom stuffs soft homemade yeast rolls with ground beef, tomato sauce and cheese to make these tasty sandwiches.

    2   packages (1/4 ounce *each*) active dry yeast
  1/2   cup warm water (110° to 115°)
  3/4   cup warm milk (110° to 115°)
  1/4   cup sugar
  1/4   cup shortening
    1   egg
    1   teaspoon salt
3-1/2   to 4 cups all-purpose flour
1-1/2   pounds ground beef
  1/4   cup chopped onion
    1   can (8 ounces) tomato sauce
    8   slices American cheese, quartered

In a mixing bowl, dissolve yeast in warm water. Add milk, sugar, shortening, egg, salt and 2 cups flour; beat until smooth. Stir in enough remaining flour to form a soft dough. Turn onto a floured surface; knead until smooth and elastic, about 4-6 minutes. Place in a greased bowl, turning once to grease top. Cover; let rise in a warm place until doubled, about 30 minutes.

In a skillet, cook beef and onion over medium heat until meat is no longer pink; drain. Stir in tomato sauce. Remove from the heat; set aside. Punch dough down; divide into 16 pieces. On a lightly floured surface, gently roll out and stretch each piece into a 5-in. circle. Top each circle with two pieces of cheese and about 3 tablespoons beef mixture. Bring dough over filling to center; pinch edges to seal.

Place seam side down on a greased baking sheet. Cover and let rise in a warm place until doubled, about

20 minutes. Bake at 400° for 8-12 minutes or until golden brown. Serve immediately. Refrigerate leftovers. **Yield:** 16 sandwiches.

Cauliflower Olive Salad

This colorful toss combines cauliflower and black and green olives with sweet peppers and red onion for a satisfying blend of flavors.

    5   to 6 cups cauliflowerets
    1   cup chopped green pepper
    1   cup stuffed olives, sliced
    1   can (4-1/2 ounces) chopped ripe olives, drained
  1/2   cup chopped sweet red pepper
  1/2   cup chopped red onion, optional
DRESSING:
    3   tablespoons lemon juice
    3   tablespoons cider vinegar
  1/2   teaspoon sugar
  1/4   teaspoon pepper
  1/2   cup vegetable oil

In a large bowl, combine the cauliflower, green pepper, olives, red pepper and onion if desired. In a small bowl, whisk the lemon juice, vinegar, sugar and pepper; gradually whisk in oil. Pour over vegetables and stir to coat. Cover; refrigerate for at least 4 hours. Serve with a slotted spoon. **Yield:** 8 servings.

Dill Pickle Potato Salad

Dill pickles add pizzazz to this old-fashioned chilled salad. The creamy, well-dressed side dish makes an attractive addition to a Fourth of July picnic or church supper.

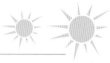

FILLING:
-     2/3 cup sugar
-     1/4 cup cornstarch
-     1/2 teaspoon salt
-       3 cups milk
-       3 egg yolks, beaten
-       1 tablespoon butter, softened
- 1-1/2 teaspoons vanilla extract

MERINGUE:
-       3 egg whites
-     1/4 teaspoon cream of tartar
-     1/8 teaspoon almond extract
-       6 tablespoons sugar

In a bowl, combine the first four ingredients; set aside 2 tablespoons. Press remaining crumb mixture onto the bottom and up the sides of an ungreased 9-in. pie plate. Bake at 350° for 10-12 minutes or until golden brown. Cool on a wire rack.

In a saucepan, combine the sugar, cornstarch and salt. Stir in milk until smooth. Bring to a boil; cook and stir for 1 minute. Remove from the heat. Stir in a small amount of hot filling into egg yolks; return all to pan, stirring constantly. Bring to a gentle boil; cook and stir for 2 minutes. Remove from the heat. Stir in butter and vanilla; keep warm.

In a small mixing bowl, beat the egg whites and cream of tartar on medium speed until foamy. Add extract; beat until soft peaks form. Beat in sugar, 1 tablespoon at a time, on high until stiff peaks form. Pour warm filling into crust. Spread meringue to edges, sealing to crust. Sprinkle with reserved crumbs.

Bake at 350° for 15 minutes or until golden. Cool on a wire rack for 1 hour. Chill for 1-2 hours before serving. **Yield:** 6-8 servings.

-       3 pounds potatoes (about 8 medium)
-       6 hard-cooked eggs, chopped
-       3 celery ribs, chopped
-       6 green onions, chopped
-       2 medium dill pickles, finely chopped
- 1-1/2 cups mayonnaise
-     1/4 cup dill pickle juice
- 4-1/2 teaspoons prepared mustard
-       1 teaspoon celery seed
-       1 teaspoon salt
-     1/2 teaspoon pepper

Leaf lettuce, optional

Place potatoes in a Dutch oven and cover with water. Bring to a boil. Reduce heat; cover and simmer for 20-30 minutes or until tender. Drain and cool.

Peel and cube potatoes; place in a large bowl. Add the eggs, celery, onions and pickles. In a small bowl, combine the mayonnaise, pickle juice, mustard, celery seed, salt and pepper. Pour over potato mixture; mix well. Cover and refrigerate for at least 4 hours. Serve in a lettuce-lined bowl if desired. **Yield:** 8-10 servings.

Custard Meringue Pie

Each bite of this light and fluffy pie will nearly melt in your mouth. The cracker-crumb crust holds a smooth vanilla filling topped with an airy meringue.

- 1-1/4 cups crushed Holland Rusks *or* graham crackers
-     1/4 cup sugar
-     1/2 teaspoon ground cinnamon
-       6 tablespoons butter, melted

The Best That Summer Offers

*By Concetta Maranto Skenfield,
Bakersfield, California*

Dinnertime holds some of my favorite childhood memories. With an Italian family, dinner was—and is—a big event. There's a lot of passing, laughing, sharing and talking…and much more food than can be consumed in one sitting!

Although my mom, Sarah Maranto (above left), owned two quilt and needlework shops when my brother, Vincent, sister, Mary, and I were kids, we never had fast food for dinner. Dad would get home first and start the meal, then Mom would finish it when she arrived. On weekends, with more time to devote to cooking, she made wonderful meals.

Her Rice Balls with Meat Sauce was always my favorite. My parents emigrated from Sicily, so we took trips to Italy as a family. I had to have rice balls while we were there. When my mom made them at home, we knew we were in for a treat.

Mom's colorful Italian Zucchini Boats make a flavorful side dish. The aroma of the cheese, tomato and garlic cooking in the kitchen is enough to make your tummy growl.

She always had plenty of fresh zucchini, tomatoes and vegetables available, thanks to my dad. He grew produce and herbs in the backyard…and still gives me pots of parsley and basil.

Basil stars in Tomato Mozzarella Salad. We sometimes like to add capers to this simple melt-in-your-mouth side dish.

And there isn't a better way to end a big Italian meal than with refreshing Lemon Ice. It's cool and light… and a welcome snack on hot summer days.

Although my brother, sister and I are married now and have careers, we all live within a couple miles of Mom and Dad. We still get together on weekends and holidays to enjoy each other's company and Mom's memorable meals.

Rice Balls with Meat Sauce, Italian Zucchini Boats, Tomato Mozzarella Salad and Lemon Ice (recipes are on pp. 192-193).

Rice Balls with Meat Sauce

My mom's deep-fried rice balls, flavored with traditional Italian cheeses, make a hearty main dish. She serves them with her special spaghetti sauce—my favorite—featuring ground beef and artichoke hearts.

- 1 **pound ground beef**
- 1 **small onion, finely chopped**
- 3 **garlic cloves, minced**
- 2 **cans (15 ounces *each*) tomato sauce**
- 1 **can (14 ounces) water-packed artichoke hearts, drained and chopped**
- 1 **cup frozen peas**
- 1 **jar (4-1/2 ounces) sliced mushrooms, drained**
- 3 **bay leaves**
- 1 **tablespoon sugar**
- 2 **teaspoons dried oregano**
- 2 **teaspoons dried basil**
- 1/4 **teaspoon pepper**

CHEESE-STUFFED RICE BALLS:
- 3 **eggs**
- 2-1/2 **cups cooked rice**
- 1/3 **cup butter, melted**

- 2/3 **cup grated Parmesan *or* Romano cheese**
- 1/4 **cup minced fresh parsley**
- 1/2 **teaspoon salt**
- 1/4 **teaspoon pepper**
- 2 **ounces mozzarella cheese, cut into 3/8-inch cubes**
- 1 **cup dry bread crumbs**

Oil for deep-fat frying

In a large saucepan, cook beef, onion and garlic over medium heat until meat is no longer pink; drain. Stir in the next nine ingredients. Bring to a boil. Reduce heat; cover and simmer for 1 hour, stirring occasionally.

In a bowl, lightly beat 2 eggs. Stir in the rice, butter, Parmesan cheese, parsley, salt and pepper. Cover and refrigerate for 20 minutes. Roll into 1-1/2-in. balls. Press a mozzarella cube into each; reshape balls.

In a small bowl, lightly beat remaining egg. Dip each ball into egg, then roll in bread crumbs. In a deep-fat fryer or electric skillet, heat oil to 375°. Fry rice balls until golden brown, about 4 minutes. Drain on paper towels. Discard bay leaf from meat sauce; serve with rice balls. **Yield:** 6-8 servings.

Italian Zucchini Boats

The tantalizing aroma of this savory side dish baking in the oven is sure to whet your appetite. Mom scoops the pulp out of zucchini halves and mixes it with tomato, Parmesan cheese, bread crumbs and parsley.

✓ Uses less fat, sugar or salt. Includes Nutritional Analysis and Diabetic Exchanges.

- 6 **medium zucchini**
- 2 **cups dry bread crumbs**
- 2 **eggs, lightly beaten**
- 1 **large tomato, diced**

1/3   cup grated Parmesan *or* Romano cheese
1/4   cup minced fresh parsley
  2   garlic cloves, minced
1/2   cup chicken broth
1/2   teaspoon salt
1/8   teaspoon pepper
  2   tablespoons butter, melted

Cut zucchini in half lengthwise. With a spoon, scoop out and reserve pulp, leaving a 3/8-in. shell. Cook shells in salted water for 2 minutes; remove and drain. Chop zucchini pulp; place in a bowl. Add the bread crumbs, eggs, tomato, Parmesan cheese, parsley and garlic. Stir in broth, salt and pepper. Stuff into zucchini shells.

Place in a greased 13-in. x 9-in. x 2-in. baking dish. Drizzle with butter. Bake, uncovered, at 350° for 20 minutes or until golden. **Yield:** 6 servings.

Nutritional Analysis: One serving (2 stuffed zucchini halves) equals 260 calories, 9 g fat (4 g saturated fat), 85 mg cholesterol, 741 mg sodium, 34 g carbohydrate, 4 g fiber, 11 g protein. **Diabetic Exchanges:** 2 starch, 1-1/2 fat, 1 vegetable.

Tomato Mozzarella Salad

Instead of tossed salad, I serve these attractive tomato and mozzarella slices, drizzled with oil and sprinkled with basil. They're especially tasty made with fresh tomatoes and basil from the garden.

  3   large tomatoes, sliced
  8   ounces mozzarella, sliced
1/4   cup olive oil
1/4   teaspoon salt
1/8   teaspoon pepper
1/4   cup minced fresh basil

On a large serving platter, alternate tomatoes and mozzarella slices. In a jar with a tight-fitting lid, combine the oil, salt and pepper; shake well. Drizzle over tomatoes and mozzarella. Sprinkle with basil. **Yield:** 6-8 servings.

Lemon Ice

Pucker up for this sweet-tart treat! The delicious lemon dessert is a perfectly refreshing way to end a summer meal…or any meal, for that matter.

  2   cups sugar
  1   cup water
  2   cups lemon juice
  1   tablespoon grated lemon peel

In a saucepan over low heat, cook and stir sugar and water until sugar is dissolved. Remove from the heat; stir in lemon juice. Pour into a freezer container. Freeze for 4 hours, stirring every 30 minutes, or until mixture becomes slushy. Sprinkle servings with lemon peel. **Yield:** 6 servings.

A Birthday Meal To Remember

By Susan Ormond, Jamestown, North Carolina

When I think about my mom, the first things that come to mind are her fabulous meals and the joy it gave her to cook for others.

My mom, Mary Ann Emrick (left), loved to entertain and hosted many baby showers and dinner parties over the years. She made each event even more special with the loving care she put into the foods she prepared.

For our birthdays, my dad, two sisters and I got to pick any meal we wanted Mom to prepare. My favorite was Round Ham Loaf, Creamed Potatoes, Fluffy Lime Salad and Texas Sheet Cake.

Her Round Ham Loaf, a nice change from the usual meat loaf, was served with a pleasantly sweet raisin sauce. She garnished the loaf with pineapple and maraschino cherries, which made it pretty enough to serve for company.

Mom's Creamed Potatoes were comforting and chunky, while the tangy Fluffy Lime Salad was cool and refreshing.

There was no better way to end a birthday meal than with her chocolaty Texas Sheet Cake. Moist like a pudding cake, it was topped with a sweet chocolate icing.

My grandmother handed down the ham, potato and salad recipes to my mother. She learned to cook from Grandma, but my mom continued to refine her skills by gathering information and recipes from magazines, newspapers, television shows and friends. There were always scraps of paper and little notebooks around the house with recipes written on them.

Mom often served my favorite meal for Easter and other holidays, too. I have continued the tradition by making the dishes during the holidays for my husband, David, and our three children.

I'm glad that I've had this chance to pay tribute to my mom by sharing this special meal with you as well.

Round Ham Loaf, Creamed Potatoes, Fluffy Lime Salad and Texas Sheet Cake (recipes are on pp. 196-197).

Bake, uncovered, at 325° for 45 minutes. Baste with reserved pineapple juice. Bake 45 minutes longer or until lightly browned and a meat thermometer reads 160°, basting occasionally with pan drippings.

For sauce, combine the sugar, cornstarch, salt and water in a saucepan; stir until smooth. Add the raisins. Bring to a boil; cook and stir for 2 minutes or until thickened. Remove from the heat; stir in butter and vanilla. Serve warm with ham loaf. Garnish with a cherry if desired. **Yield:** 6 servings.

Creamed Potatoes

These melt-in-your-mouth potatoes, baked in a mild creamy sauce, complement any meat entree, and they're a pleasant change from mashed or baked.

- **6 medium potatoes (2 pounds), peeled and cut into 1/2-inch cubes**
- **3 tablespoons butter**
- **1/4 cup all-purpose flour**
- **1 teaspoon salt**
- **1/4 teaspoon pepper**
- **2 cups milk**

Paprika and minced fresh parsley

Place potatoes in a saucepan and cover with water. Bring to a boil. Reduce heat; cover and cook for 15-20 minutes or until tender. Meanwhile, in another saucepan, melt butter. Stir in the flour, salt and pepper until smooth. Gradually add milk. Bring to a boil; cook and stir for 2 minutes or until thickened.

Drain potatoes and place in a serving bowl. Add cream sauce and toss gently. Sprinkle with paprika and parsley. **Yield:** 6 servings.

Round Ham Loaf

Slices of pineapple and a maraschino cherry make my mom's homey ham loaf pretty enough for company. The accompanying vanilla and raisin sauce lends a distinctive flavor to the meat.

- **1 egg**
- **3/4 cup milk**
- **1/4 cup crushed butter-flavored crackers (about 6 crackers)**
- **1 pound ground fully cooked ham**
- **1/2 pound ground pork**
- **1 can (8 ounces) sliced pineapple**

RAISIN SAUCE:
- **1/2 cup sugar**
- **1 tablespoon cornstarch**

Pinch salt
- **1 cup water**
- **1/3 cup golden raisins**
- **1 tablespoon butter**
- **1 teaspoon vanilla extract**
- **1 maraschino cherry, optional**

In a large bowl, combine the egg, milk and cracker crumbs. Crumble ham and pork over mixture; mix well. Form into an 8-in. round loaf in an ungreased 9-in. pie plate. Drain pineapple, reserving juice. Cut pineapple slices in half if desired; place on top of loaf.

Fluffy Lime Salad

Crunchy walnuts, plump marshmallows and tangy pineapple dot this creamy lime salad. It's a refreshing side dish for a family meal or a yummy addition to a potluck dinner. It can be made in advance, giving you one less thing to do at dinnertime.

- 1 can (8 ounces) crushed pineapple
- 1 package (3 ounces) lime gelatin
- 3 tablespoons water
- 2 packages (3 ounces *each*) cream cheese, softened
- 1 cup chopped walnuts
- 1 cup miniature marshmallows
- 1 cup heavy whipping cream, whipped

Drain pineapple, reserving juice; set the pineapple aside. In a saucepan, combine gelatin, water and reserved juice. Cook and stir over low heat until gelatin is dissolved. Refrigerate until syrupy, about 30 minutes.

In a small mixing bowl, beat cream cheese until fluffy. Stir in gelatin mixture, walnuts, marshmallows and reserved pineapple. Fold in the whipped cream. Transfer to a 1-qt. serving bowl. Cover and refrigerate for 2 hours or until set. **Yield:** 9 servings.

Texas Sheet Cake

This chocolaty delight was one of my favorites growing up. The cake is so moist and the icing so sweet that everyone who samples it wants a copy of the recipe. I'm always happy to share it.

- 1 cup butter
- 1 cup water
- 1/4 cup baking cocoa
- 2 cups all-purpose flour
- 2 cups sugar
- 1 teaspoon baking soda
- 1/2 teaspoon salt
- 1/2 cup sour cream

ICING:
- 1/2 cup butter
- 1/4 cup plus 2 tablespoons milk
- 3 tablespoons baking cocoa
- 3-3/4 cups confectioners' sugar
- 1 teaspoon vanilla extract

In a large saucepan, bring the butter, water and cocoa to a boil. Remove from the heat. Combine the flour, sugar, baking soda and salt; add to cocoa mixture. Stir in the sour cream until smooth. Pour into a greased 15-in. x 10-in. x 1-in. baking pan. Bake at 350° for 20-25 minutes or until a toothpick inserted near the center comes out clean.

In a saucepan, melt butter; add milk and cocoa. Bring to a boil. Remove from the heat. Whisk in confectioners' sugar and vanilla until smooth. Pour over warm cake. Cool completely on a wire rack. **Yield:** 15 servings.

A hearty meal with spareribs and biscuits is a fall favorite. Recipes are on pp. 210-211.

Comforting AUTUMN MEALS

Cozy Country-Style Cookin'

By Odilia Riestenberg, Elizabeth, Minnesota

Growing up on a farm, we never were afforded the luxury of sleeping in on Saturday mornings. Instead, they meant a lot of hard work both inside and out.

But one thing all seven of us looked forward to was this fit-for-a-king midday meal prepared by my mom, Odilia Riestenberg (above) of Elizabeth, Minnesota.

Her Meatball Stew was a favorite main dish at our house, especially during the cold winter months. We delighted in the aroma of the stew simmering on the stove as we came in for dinner. Mom liked that it was simple to prepare and that it satisfied all of our hearty appetites.

Sweet and tangy, Mom's Coleslaw went so well with the stew. It can be made in advance, giving you more time to complete other chores around the house or cook up another treat in the kitchen.

Like most cooks of her day, Mom was always looking for ways to use up leftovers. Older bread was never thrown away; it got recycled into Quick Garlic Toast. It never seemed like a leftover to us—we thought it was a special treat!

We didn't have dessert at every meal, but when Mom asked for suggestions, Chocolate Marshmallow Cake is what we usually requested. It was very difficult to stop at one piece.

Now Mom and Dad are semi-retired (I don't think farmers ever really retire). Mom grows flowers for dried floral arrangements, and she still invites us to dinner once in a while.

I learned most of what I know about cooking from her. As a homemaker with three children, I frequently turn to Mom's recipes like these. We hope your family will enjoy them, too.

Meatball Stew, Mom's Coleslaw, Quick Garlic Toast and Chocolate Marshmallow Cake (recipes are on pp. 202-203).

In a bowl, combine egg, bread crumbs, chopped onion, salt, marjoram and thyme. Add beef and mix well. Shape into 48 meatballs.

In a Dutch oven, brown meatballs in oil; drain. Add broth, soup, potatoes, carrots and pearl onions; bring to a boil. Reduce heat; simmer for 30 minutes or until the vegetables are tender. Sprinkle with parsley. **Yield:** 8 servings.

Mom's Coleslaw

Year-round, our family always goes for this crisp, refreshing salad. With a tangy vinegar and oil dressing, it has wonderful homemade flavor. When Mom made it years ago for our family of seven, it was rare to have leftovers.

- 1 **large head cabbage, shredded**
- 2 **medium carrots, shredded**
- 1 **teaspoon celery seed**
- 1 **cup vegetable oil**
- 1 **cup sugar**
- 1/2 **cup vinegar**
- 1 **teaspoon salt**
- 1 **teaspoon ground mustard**
- 1 **medium onion, quartered**

In a large bowl, toss cabbage, carrots and celery seed. Place the remaining ingredients in a blender or food processor; cover and process until combined. Pour over cabbage mixture and toss to coat. Cover and refrigerate for at least 2 hours. Serve with a slotted spoon. **Yield:** 10-12 servings.

Meatball Stew

The combination of tender meatballs plus potatoes, carrots and pearl onions in a golden gravy really hits the spot on chilly days after we'd worked up an appetite doing our morning chores. Mom served it with pride for Saturday dinners when I was growing up on the farm.

- 1 **egg, beaten**
- 1 **cup soft bread crumbs**
- 1/4 **cup finely chopped onion**
- 1 **teaspoon salt**
- 1 **teaspoon dried marjoram**
- 1/2 **teaspoon dried thyme**
- 1-1/2 **pounds ground beef**
- 2 **tablespoons vegetable oil**
- 2 **cans (14-1/2 ounces *each*) beef broth**
- 2 **cans (10-3/4 ounces *each*) condensed golden mushroom soup, undiluted**
- 4 **medium potatoes, peeled and quartered**
- 4 **medium carrots, cut into chunks**
- 1 **jar (16 ounces) whole pearl onions, drained**
- 1/4 **cup minced fresh parsley**

Quick Garlic Toast

Mom knew how to easily round out a meal with this crisp, cheesy garlic toast. We gobbled it up when she served it alongside slaw or salad…and used it to soak up gravy from her stew, too.

- 1/3 **cup butter, softened**
- 12 **slices bread**
- 1/2 **teaspoon garlic salt**
- 3 **tablespoons grated Parmesan cheese**

Spread butter on one side of each slice of bread. Cut each slice in half; place plain side down on a baking sheet. Sprinkle with garlic salt and Parmesan cheese. Broil 4 in. from the heat for 1-2 minutes or until lightly browned. **Yield:** 12 slices.

Chocolate Marshmallow Cake

When Mom wanted to treat us to something special, she made this awesome dessert. We could never resist the tender chocolate cake, the fluffy marshmallow layer or the fudge topping.

Marvelous Marshmallows

To keep marshmallows from turning hard, store them in the freezer. If marshmallows are already hard, tightly seal them in a plastic bag with a few slices of fresh white bread and let stand for 3 days. They'll be soft like fresh.

- 1/2 **cup butter**
- 2 **squares (1 ounce *each*) unsweetened chocolate**
- 1 **cup all-purpose flour**
- 1/2 **teaspoon baking powder**
- 1/4 **teaspoon baking soda**
- 1/4 **teaspoon salt**
- 2 **eggs**
- 1 **cup sugar**
- 1/2 **cup unsweetened applesauce**
- 1 **teaspoon vanilla extract**
- 1 **package (10-1/2 ounces) miniature marshmallows, *divided***

GLAZE:
- 1/2 **cup sugar**
- 2 **tablespoons milk**
- 2 **tablespoons butter**
- 1/4 **cup semisweet chocolate chips**

In a microwave or double boiler, melt butter and chocolate; cool for 10 minutes. Combine flour, baking powder, baking soda and salt; set aside. In a mixing bowl, beat eggs, sugar, applesauce and vanilla. Stir in chocolate mixture. Add dry ingredients; mix well.

Pour into a greased 13-in. x 9-in. x 2-in. baking pan. Bake at 350° for 20-30 minutes or until a toothpick comes out clean. Set aside 1/2 cup marshmallows for the glaze. Sprinkle remaining marshmallows over cake. Return to the oven for 2 minutes or until marshmallows are softened.

In a saucepan, combine sugar, milk and butter. Bring to a boil; boil for 1-1/2 minutes. Remove from the heat; stir in chocolate chips and reserved marshmallows until melted. Quickly drizzle over the cake (glaze will harden as it cools). **Yield:** 12-16 servings.

Sunday Meal Smells Heavenly

By Cindy Kufeldt, Orlando, Florida

I recall many wonderful things about my mom's cooking as I was growing up. My mother, Nancy Kay Woodside (left) of Flagler Beach, Florida, often had from-scratch cookies and cakes with a glass of milk ready for my younger brother and me to snack on when we got home from school.

My parents frequently hosted guests for dinner and get-togethers, and my mom is known by many to be an excellent cook. Holidays were always a deliciously special time at our house, and the best menu of the week was typically Sunday dinner.

One of my mom's best Sunday meals begins with Marinated Baked Chicken. The chicken breasts are so tender and juicy, and they produce a wonderful aroma while baking in the oven.

Mushroom Oven Rice is homey and comforting, with lots of fresh mushrooms and celery stirred in. My brother and I rushed to the table when Mom was serving this side dish, which is also wonderful alongside ham.

Special enough for company, Broccoli Casserole is another satisfying side dish. The broccoli is baked with a rich and creamy sauce, then sprinkled with cheese-flavored cracker crumbs. One helping is never enough.

Mom has a great reputation for making delectable desserts. One of my favorites is easy-to-make Cherry Cheese Pie. A lovely combination of cream cheese and cherry pie filling, it's delicious served any time of year.

I'm so thankful that my husband, Steve, and I and our two children, Seth and Abigail, live close enough to Mom to frequently enjoy her cooking. She and I are thrilled to share these recipes so you can make them for your own family, too.

Marinated Baked Chicken, Mushroom Oven Rice, Broccoli Casserole and Cherry Cheese Pie (recipes are on pp. 206-207).

Marinated Baked Chicken

This tender, flavorful chicken is one of my mom's specialties. Soy sauce and bottled Italian dressing combine in a mouth-watering marinade that nicely complements the meat.

- **1/2 cup Italian salad dressing**
- **1/2 cup soy sauce**
- **6 bone-in chicken breast halves**
- **1/8 teaspoon onion salt**
- **1/8 teaspoon garlic salt**
- **Kale and spiced apple rings, optional**

In a measuring cup, combine salad dressing and soy sauce. Pour 3/4 cup into a large resealable plastic bag; add chicken. Seal the bag and turn to coat; refrigerate for 4 hours or overnight, turning several times. Refrigerate remaining marinade for basting.

Drain chicken, discarding marinade. Place chicken, skin side up, on a rack in a roasting pan. Sprinkle with onion salt and garlic salt.

Bake, uncovered, at 350° for 45-60 minutes or until juices run clear and a meat thermometer reads 170°, brushing occasionally with reserved marinade. Garnish platter with kale and apple rings if desired. **Yield:** 6 servings.

Mushroom Oven Rice

When I was growing up, we couldn't wait to get to the table when Mom was serving this delicious rice dish. With lots of fresh mushrooms and celery stirred in, it tastes so good you're sure to want seconds!

- **1 cup uncooked long grain rice**
- **1/4 cup butter**
- **1/2 cup finely chopped celery**
- **1/2 cup finely chopped onion**
- **1 cup sliced fresh mushrooms**
- **1 can (14-1/2 ounces) chicken broth**
- **1/3 cup water**
- **1 to 2 tablespoons soy sauce**
- **1 tablespoon dried parsley flakes**

In a skillet, saute the rice in butter for 2 minutes or until golden brown. Add celery and onion; cook and stir for 2 minutes. Add mushrooms; cook and stir until the celery is tender.

Transfer to a greased 1-1/2-qt. baking dish. Stir in the broth, water, soy sauce and parsley. Cover and bake at 350° for 45-50 minutes or until liquid is absorbed and rice is tender. **Yield:** 6 servings.

Broccoli Casserole

This colorful side dish is one my mom fixes often for Christmas dinner and other special occasions. The broccoli is baked with a rich creamy sauce...and cheese-flavored cracker crumbs are sprinkled over the top. Yum!

- **2 pounds fresh broccoli, cut into florets**
- **1 can (10-3/4 ounces) condensed cream of mushroom soup, undiluted**
- **1/2 cup mayonnaise**

1/2   cup shredded cheddar cheese
1   tablespoon lemon juice
1   cup crushed cheese-flavored snack
    crackers

Place 1 in. of water and broccoli in a saucepan; bring to a boil. Reduce heat; cover and simmer for 5-8 minutes or just until crisp-tender. Drain and place in a greased 2-qt. baking dish.

In a bowl, combine the soup, mayonnaise, cheese and lemon juice. Pour over broccoli. Sprinkle with crushed crackers. Bake, uncovered, at 350° for 25-30 minutes or until heated through. **Yield:** 6-8 servings.

Cherry Cheese Pie

My mom is known for her scrumptious desserts. This easy-to-make pie is one she has served often. It's one of my favorite desserts anytime of year. I love the combination of cream cheese and cherry pie filling.

3/4   cup all-purpose flour
3   tablespoons sugar
1/4   teaspoon salt
1/4   cup butter, softened
1   can (21 ounces) cherry pie filling

1   package (8 ounces) cream cheese,
    softened
1/3   cup sugar
1   egg
1   teaspoon vanilla extract

In a bowl, combine the flour, sugar and salt. Add butter; stir until combined. Press onto the bottom and up the sides of a 9-in. pie plate. Bake at 350° for 10-12 minutes or until lightly browned. Pour pie filling into crust.

In a mixing bowl, beat cream cheese, sugar, egg and vanilla until smooth. Carefully spread around outside edges of pie, leaving a 3-in. circle of cherries exposed in the center. Bake for 30-35 minutes or until edges begin to brown. Cool on a wire rack. Refrigerate for several hours before serving. **Yield:** 8 servings.

 Cooking Chicken

When you're cooking chicken parts, remember that dark meat takes longer to cook than white meat does because of its higher fat content.

Start the dark meat a few minutes before the white—assuming the parts are about the same size; smaller pieces of chicken will cook faster than larger ones. The white meat might be too dry if it is cooked as long as the dark.

Chicken parts should be cooked within 24 hours of being purchased.

After-Harvest Meal to Enjoy

By Nancy Horsburgh, Everett, Ontario

Feeding family and seasonal farmhands for more than 20 years meant that my mother, Jean Bailey (left), spent lots of time in her huge kitchen.

During the tobacco harvest, Mom would feed our family of five, in addition to 12 to 15 workers.

All of Mom's meals were wonderful, but during the harvest, they were the best! My favorite was Barbecued Spareribs, Yukon Mashed Potatoes, Carrot Broccoli Casserole, Fluffy Biscuits and Old-Fashioned Chocolate Pie.

The aroma of those spareribs baking in the oven had us drooling long before they were ready to eat!

The garlic-seasoned Yukon Mashed Potatoes were incredibly creamy. And Carrot Broccoli Casserole complemented the ribs and potatoes so nicely. This colorful side dish can be assembled ahead of time.

Fluffy Biscuits were the result of many years of practice. Mom didn't enjoy biscuit-making, so she gave that job to me. We both learned that the secret to good biscuits is to have cold ingredients and not over-mix them.

My two brothers and I topped slices of Old-Fashioned Chocolate Pie with mounds of freshly whipped cream. It's hard to believe this yummy pie doesn't contain eggs or milk.

As I got older, I took over the harvest cooking and Mom planned the meals. I'm so thankful she gave me an early introduction to preparing nourishing foods. I've loved to cook ever since!

Every Sunday, I now prepare the big family meal. Our children, their spouses and our two grandsons live nearby. So do my brothers and their families...and Mom, of course.

I'm happy to share my mom's memorable meal with you and hope you enjoy it, too!

Barbecued Spareribs, Yukon Mashed Potatoes, Carrot Broccoli Casserole, Fluffy Biscuits and Old-Fashioned Chocolate Pie (recipes are on pp. 210-211).

Drain ribs; brush with some of the sauce. Bake, uncovered, 1 hour longer or until the meat is tender, brushing frequently with remaining sauce. **Yield:** 6 servings.

Yukon Mashed Potatoes

My mom liked to use Yukon Gold potatoes for this recipe instead of the usual white variety. These garlic-seasoned spuds are sensational served alongside spareribs.

- 8 to 9 medium Yukon Gold *or* russet potatoes, peeled and quartered
- 1/2 cup half-and-half cream
- 2 tablespoons butter
- 1/2 to 1 teaspoon garlic salt
- 1/8 teaspoon pepper

Place potatoes in a Dutch oven and cover with water. Cover and bring to a boil; cook for 20-25 minutes or until very tender. Drain well. In a mixing bowl, mash the potatoes. Add the cream, butter, garlic salt and pepper; beat until light and fluffy. **Yield:** 6 servings.

Carrot Broccoli Casserole

This colorful side dish feels right at home with any entree. The veggies are coated in a buttery cheese sauce, then layered with cracker crumbs. Even kids who turn up their noses at broccoli will eat this up.

- 1 package (16 ounces) baby carrots
- 1-1/2 pounds fresh broccoli, chopped *or* 2 packages (10 ounces *each*) frozen chopped broccoli, thawed

Barbecued Spareribs

You'll need extra dinner napkins when you serve these tender ribs because they're so finger-lickin' good. The thick and tangy sauce has bits of celery and onion as well as a cayenne pepper kick. The ribs are perfect for summer picnics.

- 6 pounds pork spareribs, cut into serving-size pieces
- 2 tablespoons vegetable oil
- 1 medium onion, finely chopped
- 2 celery ribs, finely chopped
- 2 tablespoons butter
- 1 cup water
- 1 cup ketchup
- 3 tablespoons Worcestershire sauce
- 2 tablespoons brown sugar
- 2 tablespoons cider vinegar
- 1 tablespoon lemon juice
- 1 tablespoon Dijon mustard
- 1/8 teaspoon cayenne pepper

In a large skillet, brown ribs in batches in oil. Place ribs, bone side down, on a rack in a shallow roasting pan. Cover and bake at 350° for 1 hour.

Meanwhile, in a skillet, saute onion and celery in butter until tender. Add the remaining ingredients. Bring to a boil. Reduce heat; simmer, uncovered, for 10-12 minutes or until slightly thickened.

8 ounces process cheese (Velveeta), cubed
3/4 cup butter, *divided*
1-3/4 cups crushed butter-flavored crackers
(about 40 crackers)

Place 1 in. of water in a saucepan; add carrots. Bring to a boil. Reduce heat; cover and simmer for 5-8 minutes or until crisp-tender. Add broccoli; cover and simmer 6-8 minutes longer or until vegetables are crisp-tender. Drain and set aside. In a small saucepan, cook and stir the cheese and 1/4 cup butter until smooth. Stir in the broccoli and carrots until combined.

Melt the remaining butter; toss with cracker crumbs. Sprinkle a third of the mixture in a greased 2-1/2-qt. baking dish. Top with half of the vegetable mixture. Repeat layers. Sprinkle with the remaining crumb mixture. Bake, uncovered, at 350° for 35-40 minutes or until heated through. **Yield:** 6-8 servings.

Fluffy Biscuits

If you're looking for a flaky basic biscuit, this recipe is the best. These golden-brown rolls bake up tall, light and tender. Their mild flavor tastes even better when the warm biscuits are spread with butter or jam.

2 cups all-purpose flour
4 teaspoons baking powder
3 teaspoons sugar
1/2 teaspoon salt
1/2 cup shortening
1 egg
2/3 cup milk

In a bowl, combine the flour, baking powder, sugar and salt. Cut in shortening until the mixture resembles coarse crumbs. In a small bowl, beat egg and milk; stir into dry ingredients just until moistened.

Turn onto a well-floured surface; knead 20 times. Roll to 3/4-in. thickness; cut with a 2-1/2-in. biscuit cutter. Place on a lightly greased baking sheet. Bake at 450° for 8-10 minutes or until golden brown. Serve warm. **Yield:** 1 dozen.

Old-Fashioned Chocolate Pie

Rich and oh-so-chocolaty, this silky pie is a cinch to prepare. The mouth-watering filling and flaky crust are an unbeatable combination that's sure to make this pie one of your family's favorite desserts, too.

1 cup sugar
1/3 cup baking cocoa
1/4 cup all-purpose flour
Pinch salt
2-1/4 cups water
1 tablespoon butter
1 teaspoon vanilla extract
1 pastry shell (9 inches), baked
Whipped cream and chocolate sprinkles

In a large saucepan, combine the sugar, cocoa, flour and salt; gradually add water. Cook and stir over medium heat until mixture comes to a boil. Cook and stir for 1 minute or until thickened.

Remove from the heat; stir in butter and vanilla. Pour into pastry shell. Refrigerate for 2-3 hours before slicing. Garnish with whipped cream and chocolate sprinkles. **Yield:** 6-8 servings.

Palate-Pleasing Roast Dinner

By Adeline Piscitelli, Sayreville, New Jersey

My mother loved to cook. She was well-known for her delicious everyday dinners for our family. Plus, it seemed she was always cooking for a wedding reception or some other party. My sister and I liked to help her whenever we could, and I certainly learned my way around the kitchen thanks to Mom.

Her delicious Old-Fashioned Pot Roast is a recipe she made often when I was growing up. It simmers slowly on the stove, so every mouth-watering bite of beef is moist and delicious. And we would gobble up the accompanying carrots in no time.

Sliced fresh mushrooms and simple seasonings are the secrets of success to Garlic-Buttered Green Beans. After all these years, this is still my favorite way to prepare garden-fresh green beans.

The recipe for Parsley Potatoes is simple, but the flavor is anything but plain. It's nice to have a tried-and-true recipe like this that pairs well with a variety of main dishes.

Years later, I served these same dishes in the family restaurant my husband and I ran. Our customers raved about the tasty beef, potatoes and beans—all recipes I got from Mom, prepared many times and never tired of. I was always pleased to bring a taste of my home to their table.

I'm retired from the restaurant business now, but I still like to do some catering. This pot roast meal, along with my own Peach Bavarian mold, is often requested by family, friends and customers.

I hope you enjoy this comforting meal as much as my family and I do. It has a look and aroma that just say "home cooking!"

Old-Fashioned Pot Roast, Garlic-Buttered Green Beans, Parsley Potatoes and Peach Bavarian (recipes are on pp. 214-215).

Old-Fashioned Pot Roast

My sister, dad and I loved it when Mom made her pot roast. She was such a great cook! Later, I served this dish in our restaurant for many years. It's a recipe that just says "home cooking."

1	boneless beef chuck roast (about 3 pounds)
6	tablespoons all-purpose flour, *divided*
6	tablespoons butter, *divided*
3	cups hot water
2	teaspoons beef bouillon granules
1	medium onion, quartered
1	celery rib, cut into pieces
1	teaspoon salt
1/2	teaspoon pepper
4	medium carrots, cut into 2-inch pieces

Sprinkle the roast with 1 tablespoon flour. In a Dutch oven, brown the roast on all sides in 3 tablespoons butter. Add the water, bouillon, onion, celery, salt and pepper; bring to a boil. Reduce heat; cover and simmer for 1 hour. Add carrots; cover and simmer 45-60 minutes longer or until meat is tender.

Remove meat and carrots to a serving platter and

keep warm. Strain cooking juices; set aside. In the same Dutch oven, melt remaining butter. Stir in the remaining flour; cook and stir until bubbly. Add 2 cups of the cooking juices and blend until smooth. Cook and stir until thickened; add the additional cooking juices until the gravy has reached the desired consistency. **Yield:** 6-8 servings.

Garlic-Buttered Green Beans

These dressed-up beans are simple to make but look and taste special. They're a perfect side dish for nearly any meal.

1	pound fresh *or* frozen green beans
1/2	cup sliced fresh mushrooms
6	tablespoons butter
2	to 3 teaspoons onion powder
1	to 1-1/2 teaspoons garlic powder

Salt and pepper to taste

Cook green beans in water to cover until crisp-tender. Meanwhile, in a skillet, saute mushrooms in butter until tender. Add onion powder and garlic powder. Drain beans; add to skillet and toss. Season with salt and pepper. **Yield:** 6 servings.

Parsley Potatoes

The fresh flavor of parsley is perfect with hot buttered potatoes—it adds a little extra zip. I used this recipe when I did all the cooking at our restaurant, and customers loved it.

- **2 pounds potatoes, peeled and cut into 2-inch pieces**
- **1/2 cup butter, melted**
- **1/4 cup minced fresh parsley**

Salt and pepper to taste

In a saucepan, cook potatoes in water to cover until tender; drain. Combine butter and parsley; pour over the potatoes and toss to coat. Season with salt and pepper. **Yield:** 6-8 servings.

Peach Bavarian

Fruit molds are my specialty, and I enjoy making and serving them. This one, with its refreshing peach taste, makes a colorful salad or dessert.

- **1 can (15-1/4 ounces) sliced peaches**
- **2 packages (3 ounces *each*) peach *or* apricot gelatin**
- **1/2 cup sugar**
- **2 cups boiling water**
- **1 teaspoon almond extract**

- **1 carton (8 ounces) frozen whipped topping, thawed**

Additional sliced peaches, optional

Drain peaches, reserving 2/3 cup juice. Chop peaches into small pieces; set aside. In a bowl, dissolve gelatin and sugar in boiling water. Stir in reserved syrup. Chill until slightly thickened.

Stir extract into whipped topping; gently fold into gelatin mixture. Fold in peaches. Pour into a 6-cup mold coated with nonstick cooking spray. Chill overnight. Unmold; garnish with additional peaches if desired. **Yield:** 8-10 servings.

String-Free Beans

Green beans are also called string beans or snap beans. Wax beans are the pale yellow variety. Select beans with firm, smooth, brightly colored pods. Most fresh beans today do not require stringing because the fibrous string has been bred out of the species. If you have beans that do need stringing, simply snap off the stem end and use it to pull the string down and off the pod.

A Thanksgiving To Remember

By Jacinta Ransom, South Haven, Michigan

Awesome is the best way I know to describe the Thanksgiving dinner my mom, Marsha Ransom (left), prepares.

Dinner centers on Turkey with Grandma's Stuffing, which my grandma made when my mom was growing up. The yummy stuffing is flavored with poultry seasoning, and the gravy's great over mashed potatoes.

Gelatin Ring with Cream Cheese Balls is another recipe my mom enjoyed as a child. The cream cheese balls rolled in nuts make it fancy enough for a special occasion, but it's easy to make.

Aunt Mavis used to bring Special Layered Salad to our family feasts. Now my brothers and I help prepare it when we have Thanksgiving at our house.

I can hardly wait for dessert. Pumpkin Chip Cupcakes taste so good with all the nuts and chocolate chips inside, that I'd rather have them than pumpkin pie any day!

My mom, who's a *Taste of Home* field editor, cooks mostly from scratch. Mom learned to cook while growing up in Belle Vernon, Pennsylvania. Her mom taught her how to follow a recipe, but her grandmother taught her how to add a "pinch of this or a pinch of that." My mom has passed on her skills, too…to me and my three brothers.

I really love baking and cooking with my mom. She says I've been helping her since I was 3, when I'd climb up on a stool and tear lettuce for salads. She calls me her "right-hand girl." My brothers and I pitch in if we're expecting company or having a special meal…or whenever she needs extra help.

Someday I want to be as good a cook as my mom is. I hope you'll fix one of her recipes for one of your holiday meals.

Turkey with Grandma's Stuffing, Gelatin Ring with Cream Cheese Balls, Special Layered Salad and Pumpkin Chip Cupcakes (recipes are on pp. 218-219).

3-1/2 to 4 hours or until a meat thermometer reads 180° for turkey and 165° for stuffing, basting occasionally. (Cover loosely with foil if turkey browns too quickly.)

Bake additional stuffing, covered, for 25-30 minutes. Uncover; bake 10 minutes longer. Cover turkey and let stand for 20 minutes before carving. Pour pan drippings into a 2-cup measuring cup; skim fat. Add enough remaining giblet broth to measure 2 cups.

In a saucepan, combine cornstarch and cold water until smooth. Stir in broth mixture. Bring to a boil; cook and stir for 2 minutes or until thickened. Season with salt and pepper. **Yield:** 8 servings (10 cups stuffing).

Gelatin Ring with Cream Cheese Balls

Here's a fun way to serve cranberry sauce that will please both kids and adults. The gelatin and cranberry sauce ring is dressed up with cream cheese balls rolled in walnuts.

2 packages (3 ounces *each*) raspberry gelatin
2 cups boiling water
2 cans (16 ounces *each*) whole-berry cranberry sauce
1 package (8 ounces) cream cheese
1 cup ground walnuts

In a bowl, dissolve gelatin in boiling water. Stir in cranberry sauce until well blended. Pour into a 6-cup ring mold coated with nonstick cooking spray; refrigerate overnight or until firm.

Roll cream cheese into 3/4-in. balls; coat with walnuts. Unmold gelatin onto a serving platter; place cream cheese balls in the center of ring. **Yield:** 10-12 servings.

Turkey with Grandma's Stuffing

Everyone is ready to dig in when my mom sets this impressive Thanksgiving favorite on the dinner table.

1 turkey (12 pounds) with giblets
4 celery ribs with leaves, chopped
1 small onion, finely chopped
4 tablespoons butter, *divided*
10 slices day-old white bread, cubed
10 slices day-old whole wheat bread, cubed
1/2 cup egg substitute
3/4 teaspoon poultry seasoning
1/2 teaspoon salt
Dash pepper
3 tablespoons cornstarch
1/4 cup cold water
Additional salt and pepper

Place giblets in a saucepan and cover with water; bring to a boil. Reduce heat; cover and simmer for 45-50 minutes or until tender.

Remove giblets to a cutting board; dice. Set broth and giblets aside. In a skillet, saute celery and onion in 2 tablespoons butter until tender. In a bowl, combine bread cubes, celery mixture, giblets, egg substitute and seasonings. Stir in 1 cup giblet broth.

Just before roasting, loosely stuff turkey with 8 cups stuffing. Place remaining stuffing in a greased 2-cup baking dish; refrigerate. Skewer turkey openings; tie drumsticks together with kitchen string.

Place breast side up on a rack in a roasting pan. Pour 1 cup giblet broth over turkey. Melt remaining butter; brush over turkey. Bake, uncovered, at 325° for

Special Layered Salad

Tiny shrimp make my aunt's seven-layer salad something special. This pretty salad never lasts long when my mom makes it.

- 1 **pound romaine, torn**
- 1 **medium green pepper, chopped**
- 1 **medium onion, chopped**
- 1 **package (10 ounces) frozen peas**
- 1-1/2 **cups mayonnaise**
- 2 **cups (8 ounces) shredded cheddar cheese**
- 1 **can (4-1/4 ounces) tiny shrimp, rinsed and drained**
- 4 **bacon strips, cooked and crumbled**
- 1 **medium tomato, cut into wedges**
- 3 **hard-cooked eggs, cut into wedges**

Paprika and minced fresh parsley

In a 3-qt. bowl or dish, layer the romaine, green pepper, onion, peas, mayonnaise and cheese. Cover and refrigerate for at least 2 hours or overnight. Just before serving, top with the shrimp, bacon, tomato and eggs. Sprinkle with paprika and parsley. **Yield:** 8-10 servings.

Pumpkin Chip Cupcakes

I love these cupcakes that are loaded with chocolate chips and chopped walnuts. My mom makes them for dessert on special occasions or for a sweet autumn snack.

- 1 **cup all-purpose flour**
- 3/4 **cup whole wheat flour**
- 1 **teaspoon baking powder**
- 1 **teaspoon baking soda**
- 1/2 **teaspoon salt**
- 1/2 **teaspoon ground cinnamon**
- 1/4 **teaspoon ground nutmeg**
- 2 **eggs, lightly beaten**
- 1 **cup canned pumpkin**
- 1/2 **cup vegetable oil**
- 1/2 **cup honey**
- 1/3 **cup water**
- 1/2 **cup chopped walnuts**
- 1 **cup miniature chocolate chips**

FROSTING:
- 1 **package (8 ounces) cream cheese, softened**
- 1/4 **cup butter, softened**
- 1 **teaspoon vanilla extract**
- 2 **cups confectioners' sugar**

In a large bowl, combine the first seven ingredients. Combine the eggs, pumpkin, oil, honey and water; mix well. Stir into dry ingredients just until combined; fold in walnuts and chocolate chips. Fill greased or foil-lined muffin cups three-fourths full.

Bake at 350° for 20-25 minutes or until a toothpick comes out clean. Cool for 10 minutes before removing from pans to wire racks to cool completely.

For frosting, in a small mixing bowl, beat the cream cheese, butter and vanilla until fluffy. Gradually beat in confectioners' sugar until smooth. Frost cooled cupcakes. **Yield:** 15 cupcakes.

A Special Pork Chop Supper

By Bernice Morris, Marshfield, Missouri

Thinking back to my childhood, I often wonder just how my mom ever found the time to cook three meals a day!

Not only did she tend to the children, clean the house, do laundry and help Dad milk the cows, she did her best to watch the family budget by planting a large vegetable garden each year.

Still, she somehow managed to set a pretty table laden with delicious food for the family and the hired hands at noon.

Every meal Mom prepared was wonderful because it was made with love. But I'd have to rank the meal featured here as one of my all-time favorites.

Packed with hearty ingredients and flavorful seasonings, Pork Chops with Scalloped Potatoes was always a welcome sight at the table. The thick chops in this all-in-one entree turn out moist and tender every time as they bake on top of the bubbling potatoes.

Pineapple Beets may seem unusual to you. But after one taste, their slightly sweet flavor will have you wanting more. This side dish dresses up ordinary beets with tart pineapple and adds eye-appealing color to the table.

Fresh-from-the oven Make-Ahead Butterhorns (pictured on page 223) really completed the meal. Given her hectic schedule, Mom often relied on this recipe that lets you shape and freeze the unbaked rolls until needed.

For dessert, Mom would cut hearty slices of Banana Cream Pie and top each with rich whipped cream from our own Guernsey cows.

Fortified with a meal like this, we could tackle afternoon chores with smiles on our faces!

Pork Chops with Scalloped Potatoes, Pineapple Beets and Banana Cream Pie (recipes are on pp. 222-223).

Pork Chops with Scalloped Potatoes

Mom always managed to put a delicious, hearty meal on the table for us and for our farmhands. This all-in-one main dish has a comforting flavor.

  3 **tablespoons butter**
  3 **tablespoons all-purpose flour**
1-1/2 **teaspoons salt**
  1/4 **teaspoon pepper**
  1 **can (14-1/2 ounces) chicken broth**
  6 **rib *or* loin pork chops (3/4 inch thick)**
  2 **tablespoons vegetable oil**
Additional salt and pepper, optional
  6 **cups thinly sliced peeled potatoes (about 4 pounds)**
  1 **medium onion, sliced**
Paprika and chopped fresh parsley, optional

In a saucepan, melt butter; stir in flour, salt and pepper. Add chicken broth; cook and stir constantly until mixture boils. Cook 1 minute; remove from heat; set aside.

In a skillet, brown pork chops in oil; season with additional salt and pepper if desired. In a greased 13-in. x 9-in. x 2-in. baking dish, layer potatoes and onion. Pour the broth mixture over. Place pork chops on top. Cover and bake at 350° for 1 hour; uncover and bake 30 minutes longer or until potatoes are tender. If desired, sprinkle with paprika and parsley before serving. **Yield:** 6 servings.

Pineapple Beets

This is a special way to dress up beets. Paired with pineapple, they have a fresh, slightly sweet taste that has even people who don't usually like beets taking second helpings.

  2 **tablespoons brown sugar**
  1 **tablespoon cornstarch**
  1/4 **teaspoon salt**
  1 **can (8 ounces) pineapple tidbits, undrained**
  1 **can (16 ounces) sliced beets, drained**
  1 **tablespoon butter**
  1 **tablespoon lemon juice**

In a saucepan, combine brown sugar, cornstarch and salt; add pineapple and bring to a boil, stirring constantly until thick, about 2 minutes. Add the beets, butter and lemon juice; cook over medium heat for 5 minutes, stirring occasionally. **Yield:** 4 servings.

Make-Ahead Butterhorns

Mom loved to prepare these lightly sweet, golden rolls. They're beautiful and impressive to serve and have a wonderful homemade taste. It's so handy to be able to bake and freeze them ahead.

  2 **packages (1/4 ounce *each*) active dry yeast**
  1/3 **cup warm water (110° to 115°)**
  9 **cups all-purpose flour, *divided***
  2 **cups warm milk (110° to 115°)**
  1 **cup shortening**
  1 **cup sugar**

6 **eggs**
2 **teaspoons salt**
3 **to 4 tablespoons butter, melted**

In a large mixing bowl, dissolve yeast in water. Add 4 cups flour, milk, shortening, sugar, eggs and salt; beat for 2 minutes or until smooth. Add enough remaining flour to form a soft dough. Turn onto a floured board; knead lightly. Place in a greased bowl, turning once to grease top. Cover and let rise in a warm place until doubled, about 2-3 hours.

Punch dough down; divide into four equal parts. Roll each into a 9-in. circle; brush with butter. Cut each circle into eight pie-shaped wedges; roll up each wedge from wide edge to tip of dough and pinch to seal. Place rolls with tip down on baking sheets; freeze. When frozen, place in freezer bags and seal. Store in the freezer for up to 4 weeks.

To bake, place on greased baking sheets; thaw 5 hours or until doubled in size. Bake at 375° for 12-15 minutes or until lightly browned. Remove from baking sheets and serve immediately or cool on wire racks. **Yield:** 32 rolls.

Banana Cream Pie

Made from our farm-fresh dairy products, this pie was a sensational creamy treat any time that Mom served it. Her recipe is a real treasure, and I've never found one that tastes better!

3/4 **cup sugar**
1/3 **cup all-purpose flour**
1/4 **teaspoon salt**

2 **cups milk**
3 **egg yolks, lightly beaten**
2 **tablespoons butter**
1 **teaspoon vanilla extract**
3 **medium firm bananas**
1 **pastry shell (9 inches), baked**
Whipped cream and additional sliced bananas

In a saucepan, combine sugar, flour and salt; stir in milk and mix well. Cook over medium heat, stirring constantly, until the mixture thickens and comes to a boil; boil for 2 minutes. Remove from the heat.

Stir a small amount into egg yolks; return all to saucepan. Cook for 2 minutes, stirring constantly; remove from the heat. Add butter and vanilla; cool slightly. Slice the bananas into pastry shell; pour filling over. Cool. Before serving, garnish with whipped cream and bananas. Refrigerate any leftovers. **Yield:** 6-8 servings.

Removing Beet Stains

If you get a little beet juice on your hands when making Pineapple Beets, remove the stain by rubbing your hands with half a lemon.

Teen's Favorite Birthday Menu

By Karen Wingate, Coldwater, Kansas

When I think of my mom's wonderful home cooking, one specific menu pops into my mind. It's the meal I requested for my birthday in my teen years...and the spread I missed most when graduate school took me 2,000 miles from home.

The meal, still a standby, starts with Crispy Baked Chicken, which Mom, Arlene Wise (above left), serves with baked potatoes. The chicken is moist and tender.

Her Zucchini Santa Fe, a zippy side dish made with garden vegetables, is so good with the chicken. This recipe and others Mom makes reflect her background as a third-generation Arizonian. Her cooking style revolves around the hot climate and influences from pioneer and Mexican cultures.

A frugal cook, Mom has a knack for making plain foods taste wonderful using fresh ingredients and whole grains. Her flavorful Wholesome Wheat Bread is just one example. Mom's Strawberry Shortcake is as pretty as a colorful fall day.

Now I make this memorable meal, too, for husband Jack, a minister, and our two daughters, Katherine and Christine.

I hope you enjoy this meal as much as we do. It's truly a taste of home.

Crispy Baked Chicken, Wholesome Wheat Bread, Zucchini Santa Fe and Mom's Strawberry Shortcake (recipes are on pp. 226-227).

224 Mom's Best Meals

- **2** packages (1/4 ounce *each*) active dry yeast
- **2-1/4** cups warm water (110° to 115°)
- **3** tablespoons sugar
- **1/3** cup butter, softened
- **1/3** cup honey
- **1/2** cup instant nonfat dry milk powder
- **1** tablespoon salt
- **4-1/2** cups whole wheat flour
- **2-3/4** to 3-1/2 cups all-purpose flour

In a large mixing bowl, dissolve yeast in water. Add the sugar, butter, honey, milk powder, salt and whole wheat flour; beat until smooth. Add enough all-purpose flour to form a soft dough.

Turn onto a floured surface; knead until smooth and elastic, about 10 minutes. Place in a greased bowl, turning once to grease top. Cover and let rise in a warm place until doubled, about 1 hour. Punch down.

Shape dough into traditional loaves or divide into fourths and roll each portion into a 15-in. rope. Twist two ropes together. Place in greased 9-in. x 5-in. x 3-in. loaf pans. Cover and let rise until doubled, about 30 minutes. Bake at 375° for 25-30 minutes. Remove from pans to cool on wire racks. **Yield:** 2 loaves (32 slices).

Nutritional Analysis: One slice equals 144 calories, 239 mg sodium, 0 cholesterol, 27 g carbohydrate, 4 g protein, 2 g fat. **Diabetic Exchange:** 2 starch.

Crispy Baked Chicken

My siblings and I couldn't wait to sit down to supper when Mom was making this delicious chicken. The cornmeal in the coating gives each juicy golden piece a wonderful crunch.

- **1/2** cup cornmeal
- **1/2** cup all-purpose flour
- **1-1/2** teaspoons salt
- **1-1/2** teaspoons chili powder
- **1/2** teaspoon dried oregano
- **1/4** teaspoon pepper
- **1** broiler/fryer chicken (3 to 3-1/2 pounds), cut up
- **1/2** cup milk
- **1/3** cup butter, melted

Combine the first six ingredients. Dip chicken in milk, then roll in the cornmeal mixture. Place in a greased 13-in. x 9-in. x 2-in. baking pan. Drizzle with butter. Bake, uncovered, at 375° for 50-55 minutes or until juices run clear. **Yield:** 4-6 servings.

Wholesome Wheat Bread

My sister and I were in 4-H, and Mom was our breads project leader for years. Because of that training, fresh homemade bread like this is a staple in my kitchen.

Zucchini Santa Fe

Chopped green chilies give this summer side dish lots of zip—a popular flavor around Mom's Arizona home. It's a tasty way to use up garden vegetables.

✓ Uses less fat, sugar or salt. Includes Nutritional Analysis and Diabetic Exchanges.

- 3 cups sliced zucchini
- 1/2 cup chopped onion
- 1 tablespoon vegetable oil
- 1 can (4 ounces) chopped green chilies, drained
- 1 medium tomato, chopped
- 1/2 teaspoon salt, optional
- 1/4 teaspoon pepper
- 1/4 teaspoon garlic powder
- 1/2 cup shredded cheddar *or* Monterey Jack cheese

In a large skillet, saute the zucchini and onion in oil for 3-4 minutes or until crisp-tender. Add chilies, tomato, salt if desired, pepper and garlic powder.

Cook and stir for 3-4 minutes. Spoon into a serving bowl and sprinkle with cheese. **Yield:** 6 servings.

Nutritional Analysis: One 1/2-cup serving (prepared without salt) equals 58 calories, 60 mg sodium, 2 mg cholesterol, 5 g carbohydrate, 3 g protein, 3 g fat. **Diabetic Exchanges:** 1 vegetable, 1 fat.

Mom's Strawberry Shortcake

When I was growing up, Mom sometimes experimented with different dessert recipes, but this tried-and-true spongy shortcake was always great just the way it was. It melted in my mouth!

- 2 eggs
- 1-1/2 cups sugar, *divided*
- 1 cup all-purpose flour
- 1 teaspoon baking powder
- 1/4 teaspoon salt
- 1/2 cup milk
- 1 tablespoon butter
- 1 teaspoon vanilla extract
- 1 to 1-1/2 quarts fresh strawberries, sliced
- Whipped cream
- Mint leaves, optional

In a mixing bowl, beat eggs on medium speed for 3 minutes. Gradually add 1 cup sugar, beating until thick and lemon-colored. Combine flour, baking powder and salt; beat into the egg mixture.

Heat milk and butter just until butter begins to melt. Beat into batter with vanilla (batter will be thin). Pour into a greased 8-in. square baking pan.

Bake at 350° for 25 minutes or until a toothpick inserted near the center comes out clean. Cool for at least 10 minutes. Just before serving, cut cake into serving-size pieces; cut each slice in half horizontally.

Combine strawberries and remaining sugar. Spoon strawberries between cake layers and over the top of each serving. Top with whipped cream; garnish with mint leaves if desired. **Yield:** 9 servings.

Meatballs Star In Super Supper

By Darlis Wilfer, Phelps, Wisconsin

Life wasn't as busy back when my two sisters, one brother and I were growing up.

Our mother, Lorraine Justman (left), took pride in her family, home and cooking. She always had delicious meals on the table for Dad and us kids. When we came home from school, the house had a heavenly aroma.

We sat together around the table, thanked the Lord for our blessings, ate a warm, filling meal and took time to "share our day" with one another.

One of Mom's specialties was her savory Porcupine Meatballs. The addition of rice adds a nice texture to the meatballs simmering in a lovely, rich tomato sauce.

With that delightful dish, she often served creamy Baked Mashed Potatoes. This comforting casserole featuring potatoes, sour cream and green onions is especially nice because it can be made ahead of time. So there are less dishes to put together at the last minute.

My brother would dig into the meatballs and potatoes first. But we girls started with Spinach Apple Salad. A slightly sweet dressing brings out the natural flavors of spinach and apples for a true taste sensation.

No matter how much food we piled onto our plate, we all saved room for Mom's wonderful Lazy Daisy Cake. It's an old-fashioned cake with excellent caramel and coconut topping.

Through the years, Mom has been an inspiration to me and my daughters as well. We're sure this meal will soon be a favorite at your house, too.

Porcupine Meatballs, Baked Mashed Potatoes, Spinach Apple Salad and Lazy Daisy Cake (recipes are on pp. 230-231).

Porcupine Meatballs

These well-seasoned meatballs in a rich tomato sauce are one of my mom's best main dishes. I used to love this meal when I was growing up. I made it at home for our children, and now my daughters make it for their families as well.

- 1/2 cup uncooked long grain rice
- 1/2 cup water
- 1/3 cup chopped onion
- 1 teaspoon salt
- 1/2 teaspoon celery salt
- 1/8 teaspoon pepper
- 1/8 teaspoon garlic powder
- 1 pound ground beef
- 2 tablespoons vegetable oil
- 1 can (15 ounces) tomato sauce
- 1 cup water
- 2 tablespoons brown sugar
- 2 teaspoons Worcestershire sauce

In a bowl, combine the first seven ingredients. Crumble beef over top and mix well. Shape into 1-1/2-in. balls. In a large skillet, cook meatballs in oil over medium heat until no longer pink; drain.

Combine tomato sauce, water, brown sugar and Worcestershire sauce; pour over meatballs. Reduce heat; cover and simmer for 1 hour. **Yield:** 4-6 servings.

Baked Mashed Potatoes

This is one comforting side dish that you can prepare ahead. My brother was always quick to dive into these creamy and fluffy potatoes when Mom served them with dinner. My sisters and I kept our eyes on him to be sure we'd get our fair share.

- 4 large potatoes, peeled and quartered
- 1/4 cup milk
- 1/2 teaspoon salt
- 2 tablespoons butter, melted, *divided*
- 1 egg, beaten
- 1 cup (8 ounces) sour cream
- 1 cup small-curd cottage cheese
- 5 green onions, finely chopped
- 1/2 cup crushed butter-flavored crackers

Cook potatoes until tender; drain. Place in a large bowl. Add milk, salt and 1 tablespoon butter; beat until light and fluffy. Fold in the egg, sour cream, cottage cheese and onions. Place in a greased 1-1/2-qt. baking dish. Combine cracker crumbs and remaining butter; sprinkle over potato mixture. Bake, uncovered, at 350° for 20-30 minutes or until crumbs are lightly browned. **Yield:** 4-6 servings.

Editor's Note: This dish can be made ahead and refrigerated. Remove from the refrigerator 30 minutes before baking. Sprinkle with the cracker crumbs and bake as directed.

Spinach Apple Salad

Whenever Mom made this salad, it was the first thing on my plate. With spinach, apples, raisins and a light dressing, this beautiful harvest salad is a feast for the eyes as well as the palate.

2 tablespoons cider vinegar
2 tablespoons vegetable oil
1/4 teaspoon salt
1/4 teaspoon sugar
1 cup diced unpeeled apple
1/4 cup chopped sweet onion
1/4 cup raisins
2 cups torn fresh spinach
2 cups torn romaine

In a small bowl, combine vinegar, oil, salt and sugar; mix well. Add apple, onion and raisins; toss lightly to coat. Cover and let stand for 10 minutes.

Just before serving, combine the spinach and romaine in a large salad bowl; add the dressing and toss. **Yield:** 4-6 servings.

Lazy Daisy Cake

We couldn't wait until Mom sliced this old-fashioned cake with its caramel-like frosting, loaded with chewy coconut. Even after one of Mom's delicious meals, one piece of this cake wasn't enough.

4 eggs
2 cups sugar
2 teaspoons vanilla extract
2 cups all-purpose flour

2 teaspoons baking powder
1/2 teaspoon salt
1 cup milk
1/4 cup butter
FROSTING:
1-1/2 cups packed brown sugar
3/4 cup butter, melted
1/2 cup half-and-half cream
2 cups flaked coconut

In a mixing bowl, beat the eggs, sugar and vanilla until thick, about 4 minutes. Combine the flour, baking powder and salt; add to egg mixture and beat just until combined.

In a saucepan, bring milk and butter to a boil, stirring constantly. Add to batter and beat until combined. Pour into a greased 13-in. x 9-in. x 2-in. baking pan.

Bake at 350° for 35-40 minutes or until a toothpick inserted near the center comes out clean. Combine frosting ingredients; spread over warm cake. Broil until lightly browned, about 3-4 minutes. **Yield:** 16-20 servings.

Storing Spinach

Wash fresh spinach in cold water and pat dry. Place in a plastic bag lined with paper towel; refrigerate. Use within 3 days.

An Authentic
Austrian Dinner

By Lisa Radelet, Boulder, Colorado

Energetic is the word that best describes my mother, Theresa Handlos (left) of Menomonee Falls, Wisconsin.

When my sisters and I were growing up, Mom not only cooked nightly for us girls and our dad, but also for members of our extended family who frequently joined us at the dinner table.

Mom grew up in Austria near the Hungarian border and moved to the United States at age 13. Her cooking reflects traditional Austrian dishes, those of our dad's German heritage, plus American favorites she learned over the years.

One of Mom's most memorable meals starts with Old-World Pork Roast. Now that we girls and our families are spread across the country, we prepare this savory roast and dumplings for our own families, but we all agree that no one makes it quite like Mom.

Endive Salad with Potatoes is a unique salad, with slices of cooked red potatoes nestled among the greens and a deliciously tart dressing.

Mom never had a problem getting us kids to eat our vegetables when she served Colorful Veggie Bake. The first time she made this comforting casserole, it was an instant hit with our family.

One of her wonderful desserts that never fails to draw compliments is Cherry Cheese Torte. Pretty enough to serve to company, this impressive-looking treat is easy to make and tastes absolutely scrumptious.

In 1998, Mom gave all four of us girls subscriptions to *Taste of Home* and has continued to renew them ever since. We always enjoy discovering other families' favorite recipes and are so pleased to share our mom's best meal with you!

Old-World Pork Roast, Endive Salad with Potatoes, Colorful Veggie Bake and Cherry Cheese Torte (recipes are on pp. 234-235).

dumplings. Boil, uncovered, for 15-20 minutes or until a thermometer reads 160°. Remove to a serving dish with a slotted spoon; keep warm.

Remove roast to a serving platter; keep warm. Strain pan drippings. Add enough broth to drippings to measure 1-3/4 cups. Pour into a small saucepan. Place remaining flour in a dish; stir in cold water until smooth. Stir into broth mixture.

Bring to a boil; cook and stir for 2 minutes or until thickened. Serve with roast and dumplings. **Yield:** 8-10 servings (16 dumplings).

Endive Salad with Potatoes

Endive and cooked sliced red potatoes are the unusual combo Mom tossed together in this refreshing green salad. Her tart vinaigrette dressing brings out the best of both flavors.

- 2 **bunches curly endive, torn (about 8 cups)**
- 3 **small red potatoes, cooked and sliced**
- 1/4 **cup olive oil**
- 3 **tablespoons cider vinegar**
- 2 **teaspoons sugar**
- 1 **teaspoon salt**
- 1/8 **teaspoon pepper**

In a salad bowl, combine endive and potatoes. In a jar with a tight-fitting lid, combine the remaining ingredients; shake well. Drizzle over salad; toss to coat. Serve immediately. **Yield:** 8-10 servings.

Old-World Pork Roast

No one makes this succulent pork roast and dumplings with gravy quite like my mom does. She learned how to prepare dishes like this when she was a young girl in Austria. For my sisters and me, this is truly a taste of home.

- 1 **teaspoon salt**
- 1/2 **teaspoon garlic powder**
- 1/4 **teaspoon pepper**
- 1 **boneless rolled pork loin roast (about 3-1/2 pounds)**

BREAD DUMPLINGS:
- 8 **day-old hard rolls, torn into small pieces**
- 1-1/4 **cups warm milk**
- 1 **cup plus 3 tablespoons all-purpose flour, *divided***
- 4 **eggs, lightly beaten**
- 3 **quarts water**
- 1 **can (14-1/2 ounces) beef broth**
- 6 **tablespoons cold water**

Combine the salt, garlic powder and pepper; rub over roast. Place roast fat side up on a rack in a shallow roasting pan. Bake, uncovered, at 325° for 1-1/2 to 1-3/4 hours or until a meat thermometer reads 160°.

Meanwhile, combine the rolls and milk in a large bowl. Cover and refrigerate for 1 hour. Add 1 cup flour and eggs; mix well. Shape into 2-in. balls. In a soup kettle or Dutch oven, bring 3 qts. of water to a boil. Add

Cherry Cheese Torte

We always feel special when Mom brings out this delightful dessert, whether it's for a Sunday dinner or a holiday meal. You can't help but impress people when you set this lovely cheese torte in front of them.

- 2 packages (3 ounces *each*) ladyfingers
- 1 package (8 ounces) cream cheese, softened
- 1 cup plus 1 teaspoon sugar, *divided*
- 2 teaspoons vanilla extract, *divided*
- 2 teaspoons lemon juice
- 1 teaspoon grated lemon peel
- 2 cups heavy whipping cream
- 1 can (21 ounces) cherry *or* blueberry pie filling

Place a layer of ladyfingers on the bottom and around the sides of an ungreased 9-in. springform pan. In a large mixing bowl, beat the cream cheese, 1 cup sugar and 1 teaspoon vanilla until smooth. Add lemon juice and peel; mix well.

In small mixing bowl, beat cream until it begins to thicken. Add remaining sugar and vanilla; beat until stiff peaks form. Fold into the cream cheese mixture. Spread half over crust. Arrange remaining ladyfingers in a spoke pattern over top. Evenly spread with the remaining cream cheese mixture. Top with pie filling. Cover and refrigerate overnight. Remove sides of pan just before serving. **Yield:** 12 servings.

Colorful Veggie Bake

It's impossible to resist this cheesy casserole, which has a golden crumb topping sprinkled over colorful vegetables. A versatile side that goes with any meat, Mom has relied on this favorite to round out many family meals. For a fun taste twist, try varying the veggies.

- 2 packages (16 ounces *each*) frozen California-blend vegetables
- 8 ounces process cheese (Velveeta), cubed
- 6 tablespoons butter, *divided*
- 1/2 cup crushed butter-flavored crackers (about 13 crackers)

Prepare vegetables according to package directions; drain. Place half in an ungreased 11-in. x 7-in. x 2-in. baking dish.

In a small saucepan, combine cheese and 4 tablespoons butter; cook and stir over low heat until melted. Pour half over vegetables. Repeat layers.

Melt the remaining butter and toss with cracker crumbs. Sprinkle over the top. Bake, uncovered, at 325° for 20-25 minutes or until golden brown. **Yield:** 8-10 servings.

Birthday Wish Comes True

By Dianne Esposite, New Middletown, Ohio

One of Mom's best meals is the one my three brothers and I always requested for our birthday dinners when we were growing up.

We could hardly wait for those days to come around on the calendar. (Even today when we get together, we ask her to make this memorable meal.)

Each of these treasured recipes was handed down from our great-grandmother, so the entire family has been enjoying this delicious meal for generations. And it's no wonder.

We start out with hearty slices of Swiss Steak. Smothered in mushrooms, celery and onion, it really stands out from any other versions I've tried through the years.

Crisp and golden, Mom's Potato Pancakes are an old-fashioned favorite I know I'll never tire of. I think it's the touch of onion that adds just the right amount of additional flavor. These potato pancakes always seem to disappear too fast from the plate.

Also eaten up quickly is the Creamy Coleslaw. Shredded carrots and green pepper make a nice addition. Because it needs to be prepared ahead and refrigerated, it's a perfect side dish for a busy cook.

The only way to bring Mom's meal to a fantastic finish is to dish out generous helpings of her Peach Crisp. Try topping it with sweetened whipped cream or vanilla ice cream for an even bigger indulgence.

Mom didn't leave Dad out of the meal preparation. He was employed to grate the potatoes and cabbage!

Swiss Steak, Mom's Potato Pancakes, Creamy Coleslaw and Peach Crisp (recipes are on pp. 238-239).

Swiss Steak

Mom was always glad to prepare this tender, flavorful dish for a birthday dinner when one of my three brothers or I would ask her for it. Now my family enjoys this entree when I make it for them.

- 1/4 cup all-purpose flour
- 1 teaspoon salt
- 1/4 teaspoon pepper
- 1-1/2 to 2 pounds beef round steak, trimmed
- 2 tablespoons vegetable oil
- 1 cup chopped celery
- 1 cup chopped onion
- 1/2 pound fresh mushrooms, sliced
- 1 cup water
- 1 garlic clove, minced
- 1 tablespoon steak sauce

Combine the flour, salt and pepper. Cut steak into serving-size pieces; dredge in the flour mixture. In a skillet, brown steak in oil. Drain; place in a 2-1/2-qt. casserole.

Top with celery, onion and mushrooms. Combine water, garlic and steak sauce; pour over vegetables. Cover and bake at 350° for 1-1/2 hours or until the meat is tender. **Yield:** 6 servings.

Mom's Potato Pancakes

These old-fashioned pancakes are fluffy inside and crispy on the outside. Grated onion adds nice flavor. Mom got this recipe from Grandma, so we've enjoyed it for years.

- 4 cups shredded peeled potatoes (about 4 large)
- 1 egg, lightly beaten
- 3 tablespoons all-purpose flour
- 1 tablespoon grated onion
- 1 teaspoon salt
- 1/4 teaspoon pepper

Vegetable oil

Rinse potatoes in cold water; drain well. Place in a large bowl. Add egg, flour, onion, salt and pepper; mix well. In a skillet, heat 1/4 in. of oil over medium heat.

Drop batter by 1/3 cupfuls into hot oil. Flatten to form a pancake. Fry until golden brown; turn and brown the other side. Drain on paper towels. Serve immediately. **Yield:** 6 servings.

Creamy Coleslaw

This colorful coleslaw is another longtime family favorite. Cabbage, carrots and green pepper are blended with a tasty dressing that gets its zest from a hint of mustard.

- 3 to 4 cups shredded cabbage
- 1 cup shredded carrots
- 1 cup thinly sliced green pepper
- 1/2 cup mayonnaise

1/4 cup lemon juice
  1 to 2 tablespoons sugar
  1 tablespoon prepared mustard
  1 teaspoon celery seed
  1 teaspoon salt

In a large salad bowl, toss cabbage, carrots and green pepper. In a small bowl, combine the remaining ingredients. Pour over the cabbage mixture and toss to coat. Chill for at least 2-3 hours. **Yield:** 6-8 servings.

Peach Crisp

A hearty serving of this sweet and tart treat is a mouth-watering way to end one of Mom's meals. With the comforting crust, fruit filling and crunchy topping, this dessert is as lovely as it is delicious.

    1 cup all-purpose flour
  1/2 cup packed brown sugar
  1/4 teaspoon salt
  1/2 cup cold butter

FILLING:

    2 cans (16 ounces *each*) sliced peaches
    1 cup sugar
  1/4 cup cornstarch

TOPPING:

1-1/2 cups rolled oats
  1/2 cup packed brown sugar
  1/4 cup all-purpose flour
    5 tablespoons cold butter

In a bowl, combine flour, brown sugar and salt. Cut in butter until crumbly. Pat into a greased 9-in. square baking pan. Bake at 350° for 15 minutes.

Meanwhile, drain the peaches and reserve juice in a medium saucepan. Add the sugar and cornstarch; bring to a boil, stirring constantly. Boil for 2 minutes or until thickened. Remove from the heat; stir in peaches. Pour into crust.

For topping, combine oats, brown sugar and flour. Cut in the butter until crumbly. Sprinkle over filling. Bake at 350° for 25-30 minutes or until golden and bubbly. **Yield:** 6-8 servings.

Keeping Fried Foods Warm

When foods need to be cooked in stages (such as Mom's Potato Pancakes), you can easily keep each batch warm until the entire recipe is cooked. After frying, drain the food on paper towels and then place on an ovenproof platter. Cover loosely with foil and place in a 200° oven until the entire recipe is completed.

Italian-Style Supper Satisfies

By Gina Squires, Salem, Oregon

My mother is a terrific cook who has inspired me to love working in the kitchen, too.

Ever since I was little, I've enjoyed being with my mother, Shirlee (left), when she's cooking. Over the years, she's patiently shared her skills with me. Now I enjoy making and serving complete meals for her, Dad, my older sister and brother-in-law.

Mom's Lasagna dinner has always been my favorite. For as long as I can remember, she has served her hearty lasagna with crisp Three-Green Salad and zesty homemade Italian dressing. Her Cheesy Garlic Bread is something special—I can never eat just one slice of that!

For dessert, Fluffy Pineapple Torte is a light treat that's a nice balance to this meaty main course—the perfect end to this satisfying meal.

I think Mom and I make a great team in the kitchen these days. We're excited to share our special meal with you.

We hope your family will enjoy this memorable down-home menu as much as ours does.

Mom's Lasagna, Three-Green Salad, Cheesy Garlic Bread and Fluffy Pineapple Torte (recipes are on pp. 242-243.)

Meanwhile, cook lasagna noodles according to package directions; drain and rinse in cold water. In a greased 13-in. x 9-in. x 2-in. baking dish, layer a third of the noodles and meat sauce, half of the cottage cheese, a third of the mozzarella and a third of the Parmesan. Repeat layers.

Top with remaining noodles, meat sauce, mozzarella and Parmesan. Cover and bake at 350° for 45 minutes; uncover and bake for 20 minutes. Let stand 20 minutes before cutting. **Yield:** 12 servings.

Three-Green Salad

For a crisp, refreshing side dish, this tasty salad can't be beat. The bold flavor and crunch really wake up your taste buds. It goes perfectly with lasagna.

4	cups torn iceberg lettuce
4	cups torn leaf lettuce
4	cups torn fresh spinach
1	medium cucumber, sliced
2	carrots, sliced
2	celery ribs, sliced
6	broccoli florets, sliced
3	cauliflowerets, sliced
6	radishes, sliced
4	green onions, sliced
5	fresh mushrooms, sliced

ITALIAN DRESSING:

2/3	cup olive oil
1/4	cup plus 2 tablespoons red wine vinegar
2	tablespoons grated Parmesan cheese
1	teaspoon sugar
1	to 2 garlic cloves, minced
1/4	teaspoon dried oregano
1/4	teaspoon dried basil

Pinch salt and pepper

Mom's Lasagna

We can hardly wait to dig into this cheesy, meaty lasagna. It smells great when baking and tastes even better! Watching Mom carefully make this wonderful main dish and hearing the raves she gets inspired me to learn to cook.

1/2	pound ground beef
1/2	pound bulk Italian sausage
1	large onion, chopped
3	garlic cloves, minced
1	can (28 ounces) crushed tomatoes, undrained
1	can (6 ounces) tomato paste
1-1/2	cups water
1	cup salsa
2	teaspoons sugar
1	to 2 teaspoons chili powder
1	teaspoon fennel seed
1	teaspoon dried oregano
1	teaspoon dried basil
9	lasagna noodles
1	carton (16 ounces) cottage cheese
4	cups (1 pound) shredded mozzarella cheese
3/4	cup grated Parmesan cheese

In a large kettle or Dutch oven, cook beef, sausage and onion over medium heat until the meat is no longer pink and onion is tender; drain. Stir in the next 10 ingredients. Simmer, uncovered, for 3 hours, stirring occasionally.

In a large salad bowl, toss the greens and vegetables. Cover and chill. Combine all dressing ingredients in a blender; process for 30 seconds. Pour into a jar with tight-fitting lid; chill for at least 30 minutes.

Shake dressing before serving; pour desired amount over salad and toss. **Yield:** 12 servings (about 1 cup dressing).

Cheesy Garlic Bread

Some garlic breads taste more like buttered toast. Not this one—the fresh garlic flavor really comes through. Parmesan cheese on top turns golden brown in the broiler. I enjoy the crunch of the crisp crust.

- 1/2 **cup butter, softened**
- 4 **garlic cloves, minced**
- 1/4 **teaspoon dried oregano**
- 1 **loaf (1 pound) French bread, halved lengthwise**
- 3 **tablespoons grated Parmesan cheese**

In a small bowl, combine butter, garlic and oregano; spread on cut sides of bread. Sprinkle with Parmesan cheese. Place on an ungreased baking sheet. Broil for 3 minutes or until golden brown. Slice and serve hot. **Yield:** 12 servings.

Fluffy Pineapple Torte

This fluffy dessert is so good after a hearty meal because even a big slice is as light as a feather. The cream cheese-pineapple combination makes it irresistible.

- 1-1/2 **cups graham cracker crumbs**
- 1/4 **cup butter, melted**
- 2 **tablespoons sugar**

FILLING:
- 1 **can (12 ounces) evaporated milk**
- 1 **package (3 ounces) lemon gelatin**
- 1 **cup boiling water**
- 1 **package (8 ounces) cream cheese, softened**
- 1/2 **cup sugar**
- 1 **can (8 ounces) crushed pineapple, drained**
- 1 **cup chopped walnuts, *divided***

Combine crumbs, butter and sugar; press into the bottom of a 13-in. x 9-in. x 2-in. baking dish. Bake at 325° for 10 minutes; cool.

Pour evaporated milk into a metal mixing bowl; add the beaters. Cover and chill for at least 2 hours. Meanwhile, in a small bowl, dissolve gelatin in water; chill until syrupy, about 30 minutes. Remove milk from refrigerator and beat until stiff peaks form.

In a large mixing bowl, beat cream cheese and sugar until smooth. Add the gelatin; mix well. Stir in pineapple and 3/4 cup walnuts. Fold in milk. Pour over crust. Chill for at least 3 hours or overnight. Sprinkle remaining walnuts over the top before filling is completely firm. **Yield:** 12 servings.

A Down-Home Dinner Delight

By Nancy Duty, Jacksonville, Florida

Mother taught me the value of sitting down with those who are dear for hot, home-cooked meals and warm conversation. I spent hours cooking from scratch with my mom, Nancy Herring (left). All these years later, the lesson still holds true.

She wasn't always vocal about her feelings, but Mother's love for family and friends shone through in the foods she prepared and served with such care. We love sharing one of her delicious dinners.

Her savory Pork Chop Casserole is a mouth-watering dish. We enjoy the rich sauce and the golden fried onion rings on top.

The flavorful dressing made with garlic and honey clings beautifully to the lettuce in her Greens with Vinaigrette. And my sisters and I were always glad to see refreshing Raspberry Gelatin Salad on the kitchen table.

Mama's Spice Cake, with its luscious cream cheese frosting, was one my grandmother used to make. Mother re-created this dessert from memory. She would be so pleased if you would enjoy making and serving this meal as much as she did.

Pork Chop Casserole, Raspberry Gelatin Salad, Greens with Vinaigrette and Mama's Spice Cake (recipes are on pp. 246-247).

Pork Chop Casserole

One bite of these tender pork chops smothered in a creamy sauce and we could taste the care Mother put into her cooking. She was happy to share the recipe with guests who requested it after trying this delicious dish at our house.

- 3/4 cup all-purpose flour
- 1 teaspoon salt
- 1/2 teaspoon pepper
- 6 pork chops (3/4 to 1 inch thick)
- 2 tablespoons vegetable oil
- 1 can (10-3/4 ounces) condensed cream of mushroom soup, undiluted
- 2/3 cup chicken broth
- 1/2 teaspoon ground ginger
- 1/4 teaspoon dried rosemary, crushed
- 1 cup (8 ounces) sour cream, *divided*
- 1 can (2.8 ounces) french-fried onions, *divided*

In a shallow bowl, combine the flour, salt and pepper; dredge pork chops. Heat oil in a large skillet; cook pork chops for 4-5 minutes per side or until browned. Place in a single layer in an ungreased 13-in. x 9-in. x 2-in. baking dish.

Combine soup, broth, ginger, rosemary and 1/2 cup sour cream; pour over chops. Sprinkle with half of the onions. Cover and bake at 350° for 45-50 minutes. Stir remaining sour cream into sauce. Top chops with remaining onions. Return to the oven, uncovered, for 10 minutes. **Yield:** 6 servings.

Raspberry Gelatin Salad

My sisters and I especially enjoyed Mom's cool tangy side dish, which looks so lovely on the table. The pineapple and raspberries are a delectable duo, and pecans add a hearty crunch.

- 1 can (8 ounces) crushed pineapple
- 1 package (10 ounces) frozen unsweetened raspberries, thawed
- 1 package (3 ounces) raspberry gelatin
- 1 cup applesauce
- 1/4 cup coarsely chopped pecans

Mayonnaise, optional

Drain pineapple and raspberries, reserving juices. Place fruit in a large bowl; set aside. Add enough water to the juice to measure 1 cup. Pour into a saucepan; bring to a boil. Remove from the heat; stir in gelatin until dissolved. Pour over fruit mixture.

Add the applesauce and pecans. Pour into a 1-qt. bowl. Chill until set. Spoon into individual dessert dishes; top with a dollop of mayonnaise if desired. **Yield:** 6 servings.

Greens with Vinaigrette

This colorful salad topped with a sweet and savory dressing is a refreshing addition to any meal. It's a perfect example of how Mother could turn even simple ingredients into something special.

- 6 cups torn romaine
- 1 cup sliced radishes
- 1/3 cup olive oil
- 1/4 cup honey

2 teaspoons white wine vinegar
1-1/2 teaspoons lemon juice
1 teaspoon Dijon mustard
1 teaspoon poppy seeds
2 garlic cloves, minced
1 drop hot pepper sauce
Pinch sugar
Salt and pepper to taste

In a large bowl, combine the romaine and radishes. Combine the remaining ingredients in a jar with tight-fitting lid and shake well. Just before serving, pour vinaigrette over salad and toss gently. **Yield:** 6 servings (about 2/3 cup vinaigrette).

Mama's Spice Cake

Whenever I get a craving for a tasty old-fashioned treat, I make this cake. Great cooks in my family have been baking it for generations, and their families have been enjoying the wonderful spice flavor and rich frosting.

1-1/2 cups sugar
3/4 cup butter
1 cup water
1 cup raisins, chopped
1 teaspoon ground cinnamon
1/2 teaspoon ground allspice
1/4 teaspoon ground cloves

1/4 teaspoon ground nutmeg
4 eggs, *separated*
3 cups all-purpose flour
1 tablespoon baking powder
1/2 teaspoon salt
1/4 teaspoon baking soda
3/4 cup chopped pecans
CREAM CHEESE FROSTING:
1 package (8 ounces) cream cheese, softened
1/4 cup butter, softened
1 teaspoon vanilla extract
Pinch salt
4 cups confectioners' sugar
Additional chopped pecans, optional

In a saucepan, combine the first eight ingredients; heat slowly, stirring until butter melts. Remove from the heat; cool. In a large mixing bowl, beat egg yolks lightly; gradually stir in spice mixture. Combine flour, baking powder, salt, baking soda and pecans; stir into spice mixture. Beat egg whites until soft peaks form; fold into the batter.

Pour into two greased and floured 9-in. round cake pans. Bake at 325° for 35-40 minutes or until a wooden pick inserted near the center comes out clean. Cool in pans 5 minutes before removing to a wire rack; cool completely. For frosting, beat cream cheese and butter in a mixing bowl until smooth. Add vanilla and salt. Beat in sugar until smooth and fluffy. Frost cake. Garnish with pecans if desired. Store in the refrigerator. **Yield:** 12-16 servings.

Family Recipes To Cherish

By Mildred Sherrer, Bay City, Texas

Whether she followed a recipe or just combined a "pinch of this and that," Mom had a way of making everything taste delicious.

My mother, Lillian Herman (left), enjoyed spending her every spare moment in the kitchen. She'd either try new recipes she received from others or create her own magical dishes. She especially loved cooking big meals.

But since our immediate family was small—just my parents and me—she often invited other family and friends for dinner. They were always happy to receive an invitation!

Although she worked full time as a teacher, Mom still managed to plan and prepare scrumptious meals during the week as well as on the weekends. The meal I share with you here is one I fondly remember.

One dish that always brought Mom compliments was her Brunswick Stew. Some of our friends still say it's the best they ever tasted.

The perfect side dish to go with that stew was Texas Spoon Bread. Father and I couldn't wait to dig in. Made with home-canned beets, Mom's Pickled Beets made a tangy and colorful part of the meal.

We made sure to save room for a big helping of Lemon Bread Pudding. This wonderful old-fashioned dessert was even more special topped with Mom's delightful lemon sauce.

I'm grateful I was able to learn by working with Mom in the kitchen. She not only inspired me to create fabulous foods for my family, she even taught my three sons to cook.

I'm proud to share these cherished family recipes with you.

Brunswick Stew, Texas Spoon Bread, Mom's Pickled Beets and Lemon Bread Pudding (recipes are on pp. 250-251).

Texas Spoon Bread

This Southern dish has appealing down-home flavor. A sizable serving topped with butter is a treat. When I was growing up, Mother baked it to go with soups and stews. I always thought her spoon bread was the best.

> 3 **cups milk**
> 1 **cup yellow cornmeal**
> 1 **tablespoon butter**
> 1 **teaspoon sugar**
> 1 **teaspoon salt**
> 1/4 **teaspoon baking powder**
> 3 **eggs,** *separated*

In a saucepan, scald the milk (heat to 180°); stir in cornmeal. Reduce heat; simmer for 5 minutes, stirring constantly. Remove from the heat; stir in butter, sugar, salt and baking powder.

In a small bowl, beat egg yolks. Gradually stir a small amount of the hot mixture into yolks; return all to pan and mix well. In a mixing bowl, beat egg whites until soft peaks form. Fold egg whites into hot mixture until well blended.

Pour into a greased 8-in. square baking dish. Bake at 350° for 40-45 minutes or until well puffed. Use a spoon to serve. **Yield:** 6 servings.

Brunswick Stew

Like a thick hearty soup, this stew is packed with tender chicken and an eye-catching combination of vegetables. I could never wait patiently to eat when Mother had this stew on the stove.

> 1 **broiler/fryer chicken (3 to 4 pounds), cut up**
> 1 **cup water**
> 4 **medium potatoes, peeled and cubed**
> 1 **can (15 ounces) lima beans, rinsed and drained**
> 2 **medium onions, sliced**
> 1 **teaspoon salt**
> 1/2 **teaspoon pepper**
> **Dash cayenne pepper**
> 1 **can (15-1/4 ounces) corn, drained**
> 1 **can (14-1/2 ounces) diced tomatoes, undrained**
> 1/4 **cup butter**
> 1/2 **cup dry bread crumbs**

Place the chicken and water in a Dutch oven; bring to a boil. Reduce heat; cover and simmer for 1-1/2 to 2 hours or until chicken is tender. Remove chicken and debone; cube chicken and return to broth.

Add potatoes, beans, onions and seasonings. Simmer for 30 minutes or until potatoes are tender. Stir in remaining ingredients. Simmer, uncovered, for 10 minutes or until slightly thickened. **Yield:** 6 servings.

Mom's Pickled Beets

Zesty and fresh-tasting, these bright, beautiful beet slices add spark to any meal. My mouth still begins to water when I think of how wonderful they tasted when Mother prepared them.

2 eggs
1 teaspoon vanilla extract
LEMON SAUCE:
3/4 cup sugar
2 tablespoons cornstarch
1 cup water
3 tablespoons lemon juice
2 teaspoons grated lemon peel
1 tablespoon butter

Toss the bread cubes and raisins in an ungreased 1-1/2-qt. baking dish. In a saucepan, combine milk, sugar, butter and salt; cook and stir until butter melts. Remove from the heat.

Whisk eggs and vanilla in a small bowl; gradually stir in a small amount of the hot mixture. Return all to the pan and mix well. Pour over bread and raisins. Set the dish in a larger baking pan; add 1 in. of hot water. Bake, uncovered, at 350° for 50-60 minutes or until a knife inserted near the center comes out clean.

For sauce, combine the sugar and cornstarch in a saucepan. Stir in water until smooth; bring to a boil over medium heat. Boil for 1-2 minutes, stirring constantly. Remove from the heat; stir in lemon juice, peel and butter until butter melts. Serve over warm or cold pudding. Refrigerate any leftovers. **Yield:** 6 servings.

3/4 cup sugar
3/4 cup vinegar
3/4 cup water
1-1/2 teaspoons salt
3/4 to 1 teaspoon pepper
1 large onion, thinly sliced
2 cans (13-1/4 ounces *each*) sliced beets, undrained
Sliced green onions, optional

In a saucepan, combine the first six ingredients; bring to a boil. Reduce heat; cover and simmer for 5 minutes. Remove from the heat; add beets. Let stand at room temperature for 1 hour.

Cover and chill for 6 hours or overnight. Garnish with green onions if desired. **Yield:** 6 servings.

Lemon Bread Pudding

Sweet raisins and a smooth, hot lemon sauce make this bread pudding extra special. Even today, I get requests for the recipe from people who tasted this traditional dessert years ago.

3 slices day-old bread, cubed
3/4 cup raisins
2 cups milk
1/2 cup sugar
2 tablespoons butter
1/4 teaspoon salt

Country Style And City Flavor

By Alyson Armstrong, Parkersburg, West Virginia

After moving away from home, I quickly came to appreciate all the effort my mom, Jane Forshey (left) of St. Clairsville, Ohio put into providing us with well-balanced and delicious meals.

With a family of six, we each had our favorite foods. But all of us requested this country-style meal whenever we had guests coming for dinner.

Everyone enjoys Mom's tangy Miniature Ham Loaves and creamy Cheese Potato Puff. The enticing aroma while these are baking always draws people into the kitchen.

Whoever tries the puff agrees that it's the lightest, fluffiest, tastiest potato dish they've ever tasted.

Accordion Rye Rolls warm from the oven are also wonderful. Any extra effort in making these fresh rolls is worth it.

Our favorite part of the meal is when Mom brings out dessert—Bavarian Apple Torte. This rich cheesecake topped with tender apple slices is a fitting way to end a mouth-watering meal.

These recipes are convenient, too, since much of the preparation can be done a day in advance. This is important if you enjoy visiting with your guests as much as Mom does.

My three sisters and I have learned a lot of important things from Mom over the years. Besides patiently teaching us to prepare and serve good meals, she and our father, Jim, guided us in Christian living and good work ethics, and demonstrated a strong, loving marriage.

I hope you enjoy this scrumptious meal. Good food is an important part of our lifestyle, and my mom serves only the best.

Miniature Ham Loaves, Cheese Potato Puff, Accordion Rye Rolls and Bavarian Apple Torte (recipes are on pp. 254-255).

Miniature Ham Loaves

When there's a special dinner coming, Mom will usually prepare these scrumptious loaves several days in advance and freeze them. Then she needs only to bake them before dinner. We all anticipate their wonderful aroma and flavor.

      2 **eggs**
      1 **cup evaporated milk**
  1-1/2 **cups graham cracker crumbs (about 22 squares)**
  1-1/4 **pounds ground fully cooked ham**
  1-1/4 **pounds bulk pork sausage**
      1 **can (10-3/4 ounces) condensed tomato soup, undiluted**
      1 **cup plus 2 tablespoons packed brown sugar**
    1/3 **cup vinegar**
      1 **teaspoon ground mustard**

In a bowl, combine eggs, milk and cracker crumbs; mix well. Add ham and sausage. Shape 1/2 cupfuls into individual loaves. Place in a greased 13-in. x 9-in. x 2-in. baking dish. Combine the soup, brown sugar, vinegar and mustard; mix well. Pour over loaves.

Bake, uncovered, at 350° for 1 hour, basting after 30 minutes. **Yield:** 12-14 servings.

Cheese Potato Puff

These fluffy potatoes can be made a day ahead and refrigerated until ready to bake. This dish is Mom's specialty, and we all especially love the part along the edge of the casserole dish that gets golden brown.

     12 **medium potatoes, peeled and cubed**
      2 **cups (8 ounces) shredded cheddar *or* Swiss cheese, *divided***
  1-1/4 **cups milk**
    1/3 **cup butter, softened**
      1 **to 2 teaspoons salt**
      2 **eggs, beaten**

Place the potatoes in a saucepan and cover with water; cover and bring to a boil. Cook until tender, about 15-20 minutes. Drain and mash.

Add 1-3/4 cups cheese, milk, butter and salt; cook and stir over low heat until the cheese and butter are melted. Fold in eggs. Spread into a greased 13-in. x 9-in. x 2-in. baking dish.

Bake, uncovered, at 350° for 25-30 minutes. Sprinkle with the remaining cheese. Bake 5 minutes longer or until golden brown. **Yield:** 12-14 servings.

Accordion Rye Rolls

These rolls will make anyone like rye bread. Even though Mom fixes the dough a day ahead, she bakes them right before serving so they're hot and fresh.

      2 **packages (1/4 ounce *each*) active dry yeast**
    1/2 **cup warm water (110° to 115°)**
  1-1/2 **cups warm milk (110° to 115°)**

    1/4   cup molasses
      4   tablespoons butter, softened, *divided*
      1   tablespoon sugar
      1   tablespoon plus 1/2 teaspoon salt, *divided*
      3   to 3-1/2 cups all-purpose flour
2-1/2   cups rye flour
Vegetable oil
      1   egg white
      2   teaspoons caraway seeds

In a mixing bowl, dissolve yeast in water. Add milk, molasses, 2 tablespoons butter, sugar and 1 tablespoon salt. Add 2 cups all-purpose flour; beat until smooth. Add rye flour and enough remaining all-purpose flour to form a soft dough. Turn onto a floured surface; knead until smooth and elastic, about 6-8 minutes.

Place in a greased bowl, turning once to grease top. Let stand for 20 minutes. Divide dough into four portions. On a lightly floured surface, roll each portion into a 14-in. x 6-in. rectangle. Brush with remaining butter. With the blunt edge of a knife, make creases in dough at 2-in. intervals, beginning at a short side.

Fold dough accordion-style back and forth along creased lines. Cut folded dough into 1-in. pieces. Place each piece cut side down in a greased muffin cup. Brush with the oil. Cover loosely with plastic wrap. Refrigerate for 4-24 hours. When ready to bake, uncover and let stand at room temperature for 10 minutes.

In a small mixing bowl, beat egg white until stiff peaks form; brush over dough. Sprinkle with caraway seeds and remaining salt. Bake at 375° for 20-25 minutes or until lightly browned. **Yield:** 2 dozen.

Bavarian Apple Torte

This rich, creamy torte has always been one of my favorite autumn desserts. Mom uses the freshest apples from a local orchard and bakes this treat until the apples are crisp-tender. It tastes as good as it looks.

    3/4   cup butter, softened
    1/2   cup sugar
1-1/2   cups all-purpose flour
    1/2   teaspoon vanilla extract
FILLING:
      2   packages (8 ounces *each*) cream cheese,
            softened
    1/4   cup sugar
      2   eggs
    3/4   teaspoon vanilla extract
TOPPING:
      3   cups thinly sliced peeled tart apples
    1/2   cup sugar
      1   teaspoon ground cinnamon

Combine the first four ingredients. Press onto the bottom of an ungreased 9-in. springform pan. In a mixing bowl, beat cream cheese and sugar. Add eggs and vanilla; mix well. Pour over the crust. Combine topping ingredients; spoon over filling.

Bake at 350° for 55-65 minutes or until the center is set. Cool on a wire rack. Store in the refrigerator. Cut torte into wedges with a serrated knife. **Yield:** 12-14 servings.

Editor's Note: Even a tight-fitting springform pan may leak. To prevent drips, place the pan on a baking sheet in the oven.

A Memorable Meat Loaf Meal

By Michelle Beran, Claflin, Kansas

I have fond memories of enjoying dinner at home when I was growing up. There was fun conversation between my parents, two sisters, brother and me...and Mom always served delectable food.

My mother, Linda Engemann (left), worked hard as a schoolteacher. So during her busy weeks, she often prepared casseroles ahead or had dinner simmering in the slow cooker.

The meal that's still my favorite starts with Mom's Meat Loaf. Mom frequently fixed this main dish on the weekend when she had time to put something in the oven. It's tender and flavorful with a tangy topping we love.

Cheesy Potato Bake is an excellent, hearty side dish that goes perfectly with meat loaf. Of course, we loved these potatoes so much Mom served them with a variety of main courses.

An early autumn staple on Mom's table is her Cucumbers with Dressing. Now my own family asks me to prepare this dish for our meals together.

Dessert is out of the ordinary and has wonderful old-fashioned goodness. Purple Plum Pie is one of Mom's specialties. A big slice of this sweet-tart pie still takes me back to those carefree days at home.

I gained kitchen confidence helping Mom. And she's inspired me to make dinners for my own family special by presenting great food and having good conversation.

There are 16 around Mom's table these days, and dinner there is still a treat!

Mom's Meat Loaf, Cheesy Potato Bake, Cucumbers with Dressing and Purple Plum Pie (recipes are on pp. 258-259).

In a large bowl, beat the eggs. Add milk, saltines, onion, salt, sage and pepper. Add beef and mix well. Shape into an 8-1/2-in. x 4-1/2-in. loaf in an ungreased shallow baking pan.

Combine remaining ingredients; spread 3/4 cup over meat loaf. Bake at 350° for 60-65 minutes or until meat is no longer pink; drain. Let stand 10 minutes before slicing. Serve with remaining sauce. **Yield:** 6-8 servings.

Cucumbers with Dressing

Just a few simple ingredients—mayonnaise, sugar, vinegar and salt—dress up slices of crisp cucumbers.

- 1 **cup mayonnaise**
- 1/4 **cup sugar**
- 1/4 **cup vinegar**
- 1/4 **teaspoon salt**
- 4 **cups sliced cucumbers**

In a bowl, combine mayonnaise, sugar, vinegar and salt. Add cucumbers; stir to coat. Cover and refrigerate for 2 hours. **Yield:** 6-8 servings.

Cheesy Potato Bake

This saucy side dish satisfies even hearty appetites. It's easy to fix since there's no need to peel the potatoes. The mild, comforting flavor goes nicely with any meat—I especially like it with meat loaf.

- 4 **large unpeeled baking potatoes**
- 1/4 **cup butter**
- 1 **tablespoon grated onion**

Mom's Meat Loaf

Mom made this scrumptious main dish frequently when I was growing up. When I first met my husband, he wasn't fond of meat loaf. This is the first meal I prepared for him, and now he requests it often.

- 2 **eggs**
- 3/4 **cup milk**
- 2/3 **cup finely crushed saltines**
- 1/2 **cup chopped onion**
- 1 **teaspoon salt**
- 1/2 **teaspoon rubbed sage**
- **Dash pepper**
- 1-1/2 **pounds ground beef**
- 1 **cup ketchup**
- 1/2 **cup packed brown sugar**
- 1 **teaspoon Worcestershire sauce**

Cues for Storing Cukes

Store whole cucumbers, unwashed, in a plastic bag in the refrigerator for up to 10 days. Cut cucumbers can be wrapped and refrigerated for up to 5 days.

> 1 tablespoon lemon juice
> 1 unbaked deep-dish pastry shell (9 inches)
> TOPPING:
> 1/2 cup sugar
> 1/2 cup all-purpose flour
> 1/4 teaspoon ground cinnamon
> 1/4 teaspoon ground nutmeg
> 3 tablespoons cold butter

In a bowl, combine the first six ingredients; pour into pastry shell. For topping, combine sugar, flour, cinnamon and nutmeg in a small bowl; cut in butter until the mixture resembles coarse crumbs. Sprinkle over filling. Bake at 375° for 50-60 minutes or until bubbly and golden brown. Cover edges of crust with foil during the last 20 minutes to prevent overbrowning. Cool on a wire rack. **Yield:** 8 servings.

> 1 teaspoon salt
> 1/2 teaspoon dried thyme
> 1/8 teaspoon pepper
> 1 cup (4 ounces) shredded cheddar cheese
> 1 tablespoon chopped fresh parsley

Thinly slice the potatoes and place in a greased shallow 2-qt. baking dish. In a small saucepan, heat butter, onion, salt, thyme and pepper until the butter is melted. Drizzle over potatoes.

Cover and bake at 425° for 45 minutes or until tender. Sprinkle with cheese and parsley. Bake, uncovered, 15 minutes longer or until the cheese melts. **Yield:** 6-8 servings.

Purple Plum Pie

I can never resist a tart, tempting slice of this beautiful pie. It's a down-home dessert that makes any meal special. This pie is a terrific way to put fresh plums to use.

> 4 cups sliced fresh plums (about 1-1/2 pounds)
> 1/2 cup sugar
> 1/4 cup all-purpose flour
> 1/4 teaspoon salt
> 1/4 teaspoon ground cinnamon

Spaghetti Is Requested Most

By Grace Yaskovic, Branchville, New Jersey

Born during the Depression, Mom learned early how to cook and bake. She became an expert at making a little taste like a lot.

My mother, Joan Mulholland Schweer (left), married young and raised five kids. Those kitchen skills served her well over the years.

When we were growing up, Mom got involved in all our activities. Still, she managed to provide terrific meals and treats. She frequently hosted big Sunday dinners for the family and was famous for her Christmas cookies.

My brother, three sisters and I agree that of all the good foods she served, Mom's Hearty Spaghetti was definitely her best meal. It was also the most requested—by family and guests.

Her special spaghetti sauce features both Italian sausage and big ground beef meatballs. As it simmered, the bubbling sauce filled the house with a mouth-watering aroma.

It tasted even better than it smelled. It was hard to wait for dinner!

Alongside her steaming spaghetti, Mom served crusty Garlic Bread. She made it with freshly minced garlic that produced a robust flavor.

Her Salad with Creamy Dressing was a cool accompaniment to the savory main dish.

All five kids remembered to save room for dessert whenever Mom made buttery Pecan Crescent Cookies. With their sugar coating, the cookies looked like brightly lit moons in a dark fall sky. These old-fashioned treats would melt in our mouths.

I cherish the memory of all of Mom's great meals. It's a pleasure to share these recipes as a special tribute to her.

Mom's Hearty Spaghetti, Garlic Bread, Salad with Creamy Dressing and Pecan Crescent Cookies (recipes are on pp. 262-263).

Mom's Hearty Spaghetti

Flavored with Italian sausage and dotted with juicy meatballs, the savory from-scratch sauce made this dish one of my mom's most-requested. We five kids were always thrilled when it was on the menu.

- 1 egg
- 1/4 cup milk
- 1 cup soft bread crumbs
- 1/2 teaspoon salt
- 1/2 teaspoon garlic powder
- 1/2 teaspoon minced fresh parsley
- 1 pound ground beef

SAUCE:

- 1 pound Italian sausage links, cut into 2-inch pieces
- 1 large onion, chopped
- 1 medium green pepper, chopped
- 2 cans (28 ounces *each*) plum *or* whole tomatoes, drained and diced
- 2 cans (8 ounces *each*) tomato sauce
- 1 can (14-1/2 ounces) beef broth
- 1 can (6 ounces) tomato paste
- 2 garlic cloves, minced

- 2 teaspoons *each* dried basil, oregano and parsley flakes
- 2 teaspoons sugar

Salt and pepper to taste
Hot cooked spaghetti
Grated Parmesan cheese

In a bowl, combine the first six ingredients. Add beef and mix well. Shape into eight meatballs. Brown in a Dutch oven over medium heat; drain and set meatballs aside.

In the same pan, cook sausage, onion and green pepper until vegetables are tender; drain. Add the tomatoes, tomato sauce, broth, tomato paste, garlic and seasonings. Add meatballs; stir gently.

Bring to a boil. Reduce heat; cover and simmer for 2-3 hours. Serve over spaghetti; sprinkle with Parmesan cheese. **Yield:** 8 servings.

Garlic Bread

This wonderful accompaniment could not be tastier or simpler to make. Minced fresh garlic is key to these flavor-packed crusty slices, which our big family would snatch up before they even had a chance to cool.

- 1/2 cup butter, melted
- 3 to 4 garlic cloves, minced
- 1 loaf (1 pound) French bread, halved lengthwise
- 2 tablespoons minced fresh parsley

In a small bowl, combine butter and garlic. Brush over cut sides of bread; sprinkle with parsley. Place, cut side up, on a baking sheet.

Bake at 350° for 8 minutes. Broil 4-6 in. from the heat for 2 minutes or until golden brown. Cut into 2-in. slices. Serve warm. **Yield:** 8 servings.

Salad with Creamy Dressing

Mom had a magic way of combining ordinary ingredients into something extraordinary. In this refreshing salad, lettuce and vegetables are deliciously topped with a thick, hearty dressing.

- 12 **cups mixed salad greens**
- 2 **large tomatoes, chopped**
- 1 **large cucumber, chopped**
- 1 **cup mayonnaise**
- 1 **cup Thousand Island salad dressing**
- 2 **tablespoons milk**
- 2 **hard-cooked eggs, chopped, optional**

In a large bowl, toss the salad greens, tomatoes and cucumber; set aside. In a small bowl, combine mayonnaise, Thousand Island dressing and milk; mix well.

If desired, gently stir in eggs. Serve over salad. Store any leftover dressing in the refrigerator. **Yield:** 8 servings (2 cups dressing).

Pecan Crescent Cookies

Rich, buttery and absolutely irresistible, these old-fashioned nut cookies were one of Mom's specialties. Any meal was a memorable event when she served this scrumptious treat.

- 1 **cup butter, softened**
- 1/2 **cup sugar**
- 1 **teaspoon vanilla extract**
- 2 **cups all-purpose flour**
- 1 **cup finely chopped pecans**
Confectioners' sugar

In a mixing bowl, cream butter, sugar and vanilla. Gradually add flour. Stir in pecans. Shape rounded teaspoonfuls of dough into 2-1/2-in. logs and shape into crescents.

Place 1 in. apart on ungreased baking sheets. Bake at 325° for 20-22 minutes or until set and bottoms are lightly browned. Let stand for 2-3 minutes before removing to wire racks to cool. Dust with confectioners' sugar before serving. **Yield:** 6 dozen.

 Lowdown on Leftovers

For an interesting side dish, stir-fry leftover spaghetti noodles until golden, then add uncooked scrambled eggs. Cook until eggs are firm.

Leftover sausage and vegetables make a quick and tasty meal when stirred into prepared macaroni and cheese.

Mix leftover crushed pineapple with applesauce for a quick, refreshing salad.

An Old-World Dinner to Savor

By Cathy Eland, Hightstown, New Jersey

Mom is known throughout our family as an excellent cook, and with good reason.

When I was growing up, my mother, Norma Wyckoff (left) from Brick, New Jersey, worked for a deli preparing all sorts of salads and sandwiches. But she still loved to make special dinners for my father, brother, sister and me.

Her family was German, and Mom learned a lot by working in the kitchen with *her* mom, who also loved to cook. Oma (that's German for grandmother) was a good teacher, and the two created many happy memories as well as delicious meals.

Now whenever we all get together, we unanimously request that Mom fix our favorite old-world meal.

German Sauerbraten is a traditional main dish that is tender and flavorful when it's cooked to perfection. The tempting aroma of the spiced beef roast always draws us into the kitchen.

Ginger, vinegar, onions, cloves and pickling spices create a marinade that turns into a rich, tasty gravy. Dad especially enjoys pouring the gravy over Mom's Potato Dumplings. These mild little dumplings are hearty and delightful with just a hint of nutmeg.

Sweet-Sour Red Cabbage is a colorful and crunchy side dish that really tingles your taste buds. We always go back for seconds.

It's not easy, but we try to save room for dessert when Mom makes her wonderful Sour Cream Peach Kuchen. The crust is tender, and the filling is fresh-tasting and lightly sweet. It can even be made with canned peaches when fresh ones are not in season.

This meal takes a bit of effort to prepare, but Mom doesn't mind since she knows we savor every bite. Mom and I are thrilled to share these recipes so your family can enjoy what is, for us, a true taste of home.

German Sauerbraten, Sweet-Sour Red Cabbage, Potato Dumplings and Sour Cream Peach Kuchen (recipes are on pp. 266-267).

Strain cooking liquid, discarding the onions and seasonings. Measure liquid; if necessary, add enough reserved marinade to equal 3 cups. Pour mixture into a saucepan; bring to a rolling boil. Add gingersnaps; simmer until gravy is thickened. Slice roast and serve with gravy. **Yield:** 12-14 servings.

Sweet-Sour Red Cabbage

This crunchy, eye-catching cooked cabbage is seasoned with a flavorful blend of vinegar, spices and bacon.

1/2	cup cider vinegar
1/4	cup sugar
1/4	cup packed brown sugar
1	medium head red cabbage, shredded (10 cups)
2	bacon strips, diced
1	medium tart apple, peeled and chopped
1/2	cup chopped onion
1/4	cup water
2	tablespoons white wine vinegar *or* additional cider vinegar
1/2	teaspoon salt
1/4	teaspoon pepper
1/8	teaspoon ground cloves

In a large bowl, stir the cider vinegar and sugars until sugars are dissolved. Add cabbage; toss to coat. Let stand for 5-10 minutes. Meanwhile, in a large skillet over medium heat, cook bacon until crisp. Remove with a slotted spoon, reserving drippings.

German Sauerbraten

Our family loves it when Mom prepares this wonderful old-world dish. The tender beef has a bold blend of mouth-watering seasonings. It smells so good in the oven and tastes even better!

2	teaspoons salt
1	teaspoon ground ginger
1	beef top round roast (about 4 pounds)
2-1/2	cups water
2	cups cider vinegar
2	medium onions, sliced
1/3	cup sugar
2	tablespoons mixed pickling spices
1	teaspoon whole peppercorns
8	whole cloves
2	bay leaves
2	tablespoons vegetable oil
14	to 16 gingersnaps, crushed

Combine salt and ginger; rub over the roast. Place in a deep glass bowl. In a saucepan, combine water, vinegar, onions, sugar, pickling spices, peppercorns, cloves and bay leaves; bring to a boil. Pour over the roast; turn to coat.

Cover and refrigerate for 2 days, turning twice a day. Remove roast, reserving marinade; pat roast dry. In a large kettle or Dutch oven, brown roast on all sides in oil. Strain marinade, reserving half of the onions and seasonings.

Pour 1 cup of marinade and reserved onions and seasonings over roast (cover and refrigerate remaining marinade). Bring to a boil. Reduce heat; cover and simmer for 3 hours or until meat is tender.

Sour Cream Peach Kuchen

For an old-fashioned treat, there's nothing that beats my mom's peach kuchen. With a melt-in-your-mouth crust and a lightly sweet filling, this dessert is perfect after a big meal. Sweetened sour cream tops it off.

- 3 **cups all-purpose flour**
- 1-1/4 **cups sugar,** *divided*
- 1/2 **teaspoon baking powder**
- 1/4 **teaspoon salt**
- 1 **cup cold butter**
- 2 **cans (29 ounces** *each***) sliced peaches, drained** *or* **13 small fresh peaches, peeled and sliced**
- 1 **teaspoon ground cinnamon**

TOPPING:
- 4 **egg yolks**
- 2 **cups (16 ounces) sour cream**
- 2 **to 3 tablespoons sugar**
- 1/4 **teaspoon ground cinnamon**

In a bowl, combine the flour, 1/4 cup sugar, baking powder and salt; cut in butter until mixture resembles coarse crumbs. Press onto the bottom and 1 in. up the sides of a greased 13-in. x 9-in. x 2-in. baking dish. Arrange peaches over crust. Combine cinnamon and remaining sugar; sprinkle over peaches. Bake at 400° for 15 minutes.

Meanwhile, in a bowl, combine egg yolks and sour cream. Spread over peaches. Combine sugar and cinnamon; sprinkle over top. Bake 30-35 minutes longer or until golden. Serve warm or cold. Store leftovers in the refrigerator. **Yield:** 12 servings.

In the drippings, saute the apple and onion until tender. Add the water and cabbage mixture. Bring to a boil. Reduce heat; cover and simmer for 30-35 minutes. Stir in the remaining ingredients. Simmer, uncovered, for 5 minutes or until tender. Sprinkle with the reserved bacon just before serving. **Yield:** 8-10 servings.

Potato Dumplings

With a few additional basic ingredients, my mom transforms potatoes into these delightful dumplings. This authentic German side dish is so hearty and comforting. We love the dumplings in sauerbraten gravy.

- 3 **pounds russet potatoes**
- 2 **eggs**
- 1 **cup all-purpose flour,** *divided*
- 1/2 **cup dry bread crumbs**
- 1 **teaspoon salt**
- 1/4 **teaspoon ground nutmeg**

Dash pepper
Minced fresh parsley, optional

Place potatoes in a saucepan and cover with water; bring to a boil. Reduce heat; cover and simmer for 30-35 minutes or until tender. Drain well. Refrigerate for 2 hours or overnight. Peel and grate potatoes. In a bowl, combine the eggs, 3/4 cup flour, bread crumbs, salt, nutmeg and pepper. Add potatoes; mix with hands until well blended. Shape into 1-1/2-in. balls; roll in remaining flour.

In a large kettle, bring salted water to a boil. Add the dumplings, a few at a time, to boiling water. Simmer, uncovered, until the dumplings rise to the top; cook 2 minutes longer. Remove dumplings with a slotted spoon to a serving bowl. Sprinkle with parsley if desired. **Yield:** 10 servings.

An Italian-Style Rib Dinner

By Jeanne Voss, Anaheim Hills, California

My mother, Pat Voss (left), has been a proud homemaker since the day she and my dad got married more than 40 years ago.

Of Italian descent, Mom can make a full day of meal planning, grocery shopping and cooking. She thinks nothing of working hours in the kitchen preparing a meal for her family in La Mirada, California.

When my two brothers and I were growing up, we'd walk in the door after school and always be greeted by wonderful aromas wafting from the kitchen.

She taught us kids to cook at an early age. When most of my friends were earning their Girl Scout cooking badges by making something simple like hamburgers, Mom insisted I prepare chicken tetrazzini, antipasto salad and cream puffs!

Mom has many specialties, but my absolute favorite meal starts with her flavorful Tangy Country-Style Ribs. Smothered in a sweet and zesty sauce, those tender ribs are irresistible.

In Bacon-Tomato Spinach Salad, oregano perks up the creamy homemade dressing. It's served with a pretty mixture of spinach, red onion, tomatoes and bacon.

Her golden Sally Lunn Batter Bread bakes up high and as light as a feather. It tastes as good as it smells.

Cream Cheese Finger Cookies are sure to melt in your mouth. They're a nutty old-fashioned treat.

The love of cooking is one of the best gifts Mom could have given me. I enjoy fixing meals for my husband, Robert, and our son, Andrew. We're fortunate to live close to my parents so we can still have dinner at their house regularly.

Mom and I enjoyed sharing our favorite recipes with you, and we hope they will become part of your treasured collection, too.

Tangy Country-Style Ribs, Bacon-Tomato Spinach Salad, Sally Lunn Batter Bread and Cream Cheese Finger Cookies (recipes are on pp. 270-271).

Tangy Country-Style Ribs

There are never any leftovers when my mom fixes these tender sweet-and-sour ribs. She doubles the batch when our family gets together so there'll be enough for each of us to take some home for our freezers.

- **4 pounds boneless country-style pork ribs**
- **1 medium onion, chopped**
- **2 tablespoons vegetable oil**
- **1 cup chili sauce**
- **1/2 cup water**
- **1/4 cup lemon juice**
- **2 tablespoons brown sugar**
- **2 tablespoons white vinegar**
- **2 tablespoons ketchup**
- **1 tablespoon Worcestershire sauce**

Dash salt and pepper
Hot cooked rice

Place ribs on a rack in a shallow roasting pan. Cover and bake at 325° for 1 hour and 15 minutes. Meanwhile, in a skillet, saute onion in oil until tender. Add the chili sauce, water, lemon juice, brown sugar, vinegar, ketchup, Worcestershire sauce, salt and pepper. Reduce heat; simmer, uncovered, for 5 minutes or until slightly thickened.

Drain ribs; brush with half of the sauce. Cover and bake 30 minutes. Uncover; baste with remaining sauce. Bake 15-20 minutes longer or until the ribs are tender. Serve with hot cooked rice. **Yield:** 8 servings.

Bacon-Tomato Spinach Salad

Mom always knew how to get us kids to eat our vegetables! This lovely salad combines spinach, tomatoes, red onions and bacon, served with a creamy homemade dressing.

- **16 cups torn fresh spinach (about 12 ounces)**
- **12 cherry tomatoes, halved**
- **6 bacon strips, cooked and crumbled**
- **1/4 cup julienned red onion**

CREAMY OREGANO DRESSING:

- **1 cup mayonnaise**
- **1 to 2 tablespoons white vinegar**
- **2 teaspoons dried oregano**

Salt and pepper to taste

In a large bowl, combine the spinach, tomatoes, bacon and onion. In a small bowl, whisk the dressing ingredients until smooth. Serve with salad. **Yield:** 8 servings.

Sally Lunn Batter Bread

The tantalizing aroma of this golden loaf baking always draws people into my mother's kitchen. With its circular shape, it's a pretty bread, too. I've never seen it last more than 2 hours out of the oven!

1 package (1/4 ounce) active dry yeast
1/2 cup warm water (110° to 115°)
1 cup warm milk (110° to 115°)
1/2 cup butter, softened
1/4 cup sugar
2 teaspoons salt
3 eggs
5-1/2 to 6 cups all-purpose flour
HONEY BUTTER:
1/2 cup butter, softened
1/2 cup honey

In a mixing bowl, dissolve yeast in warm water. Add the milk, butter, sugar, salt, eggs and 3 cups flour. Beat until smooth. Stir in enough remaining flour to form a soft dough (do not knead). Place in a greased bowl, turning once to grease top. Cover and let rise in a warm place until doubled, about 1 hour.

Stir dough down. Spoon into a greased and floured 10-in. tube pan. Cover and let rise until doubled, about 1 hour. Bake at 400° for 25-30 minutes or until golden brown. Remove from pan to a wire rack.

Combine the honey butter ingredients until smooth. Serve with bread. **Yield:** 12-16 servings.

Cream Cheese Finger Cookies

These melt-in-your-mouth cookies are one of my mom's specialties. Made with cream cheese and butter, they're very rich…and the pecans add wonderful flavor. They're great with a hot cup of coffee or a tall glass of cold milk.

1/2 cup butter, softened
4 ounces cream cheese, softened
1 teaspoon vanilla extract
1-3/4 cups all-purpose flour
1 tablespoon sugar
Dash salt
1 cup finely chopped pecans
Confectioners' sugar

In a mixing bowl, cream butter and cream cheese. Beat in vanilla. Combine the flour, sugar and salt; gradually add to creamed mixture. Stir in pecans (dough will be crumbly). Shape tablespoonfuls into 2-in. logs. Place 2 in. apart on ungreased baking sheets.

Bake at 375° for 12-14 minutes or until lightly browned. Roll warm cookies in confectioners' sugar; cool on wire racks. **Yield:** 2 dozen.

Perfect Cookies

For accurate temperatures, always use a good oven thermometer. A mercury thermometer will outlast metal spring-style thermometers, which are less expensive but can become unreliable after a jolt. Mercury thermometers can be found in kitchen-supply stores. If you're baking more than one sheet at a time, ensure even browning by switching the sheets from top to bottom and front to back halfway through the baking time.

Family-Favorite Steak Dinner

By Gina Mueller, Converse, Texas

As children, my brothers and I loved watching our mother, Kathy Lehman (left) of San Antonio, Texas, work magic in the kitchen.

We'd spend hours by her side, mesmerized by the sweet and savory aromas escaping from stovetop pots. But it wasn't just the lure of simmering foods that drew us near. We lingered because we sensed Mom's pleasure in caring for her family and preparing delectable dishes for us to enjoy.

Our only difficulty during those long afternoons with Mom was waiting until dinner was served. Our taste buds would tingle and our stomachs growled in happy anticipation.

Mom never disappointed us. One meal we especially enjoyed included her Squash and Pepper Skillet. She'd stir-fry zucchini and summer squash with onion, bell pepper and garlic for a marvelous blend.

The only way to distract us from this bounty of flavor was to serve something equally delicious. Mom accomplished this by dishing up plates of her Breaded Steaks. The golden coating was so good that we'd relish every bite.

Lightly seasoned, the steaks were perfectly matched with Mom's Olive Lover's Salad. It was such a family favorite that the bowl was always scraped clean!

Finally, just as we thought our stomachs might burst, Mom would bring out a luscious dessert like her tender Prune Bundt Cake. What else could we do but smile and dig in?

Mom and Dad are retired now, and I like to return to them all the wonderful gifts they shared with me—love, support and many, many fabulous meals.

One day, I even hope to compile a cookbook containing all of my mother's recipes. Mom's Best Meal will be included, of course!

Breaded Steaks, Squash and Pepper Skillet, Olive Lover's Salad and Prune Bundt Cake (recipes are on pp. 274-275).

Squash and Pepper Skillet

Mom knew how to get us to eat our vegetables—she'd serve this colorful blend of fresh zucchini, summer squash and bell pepper! It's tasty enough to please the whole family, and it makes a wonderful addition to any potluck.

☑ Uses less fat, sugar or salt. Includes Nutritional Analysis and Diabetic Exchanges.

- 1 medium onion, thinly sliced
- 1 tablespoon olive oil
- 5 medium zucchini, sliced
- 3 medium yellow summer squash, sliced
- 1 small sweet red *or* green pepper, julienned
- 1 garlic clove, minced

Salt and pepper to taste

In a skillet, saute onion in oil until tender. Add squash, red pepper and garlic; stir-fry for 12-15 minutes or until vegetables are crisp-tender. Season with salt and pepper. **Yield:** 8 servings.

Nutritional Analysis: One serving (prepared without salt) equals 53 calories, 7 mg sodium, 0 cholesterol, 8 g carbohydrate, 3 g protein, 2 g fat, 3 g fiber. **Diabetic Exchanges:** 1 vegetable, 1/2 fat.

Olive Lover's Salad

Mom concocted this creative salad with only a handful of ingredients. Chopped olives, celery and garlic are tossed with oil and chilled for a cool refreshing side dish that's perfect with any warm meal.

Breaded Steaks

This homespun, stick-to-your-ribs steak supper was always a favorite with us kids. Mom coated tender steaks with lightly seasoned bread crumbs and fried them in oil until golden brown.

- 2 pounds sirloin tip steaks
- 1/2 cup all-purpose flour
- 2 eggs
- 1 cup milk
- 1/4 teaspoon salt
- 1/8 teaspoon pepper
- 1 package (15 ounces) seasoned bread crumbs
- 1/4 cup vegetable oil

Flatten steaks to 1/2-in. thickness. Cut into serving-size pieces; set aside. Place flour in a large resealable plastic bag. In a shallow bowl, combine the eggs, milk, salt and pepper. Place bread crumbs in another shallow bowl.

Coat steaks with flour, then dip into egg mixture and coat with crumbs. In a large skillet over medium-high heat, cook steaks in oil for 2-3 minutes on each side or until golden brown and cooked to desired doneness. **Yield:** 8 servings.

Prune Bundt Cake

Moist and flavorful, this old-fashioned fruity cake was one of Mom's best desserts. Top with confectioners' sugar or frosting for a sweet treat that rounds out any menu.

- 1/2 **cup butter-flavored shortening**
- 1 **cup sugar**
- 2 **eggs**
- 2 **cups all-purpose flour**
- 1 **teaspoon baking soda**
- 1 **teaspoon ground cinnamon**
- 3/4 **teaspoon salt**
- 1/4 **teaspoon** *each* **ground allspice, cloves and nutmeg**
- 1 **cup prune juice**
- 1 **cup finely chopped prunes, drained**

Confectioners' sugar, optional

In a mixing bowl, cream shortening and sugar until light and fluffy. Add eggs, one at a time, beating well after each addition.

Combine the dry ingredients; add to the creamed mixture alternately with prune juice. Stir in the prunes. Pour into a greased 10-in. fluted tube pan.

Bake at 350° for 40-45 minutes or until a toothpick inserted near the center comes out clean. Cool for 10 minutes before removing to a wire rack to cool completely. Dust with confectioners' sugar if desired. **Yield:** 12 servings.

- 1 **can (6 ounces) pitted ripe olives, drained and chopped**
- 1 **jar (5-3/4 ounces) stuffed olives, drained and chopped**
- 2 **celery ribs, chopped**
- 2 **garlic cloves, minced**
- 2 **tablespoons olive oil**

In a bowl, combine olives, celery and garlic. Drizzle with oil; toss to coat. Cover and refrigerate for 4 hours or overnight. **Yield:** 3-1/2 cups.

Zucchini Secrets

It's almost impossible to find zucchini without any blemishes because of its tender skin. But look for small ones that are firm and free of cuts.

Refrigerate zucchini in a plastic bag for about a week. Make sure there is no moisture on the zucchini or in the plastic bag.

Substitutions & Equivalents

EQUIVALENT MEASURES

3 teaspoons	= 1 tablespoon	**16 tablespoons**	= 1 cup
4 tablespoons	= 1/4 cup	**2 cups**	= 1 pint
5-1/3 tablespoons	= 1/3 cup	**4 cups**	= 1 quart
8 tablespoons	= 1/2 cup	**4 quarts**	= 1 gallon

FOOD EQUIVALENTS

Grains

Macaroni	1 cup (3-1/2 ounces) uncooked	= 2-1/2 cups cooked
Noodles, Medium	3 cups (4 ounces) uncooked	= 4 cups cooked
Popcorn	1/3 to 1/2 cup unpopped	= 8 cups popped
Rice, Long Grain	1 cup uncooked	= 3 cups cooked
Rice, Quick-Cooking	1 cup uncooked	= 2 cups cooked
Spaghetti	8 ounces uncooked	= 4 cups cooked

Crumbs

Bread	1 slice	= 3/4 cup soft crumbs, 1/4 cup fine dry crumbs
Graham Crackers	7 squares	= 1/2 cup finely crushed
Buttery Round Crackers	12 crackers	= 1/2 cup finely crushed
Saltine Crackers	14 crackers	= 1/2 cup finely crushed

Fruits

Bananas	1 medium	= 1/3 cup mashed
Lemons	1 medium	= 3 tablespoons juice, 2 teaspoons grated peel
Limes	1 medium	= 2 tablespoons juice, 1-1/2 teaspoons grated peel
Oranges	1 medium	= 1/4 to 1/3 cup juice, 4 teaspoons grated peel

Vegetables

Cabbage	1 head	= 5 cups shredded	**Green Pepper**	1 large	= 1 cup chopped
Carrots	1 pound	= 3 cups shredded	**Mushrooms**	1/2 pound	= 3 cups sliced
Celery	1 rib	= 1/2 cup chopped	**Onions**	1 medium	= 1/2 cup chopped
Corn	1 ear fresh	= 2/3 cup kernels	**Potatoes**	3 medium	= 2 cups cubed

Nuts

Almonds	1 pound	= 3 cups chopped	**Pecan Halves**	1 pound	= 4-1/2 cups chopped
Ground Nuts	3-3/4 ounces	= 1 cup	**Walnuts**	1 pound	= 3-3/4 cups chopped

EASY SUBSTITUTIONS

When you need...		Use...
Baking Powder	1 teaspoon	1/2 teaspoon cream of tartar + 1/4 teaspoon baking soda
Buttermilk	1 cup	1 tablespoon lemon juice *or* vinegar + enough milk to measure 1 cup (let stand 5 minutes before using)
Cornstarch	1 tablespoon	2 tablespoons all-purpose flour
Honey	1 cup	1-1/4 cups sugar + 1/4 cup water
Half-and-Half Cream	1 cup	1 tablespoon melted butter + enough whole milk to measure 1 cup
Onion	1 small, chopped (1/3 cup)	1 teaspoon onion powder *or* 1 tablespoon dried minced onion
Tomato Juice	1 cup	1/2 cup tomato sauce + 1/2 cup water
Tomato Sauce	2 cups	3/4 cup tomato paste + 1 cup water
Unsweetened Chocolate	1 square (1 ounce)	3 tablespoons baking cocoa + 1 tablespoon shortening *or* oil
Whole Milk	1 cup	1/2 cup evaporated milk + 1/2 cup water

General Recipe Index

This handy index lists every recipe by food category, major ingredient and/or cooking method, so you can easily locate recipes to suit your needs.

CAKES, CUPCAKES & TORTES (continued)

Fluffy Pineapple Torte, 243
Frozen Mocha Torte, 161
German Chocolate Birthday
   Cake, 53
Hot Fudge Cake, 137
Hot Milk Cake, 13
Lazy Daisy Cake, 231
Mama's Spice Cake, 247
Mom's Chocolate Cake, 127
Mom's Strawberry Shortcake, 227
Mother's Walnut Cake, 115
Old-Fashioned Carrot Cake, 119
Orange Dream Cake, 103
Pistachio Cake, 33
Prune Bundt Cake, 275
Pumpkin Chip Cupcakes, 219
Pumpkin Raisin Cake, 21
Sour Cream Peach Kuchen, 267
Texas Sheet Cake, 197
Zucchini Chip Snack Cake, 185

CANDY

Chocolate Easter Eggs, 99

CARROTS

Candied Carrots, 114
Carrot Broccoli Casserole, 210
Carrot Raisin Salad, 82
Cheesy Turnips and Carrots, 40
Mom's Beef Stew, 106
Mom's Carrot Casserole, 56
Old-Fashioned Beef Stew, 36
Old-Fashioned Carrot Cake, 119

CASSEROLES (also see

Oven Entrees)
Main Dishes
Chicken Macaroni Casserole, 148
Chicken Tortilla Bake, 110
Pork Chop Casserole, 246
Sausage Pie, 140
Side Dishes
Almond Celery Bake, 172
Broccoli Casserole, 206
Cabbage Casserole, 20
Carrot Broccoli Casserole, 210

Cauliflower Casserole, 126
Cheesy Potato Bake, 258
Colorful Veggie Bake, 235
Creamy Spinach Bake, 176
Mom's Carrot Casserole, 56
Mom's Macaroni and Cheese, 90
Mom's Sweet Potato Bake, 64
Mushroom Oven Rice, 206
Roasted Root Vegetables, 16
Sauerkraut Casserole, 12
Scalloped Corn, 68

CAULIFLOWER

Cauliflower Casserole, 126
Cauliflower Olive Salad, 188
Colorful Vegetable Salad, 78
Fresh Vegetable Salad, 99

CELERY

Almond Celery Bake, 172

CHEESE

Breads
Cheesy Garlic Bread, 243
Cheesy Italian Bread, 48
Swiss-Onion Bread Ring, 172
Desserts
Cherry Cheese Pie, 207
Cherry Cheese Torte, 235
Cream Cheese Finger
   Cookies, 271
Salads
Cottage Cheese Spinach
   Salad, 160
Gelatin Ring with Cream
   Cheese Balls, 218
Hawaiian Salad, 52
Tomato Mozzarella Salad, 193
Sandwiches
Cheeseburger Buns, 188
Side Dishes
Au Gratin Potatoes, 130
Cheese Potato Puff, 254
Cheese Potatoes, 86
Cheesy Potato Bake, 258
Cheesy Turnips and Carrots, 40
Creamy Spinach Bake, 176
Mom's Macaroni and Cheese, 90

CHERRIES

Cheery Cherry Cookies, 145
Cherry Cheese Pie, 207
Cherry Cheese Torte, 235
Chocolate Cherry Torte, 157
Duck with Cherry Sauce, 68

CHICKEN

Main Dishes
Baked Chicken, 122
Brunswick Stew, 250
Buttermilk Fried Chicken and
   Gravy, 136
Chicken and Dumplings, 102
Chicken and Rice Dinner, 82
Chicken Macaroni
   Casserole, 148
Chicken Tortilla Bake, 110
Cranberry-Stuffed Chicken, 60
Creamed Chicken in Patty
   Shells, 184
Crispy Baked Chicken, 226
Marinated Baked Chicken, 206
Roasted Chicken and
   Potatoes, 40
Soup
Mom's Special Chicken Soup, 48

CHOCOLATE

Bars
Frosted Shortbread, 181
Cakes, Cupcakes & Tortes
Chocolate Cake Roll, 131
Chocolate Cherry Torte, 157
Chocolate Marshmallow
   Cake, 203
Chocolate Mayonnaise Cake, 87
Chocolate Picnic Cake, 123
Frozen Mocha Torte, 161
German Chocolate Birthday
   Cake, 53
Hot Fudge Cake, 137
Mom's Chocolate Cake, 127
Pumpkin Chip Cupcakes, 219
Texas Sheet Cake, 197
Upside-Down Strawberry
   Shortcake, 177
Zucchini Chip Snack Cake, 185

OVEN ENTREES

Pork, Ham & Bacon (continued)
Pineapple Mustard Ham, 78
Pork Chop Casserole, 246
Pork Chops with Scalloped
    Potatoes, 222
Round Ham Loaf, 196
Sausage Pie, 140
Sunday Pork Roast, 64
Sweet-and-Sour Spareribs, 94
Tangy Country-Style Ribs, 270
Tangy Spareribs, 144
Turkey
Turkey with Grandma's
    Stuffing, 218

PANCAKES

Mom's Potato Pancakes, 238

PASTA & NOODLES (also see Lasagna; Spaghetti)

Chuck Roast with Homemade
    Noodles, 56
Mom's Hearty Spaghetti, 262
Mom's Macaroni and Cheese, 90
Mushroom Pasta Pilaf, 152

PEACHES

Mom's Peach Pie, 141
Peach Bavarian, 215
Peach Crisp, 239
Peachy Pork Chops, 164
Sour Cream Peach
    Kuchen, 267

PEANUT BUTTER

Chocolate Easter Eggs, 99
Peanut Butter Pie, 149

PEARS

Pear Lime Gelatin, 68
Strawberry Pear Gelatin, 127

PEAS

Creamed Peas and Potatoes, 28

PEPPERS & CHILIES

Bell Peppers
Squash and Pepper Skillet, 274
Sweet Red Pepper Salad, 49
Green Chilies
Zucchini Santa Fe, 227

PIES

Banana Cream Pie, 223
Cherry Cheese Pie, 207
Coconut Pie, 25
Cranberry Raisin Pie, 69
Custard Meringue Pie, 189
Dixie Pie, 65
Dutch Apple Pie, 165
Frozen Hawaiian Pie, 152
Mom's Custard Pie, 169
Mom's Peach Pie, 141
Old-Fashioned Chocolate
    Pie, 211
Peanut Butter Pie, 149
Purple Plum Pie, 259
Raisin Custard Pie, 95
Strawberry Satin Pie, 79
Summer Berry Pie, 173

PINEAPPLE

Christmas Wreath Salad, 33
Creamy Pineapple Salad, 94
Fluffy Lime Salad, 197
Fluffy Pineapple Torte, 243
Frozen Hawaiian Pie, 152
Ham with Pineapple Sauce, 176
Hawaiian Salad, 52
Old-Fashioned Baked Ham, 12
Molded Strawberry Salad, 56
Pineapple Beets, 222
Pineapple Mustard Ham, 78
Raspberry Gelatin Salad, 246
Round Ham Loaf, 196

PLUMS

Purple Plum Pie, 259

PORK (also see Bacon & Canadian Bacon; Ham; Sausage)

Main Dishes
Barbecued Spareribs, 210
Breaded Pork Chops, 86
Broiled Pork Chops, 52
City Kabobs, 168
Favorite Pork Chops, 130
Garlic Pork Roast, 20
Old-World Pork Roast, 234
Peachy Pork Chops, 164
Pork Chop Casserole, 246
Pork Chops with Scalloped
    Potatoes, 222
Sunday Pork Roast, 64
Sweet-and-Sour Spareribs, 94
Tangy Country-Style Ribs, 270
Tangy Spareribs, 144
Sandwiches
Betty's Barbecue, 180

POTATOES (also see Sweet Potatoes)

Main Dishes
Mom's Beef Stew, 106
Old-Fashioned Beef Stew, 36
Pork Chops with Scalloped
    Potatoes, 222
Roasted Chicken and
    Potatoes, 40
Salads
Creamy Potato Salad, 180
Dill Pickle Potato Salad, 188
Endive Salad with Potatoes, 234
Garden Potato Salad, 148
Side Dishes
Au Gratin Potatoes, 130
Baked Mashed Potatoes, 230
Cheese Potato Puff, 254
Cheese Potatoes, 86
Cheesy Potato Bake, 258
Creamed Beans and Potatoes, 52
Creamed Peas and Potatoes, 28
Creamed Potatoes, 196
Herbed Oven Potatoes, 161
Mom's Potato Dumplings, 44
Mom's Potato Pancakes, 238
Oven-Roasted Potatoes, 72
Parmesan Baked Potatoes, 98
Parsley Potatoes, 215
Peppery Scalloped Potatoes, 114
Potato Dumplings, 267
Scored Potatoes, 122

Alphabetical Index

This handy index lists every recipe in alphabetical order
so you can easily find your favorite dish.

Metric Conversion Chart

VOLUME MEASUREMENTS (DRY)

1/8 teaspoon	= 0.5 mL
1/4 teaspoon	= 1 mL
1/2 teaspoon	= 2 mL
3/4 teaspoon	= 4 mL
1 teaspoon	= 5 mL
1 tablespoon	= 15 mL
2 tablespoons	= 30 mL
1/4 cup	= 60 mL
1/3 cup	= 75 mL
1/2 cup	= 125 mL
2/3 cup	= 150 mL
3/4 cup	= 175 mL
1 cup	= 250 mL
2 cups	= 1 pint	= 500 mL
3 cups	= 750 mL
4 cups	= 1 quart	= 1 L

VOLUME MEASUREMENTS (FLUID)

1 fluid ounce (2 tablespoons)	= 30 mL
4 fluid ounces (1/2 cup)	= 125 mL
8 fluid ounces (1 cup)	= 250 mL
12 fluid ounces (1-1/2 cups)	= 375 mL
16 fluid ounces (2 cups)	= 500 mL

WEIGHTS (MASS)

1/2 ounce	= 15 g	
1 ounce	= 30 g	
3 ounces	= 90 g	
4 ounces	= 120 g	
8 ounces	= 225 g	
10 ounces	= 285 g	
12 ounces	= 360 g	
16 ounces	= 1 pound	= 450 g

DIMENSIONS

1/16 inch	= 2 mm
1/8 inch	= 3 mm
1/4 inch	= 6 mm
1/2 inch	= 1.5 cm
3/4 inch	= 2 cm
1 inch	= 2.5 cm

OVEN TEMPERATURES

250° F	= 120° C
275° F	= 140° C
300° F	= 150° C
325° F	= 160° C
350° F	= 180° C
375° F	= 190° C
400° F	= 200° C
425° F	= 220° C
450° F	= 230° C

BAKING PAN SIZES

Utensil	Size in Inches/Quarts	Metric Volume	Size in Centimeters
Baking or	8x8x2	2 L	20x20x5
Cake Pan	9x9x2	2.5 L	23x23x5
(square or	12x8x2	3 L	30x20x5
rectangular)	13x9x2	3.5 L	33x23x5
Loaf Pan	8x4x3	1.5 L	20x10x7
	9x5x3	2 L	23x13x7
Round Layer	8x1-1/2	1.2 L	20x4
Cake pan	9x1-1/2	1.5 L	23x4
Pie Plate	8x1-1/4	750 mL	20x3
	9x1-1/4	1 L	23x3
Baking Dish	1 quart	1 L	—
or Casserole	1-1/2 quart	1.5 L	—
	2 quart	2 L	—